WHAT WOMEN REPRESENT

I0803502

What Women Represent

The Impact of Women in Parliament

ERICA RAYMENT

McGill-Queen's University Press
Montreal & Kingston • London • Chicago

© McGill-Queen's University Press 2024

ISBN 978-0-2280-2094-3 (cloth)
ISBN 978-0-2280-2095-0 (paper)
ISBN 978-0-2280-2096-7 (ePDF)
ISBN 978-0-2280-2097-4 (ePUB)

Legal deposit second quarter 2024
Bibliothèque nationale du Québec

Printed in Canada on acid-free paper that is 100% ancient forest free (100% post-consumer recycled), processed chlorine free

This book has been published with the help of a grant from the Canadian Federation for the Humanities and Social Sciences, through the Awards to Scholarly Publications Program, using funds provided by the Social Sciences and Humanities Research Council of Canada.

Financé par le gouvernement du Canada | Funded by the Government of Canada | Canada | Conseil des arts du Canada | Canada Council for the Arts

We acknowledge the support of the Canada Council for the Arts.

Nous remercions le Conseil des arts du Canada de son soutien.

McGill-Queen's University Press in Montreal is on land which long served as a site of meeting and exchange amongst Indigenous Peoples, including the Haudenosaunee and Anishinabeg nations. In Kingston it is situated on the territory of the Haudenosaunee and Anishinaabek. We acknowledge and thank the diverse Indigenous Peoples whose footsteps have marked these territories on which peoples of the world now gather.

Library and Archives Canada Cataloguing in Publication

Title: What women represent: the impact of women in Parliament / Erica Rayment.

Names: Rayment, Erica, author.

Description: Includes bibliographical references and index.

Identifiers: Canadiana (print) 20230572316 | Canadiana (ebook) 20230572359 | ISBN 9780228020943 (cloth) | ISBN 9780228020950 (paper) | ISBN 9780228020974 (ePUB) | ISBN 9780228020967 (ePDF)

Subjects: LCSH: Women—Political activity—Canada. | LCSH: Women politicians—Canada. | LCSH: Canada. Parliament.

Classification: LCC HQ1236.5.C2 R39 2024 | DDC 320.90082—dc23

This book was typeset by Marquis Interscript in 10.5/13 Sabon.

For Philippa

Contents

Tables and Figures

TABLES

FIGURES

Acknowledgments

This book has been a long time in the making and has benefited from the feedback and support of many distinguished scholars. At the University of Toronto, Sylvia Bashevkin's wisdom, encouragement, and willingness to talk through the details of the project helped me to grow as a researcher. It was a privilege and an honour to work with her. Ludovic Rheault's methodological expertise and genuine enthusiasm for sharing it are the only reason I know anything about computational text analysis. I couldn't have undertaken this project without his guidance. Erin Tolley consistently provided insightful, detailed feedback on drafts that never lost sight of the big picture, and connected me to opportunities for research collaboration and teaching. I am so fortunate to have benefitted from the guidance of all three of these outstanding mentors.

I am immeasurably grateful to the Linked Parliamentary Data Project team for their extraordinary work digitizing Hansard and making the Lipad dataset available. I am especially grateful to Chris Cochrane for first pointing me towards this invaluable resource. Without the Lipad dataset this book would not exist.

I would also like to acknowledge financial support from the Social Sciences and Humanities Research Council, both in the form of a Canada Graduate Scholarship and then as a book grant.

I presented much (much) earlier versions of the research in some of the chapters at annual meetings of the Canadian Political Science Association in 2018 and 2019 and at the European Conference on Politics and Gender in 2019. I am grateful to paper discussants and others who attended the sessions for helpful feedback and advice. John Scherpereel's comments at ECPG were especially useful in helping me think through some of the conceptual refinements to the substantive representation of women that appear in this book.

I am grateful for wonderful colleagues at the University of Calgary. In particular, Melanee Thomas and Susan Franceschet believed in this project from the very beginning and provided sage advice on the big picture and technical details as I worked through final revisions. Jack Lucas provided encouragement and helpful advice on how to frame the project for a job talk that made its way into the book. Meagan Cloutier provided vital research assistance as I wrapped up the final version of the manuscript. Not at the University of Calgary but also very wonderful, I couldn't have asked for a better collaborator than Elizabeth McCallion. Work on our co-authored article and her feedback on final revisions were invaluable in helping me refine the theoretical details of this project.

I am grateful for the support and enthusiasm of Emily Andrew at McGill-Queen's University Press. She guided me through the process with clarity, kindness, and patience. I am grateful as well for the anonymous reviewers whose encouraging feedback helped improve the final version of the manuscript.

I submitted this manuscript for review less than a month before giving birth (the hardest of hard deadlines) and muddled through revisions while Philippa muddled through learning how to nap. In her short life, she has taught me important lessons about patience, priorities, and the utter futility of my perfectionist impulses. I am proud of this book but infinitely prouder to be her mum.

It takes an extraordinary amount of patience to be married to a person who is completing a PhD (and then, God help us, writing a book). My partner, Reynold Caskey, has put up with my long days and nights at Robarts and at my desk in Toronto and in Calgary. He has cheered me on, talked me off the ledge, reminded me to live a little, moved across the country with me in the middle of a global pandemic, and kept everything running smoothly in the background so that I could focus on finishing. This book could not exist without his support. Thank you is woefully inadequate.

WHAT WOMEN REPRESENT

Introduction

Imagine a House of Commons in which 70 per cent of the seats were occupied by women MPs instead of men. Would parliamentary politics in Canada look different? Intuitively, many of us would say yes. This intuition is part of why advocacy organizations have pushed for the election of more women in Canada for decades. It is also part of why gender and politics scholars have been studying the barriers to women's political inclusion for just as long. But, of course, the presence of more women in parliament is no guarantee that political processes or outcomes will be transformed – institutional rules and norms are deeply entrenched and resistant to change. Moreover, the diversity of the identities, experiences, and perspectives of the women who might participate in formal politics is such that the specifics of what that potential transformation might look like remain unclear. And yet, this intuition that the inclusion of more women might somehow change politics persists.

Women's share of parliamentary seats lags stubbornly behind our share of the population. Numbers have increased steadily but slowly since the first woman was elected in 1921 and reached a high of just over 30 per cent following the 2021 federal election – still nowhere near parity. But how exactly might Canadian politics look different if more women were elected? How (if at all) might women MPs behave differently from the men who have dominated the House of Commons since Confederation? And, if they do act differently, what kind of an impact might these women have on how politics gets done – in terms of the issues that are put on the parliamentary agenda, the decisions that get made, and the policy outcomes that follow from them? These are the questions that motivate this book. They are important questions for our understanding of women's political representation and of how parliamentary institutions operate to facilitate and constrain legislator behaviour, but we still don't have clear answers to them.

To address the question of whether and how elected women might have an impact on political debate and decision making in Canada, this book begins with the assumption that our democratic institutions and the people who occupy them matter for how we are governed. It takes seriously the possibility that greater diversity in terms of who our political representatives are will have an impact on the types of decisions that get made and the policies that get implemented. This starting point is perhaps at odds with the conventional view of the Canadian parliamentary system, which, like most Westminster parliaments, is understood to be dominated by the executive branch and political parties. Within such a system there are limited opportunities for individual MPs to influence political agendas or policy outcomes, and the identities, preferences, and priorities of individual MPs are often seen as irrelevant. This view of parliamentary politics, however, ignores the very real possibility that individual MPs might in fact try to influence politics and policy in Canada and, indeed, occasionally succeed in doing so. It also neglects the possibility that diversifying and expanding the range of views that are brought into parliamentary institutions has transformative potential. Opportunities for influence may be limited, but they are nonetheless worth investigating. Indeed, by exploring the details of what these opportunities look like and how they can be leveraged, we can shed light on the ways in which our core democratic institutions can be made more reflective of and responsive to the full diversity of the population.

Stepping into these under-explored possibilities, this book empirically investigates the impact of elected women in Canada across a range of representational dimensions. Looking at representational impacts in parliamentary debate, it asks who speaks for and about women, what issues are addressed in connection with women, and how those patterns of issue attention change over time. When it comes to policy decision making and outcomes, it asks if women MPs advocate for women, what strategies they use to navigate their institutional and political context to do so, and what determines whether they succeed in achieving their desired outcomes. The focus of the empirical analysis is on the Canadian case, but the observed patterns and the theoretical insights developed here are relevant to other Westminster parliamentary systems in which MPs face similar institutional constraints. In the pages that follow,

I argue that, even though they operate within an institutional context that works against their capacity for influence, elected women in Canada nonetheless navigate this context and have an impact on what gets discussed and the policy decisions that get made in parliament. Through a large-scale systematic examination of Canadian parliamentary debate and qualitative analysis of the role elected women play in representing women's interests in specific instances of parliamentary policymaking, I show that women's presence in parliament matters for the effective representation of women's interests, particularly when governments threaten to curtail previous equality gains.

WOMEN'S POLITICAL REPRESENTATION

One of the central ways in which the presence of women might have an impact on politics – and the focus of this study – is through improved representation of women citizens' interests in legislative debate and decision making. The "poverty of women's political representation" has been well documented (Celis and Childs 2020, 28). A generation of gender and politics scholars has made the case for the importance of women's presence in politics for the substantive representation of women's interests (Phillips 1995; Mansbridge 1999; Dovi 2002). These arguments link Pitkin's (1967) foundational concepts of descriptive representation and substantive representation. Descriptive representation refers to "what a representative is, what he must be like in order to represent," and conceives of representation in terms of *standing for* the population they represent (59). Substantive representation refers to "what a representative does, what constitutes the act of representing" (ibid.) and conceives of representation as *acting for* a larger collectivity or interest. The descriptive representation of women in politics is manifested by women's numerical presence in positions of elected office, whereas substantive representation occurs through action to promote and advance the interests of women. These actions can include anything from prioritizing women's policy issues, to patterns of issue attention in debate, to bill introduction and legislative voting, to concrete policy changes.

Although women's presence is typically understood to be an important factor for improving the substantive representation of women's interests in politics, descriptive representation does not lead automatically to better substantive representation. Women's interests are diverse and not universally shared. Moreover, women's ability to influence politics will be contingent upon the opportunities and constraints created by the institutional context in which they operate. Despite these limitations, women are nonetheless viewed as better equipped to act for women by virtue of the shared experience of existing in the world *as women* and the possibility of shared interests that result from that. The descriptive representation of women is particularly important for facilitating substantive representation in the case of uncrystallized interests – that is, on issues for which there is no clear-cut set of policy demands. Under these conditions, representatives who share the identity of those they represent will be better representatives because they can draw on their own experiences and perspectives to inform their decision making (Mansbridge 1999). The increased presence of women is thus likely but not guaranteed to improve the substantive representation of women in politics (Childs and Krook 2006; Mackay 2008; Wängnerud 2009).

THE IMPACT OF ELECTED WOMEN

Despite the complexity of the relationship between women's presence and the substantive representation of women in politics, tentative evidence from Canada and beyond suggests that women's presence does have an impact on substantive representation. Foundationally, women legislators consistently report a sense of obligation to act on behalf of women (see Tremblay 2003, 2007; Carroll 2002; Dittmar et al. 2018). In survey research, women legislators also report higher levels of interest in women's issues than do male legislators. Surveys of the attitudes of parliamentary candidates and MPs in the United Kingdom have found that women are more supportive of gender equality and policy measures that address these inequalities than are their male counterparts, even when controlling for party differences (Campbell et al. 2010; Lovenduski and Norris 2003). In Sweden, women parliamentarians have been found to prioritize the promotion of women's views in their parliamentary work and are more supportive of gender equality and policy efforts to promote it than are men (Wängnerud 2000). Surveys of parliamentary candidates in Canada have found that women were more interested in issues related to gender equality and supportive of policy interventions to address inequalities than were their male colleagues (Erickson 1997) – although feminist group consciousness appears to be the more powerful predictor of attitudes on these issues (Tremblay and Pelletier 2000). While these attitudes and priorities provide an important foundation for the substantive representation of women, they do not necessarily or independently lead to concrete actions or impacts on politics.

More concretely, there is evidence that elected women raise different issues than do men in parliamentary debate, which has the potential to shift the political agenda. In the United Kingdom, women MPs were more likely to ask parliamentary oral questions that addressed women specifically, and these questions tended to focus on "women's employment, domestic violence, politics and representation, and women's health" (Bird 2005, 361). Women MPs in the UK also participated more frequently than did their male colleagues in legislative debates on health care bills and, when doing so, actively voiced women's distinctive concerns in their interventions (Catalano 2009). In a longitudinal analysis of all elements of UK parliamentary debates, Blaxill and Beelen (2016) found that women were more likely to make parliamentary speeches about women and that women's parliamentary interventions focused on different issues than did those of their male colleagues. In the Welsh assembly, elected women tended to make more speeches about issues relating to domestic violence, childcare, and pay equity than did their male colleagues (Chaney 2006). In the Belgian Parliament, analyses of the content of budget debates (Celis 2006) and of oral questions (Erzeel 2012) found that women MPs made far more interventions about women in parliamentary debate than did their male colleagues. In Canada, less is known about the representation of women in parliamentary debate, but one study examining the topics addressed in parliamentary speeches in a single session of the 35th Parliament found that women MPs spoke more frequently than did their male colleagues about women's issues – understood to include women's rights and feminist issues as well as issues related to women's traditional role as caregivers (Tremblay 1998).

Research has also found that women MPs find ways to leverage the procedural tools available to them to advocate for and advance women's equality issues. For example, in the UK, Childs and Withey (2004) found that women MPs were more likely to introduce and sign Early Day Motions that were about women or about "'issues that bear on women' for either 'biological' or 'social' reasons" (555). In Canada, Tremblay (1998) found that women were more likely than their male colleagues to introduce private members' bills and motions relating to women's issues. Although Early Day Motions and private members' business are both typically seen as unlikely to lead to policy change, they can in some cases influence government policy decision making (see Childs and Withey 2006; Blidook 2010). In presidential systems, in which legislators have greater opportunity to influence policy agendas than in Westminster parliaments, there is evidence that women are more likely to introduce, support, and collaborate on legislation that has an impact on women (Barnes 2016; Swers 2002, 2013; Osborn 2012).

There is also evidence to suggest that women's presence has an impact on policy decisions and outputs. Quantitative analyses of the relationship between the proportion of women in parliaments and the presence of women's equality policy provisions, such as childcare or parental leave across multiple jurisdictions, suggest that the proportion of women legislators has a positive and statistically significant effect on the adoption of policies that support women's equality (e.g., O'Regan 2000; Schwindt-Bayer and Mishler 2005; Bratton and Ray 2002; Kittilson 2008). In parliamentary systems, in which legislation generally originates in the political executive, it is reasonable to expect that the number of women in cabinet might be a more relevant factor in determining pro-equality policy outcomes than the presence of women legislators. In a study of eighteen advanced industrial parliamentary democracies, Atchison and Down (2009) found a positive correlation between the proportion of women cabinet ministers and the generosity of a country's maternity and parental leave provisions. In a nineteen-country study, Atchison (2015) again found a positive relationship between the proportion of cabinet seats held by women and the extent to which a country's policy landscape supports women's labour force participation, measured using an index that captures issues relating to family leave, working time, and childcare. These studies suggest there is indeed a connection between the presence of women and policy outcomes that address women's interests, but they tend to focus on static outputs, often at a single moment in time. As a result, they are unable to explain how women's presence translates into policy impact.

INSTITUTIONAL CONSTRAINTS

Key to understanding how women's presence might translate into impact is accounting for the institutional context in which legislators operate. In the Canadian context, parliamentary institutions are structured in a way that works against the capacity of individual MPs to act independently or to influence policymaking, thus limiting the extent to which we might reasonably expect women parliamentarians to represent women in parliamentary speech or for their presence to shape policy outcomes. The standard view of Canadian politics suggests that the opportunities for individual MPs to influence government legislation or policy initiatives are limited at best. Strong party discipline constrains MPs' capacity for independent action while executive dominance of the legislative policy agenda limits opportunities for individual MPs to influence policy. There are thus reasons to doubt the extent to which women's presence might translate into political impact in Canada. Opportunities for gender differences in preferences to be expressed in parliamentary activity and for those differences to have an impact on policy action are more constrained in the Canadian political system than in contexts in which individual legislators have greater independence from party control or greater opportunity to influence legislative policymaking.

Canadian MPs have limited capacity for independent action due to the constraints placed on their behavior by strong norms of party discipline (Franks 1987; Docherty 1997; Malloy 2003). Political parties are the "basic unit of organization" around which Canadian parliamentary debates and activity are structured (Franks 1987, 101). MPs operate within unified partisan blocs directed by the party leader rather than as independent actors. Party discipline in the Canadian context is strong even when compared with other Westminster parliamentary systems, with MPs rarely voting against their party on government legislation and defeats of government bills even rarer, especially within the past century (Franks 1987; Malloy 2003; Godbout 2020). Strong party discipline is typically understood to be a consequence of the institutional structure of Westminster parliaments, the central operating principle of which is that the government must maintain the confidence of a majority of members in the legislature in order to remain the government. To maintain confidence and ensure that its core program is approved by a majority of MPs, the government must be able to rely, at a minimum, on the support of the members of its party's caucus. MPs can express their opposition to their party's position behind closed doors in caucus meetings, but there is an expectation that the party will vote together, providing the government with the stability it needs to govern without the constant threat of defeat (Franks 1987; Docherty 1997; Marland 2020). Strong party discipline is thus not a strict requirement of responsible government, but it makes its operation run more smoothly (Smith 2003).

Related to these constraints on independent behaviour is the limited opportunity for individual MPs to influence the development and implementation of policy that results from a strong executive. As Docherty (1997, 95–6) notes, "given the executive-centered nature of Canada's parliamentary system, opportunities for significant influence in policy are limited to those individuals in or close to the political executive. Government policy and legislation are initiated in cabinet or cabinet committees." A central feature of responsible government is that "the prime minister and cabinet have the responsibility of governing, not the individual members of parliament or the opposition parties" (Franks 1987, 212). Only ministers of the Crown are permitted to "introduce legislation that raises or spends public money" (Docherty 2014, 161). While private members can introduce bills that do not have fiscal implications, these bills are passed into law much less frequently than is government legislation (Blidook 2010). Instead, the policy agenda is established by the government. Policy proposals are raised, discussed, and debated around the cabinet table – although even cabinet's influence has been called into question in recent years as power has been increasingly concentrated in the office of the prime minister, with limited opportunity for ministerial influence over policy decision making (Savoie 1999; for a counterargument see Brodie 2018). Legislation is presented to parliament for approval as a final legitimating step rather than as an opportunity for meaningful consideration or input. The scope of opportunity for individual MPs to influence policy outcomes independent of partisan agendas is thus quite narrow.

There are nonetheless opportunities, albeit limited, for MPs to influence government policymaking. Committees are important spaces for policy initiation, deliberation, and influence (Franks 1987), although their ability to influence policy outcomes is "highly dependent on the willingness of the government to respond to committee reports" (Docherty 1997, 97). Private members' business is often seen as a tool through which parliamentarians can shift government policymaking even if bills or motions are not passed (Franks 1987; Docherty 1997). Similarly, question period can be used by opposition members to bring attention to issues or to generate pressure to influence government agendas and actions (Franks 1987). Somewhat less visibly, backbenchers and opposition members can lobby their caucus colleagues or cabinet ministers to support or oppose government initiatives (Franks 1987). Opportunities for MPs to influence policy thus do exist, but they are generally considered to be minor relative to the overall policy power and direction set by the executive.

More recent scholarship from Canada and other Westminster systems has begun to examine the ways in which MPs leverage these often overlooked aspects of parliamentary proceedings to influence policymaking in executive-dominated parliaments and to exercise greater independence and influence than is typically assumed. In Canada, MPs have been found to use question period to represent constituency concerns (Soroka et al. 2009) and leverage private members' business to influence government policymaking (Blidook 2010, 2012). In the United Kingdom, there is evidence to suggest that MPs exert indirect influence over government decision making, particularly at the earlier stages of the policy process (Russell and Cowley 2016; Russell et at. 2016; Russell et al. 2017). One important mechanism through which parliamentarians influence policymaking is through anticipated reactions (Russell and Cowley 2016). Anticipating resistance, the executive avoids introducing legislation it knows will be rejected by the backbench or an upper house, or makes pre-emptive changes to draft legislation behind the scenes. Since governments must secure the votes of backbenchers to ensure that legislation passes, they "are willing to do deals with their backbenchers" to minimize dissent (Russell and Cowley 2016, 125). MPs can thus influence policy direction and decision making through caucus discussions and behind-the-scenes lobbying, but these impacts are difficult for researchers to observe. Despite these limited opportunities for MP influence and increased scholarly attention to them, the predominant view remains that parliament and parliamentarians are largely powerless.

UNDERSTANDING THE IMPACT OF ELECTED WOMEN IN CANADA

Despite sustained attention to the relationship between women's presence and substantive representation among gender and politics scholars over the past several decades, we still know very little about the impact that elected women have in Canadian politics. Do they act as substantive representatives of women, advocating for women's interests and concerns in parliamentary debate? Does the presence of a more diverse group of legislators change the issues that get discussed and debated? Do elected women push for and achieve policy changes that promote women's equality? These are important questions – not only for research on gender and politics but also for our understanding of the operations of parliamentary institutions, patterns of representation, and the role of MPs in Canada and in other Westminster systems. But, for conceptual and methodological reasons, as well as for reasons of focus and priority in the study of Canadian parliamentary politics, they are stubbornly difficult to answer.

Conceptually, addressing the question of whether elected women in Canada act as substantive representatives of women is challenging because there is a lack of consensus in the gender and politics literature about what the concept of substantive representation itself encompasses. The idea of acting for women can entail any number of activities – sharing policy priorities, speaking out in debate, introducing or supporting legislation, or achieving policy outcomes. Perhaps more important, there is contention as to what the content and direction of those activities must look like to constitute the substantive representation of women. Must these activities be focused on certain "women's issues," feminist priorities, or the promotion of gender equality (e.g., Tremblay 1998; Swers 2005; Kittilson 2008)? If so, which issues are relevant and what initiatives meet the requirement of being equality-promoting? What about anti-feminist or anti-equality claims (Celis and Childs 2012)? An alternative approach focuses on representative claims about women and allows the specific issue content of substantive representation to emerge through the process of making those claims (Celis et al. 2014; Erzeel 2012). This conceptual disagreement means that it is difficult for researchers to pin down precisely what they should be looking for when making empirical assessments about legislators' impact on the substantive representation of women.

Responding to this conceptual challenge, this book proposes a disaggregation of the concept of the substantive representation of women in order to provide additional clarity and to increase analytical leverage. This new framework builds on the insight advanced by Franceschet and Piscopo (2008) that we must distinguish between two distinct aspects of the substantive representation of women: (1) those that are process-oriented, such as bill introduction, advocacy, or raising new issues for debate, and (2) those that are outcome-oriented, such as policy changes and outputs. This process/outcome distinction focuses on the *form* that substantive representation takes, but we must also consider the *content* and direction of those activities. Thinking about the form of substantive representation, I distinguish between parliamentary speech, policy advocacy, and policy outcomes. Thinking about the content and direction of those activities and outcomes, I distinguish between pro-equality and more traditionally oriented issues and advocacy. This builds on the approach to substantive representation that focuses on representative claims and makes space for greater diversity in terms of which women and whose interests count as manifestations of the representation of women and who the representatives of women might be. Within this conception, pro-equality and more traditionally oriented claims are both included as part of the broad concept of the substantive representation of women. In addition to this conceptual disaggregation, I also expand the scope of what counts as substantive representation of women to more explicitly include actions that defend or push back against government policy initiatives, in addition to actions that advance new policy proposals – a dimension that has often been overlooked by scholars of women's political representation.

Related to the conceptual challenge is a methodological one. If there is a lack of conceptual clarity in terms of what we should be looking for to make empirical assessments about the impact of elected women, then the details of how to measure and analyze that concept will also be challenging. Which activities, assessed at what scale, should be used as indicators of impact? In the Canadian context, a focus on actions such as voting records or bill introduction are not especially instructive given the realities of party cohesion and executive dominance of the legislative process in our Westminster parliamentary system. Patterns of parliamentary debate emerge as a promising indicator of at least part of the broader concept of substantive representation because they are less constrained by party discipline. As Proksch and Slapin (2015) note, parliamentary speech-making constitutes a lower-stakes venue through which MPs can register disagreement with their party, even in institutional contexts that are characterized by strong partisan control over individual MPs. Legislative debates serve an important public communication function, inform decision making, and have the potential to influence policy outcomes (Bäck et al 2021). MPs' ability to speak in parliament may be limited by party leaders and whips (Cochrane et al. 2021). But MPs nonetheless enjoy some degree of autonomy when it comes to whether and how they speak on certain issues in the House and "can still bring nuances to these themes in the form of context or examples, without deviating from the party line" (Tremblay 1998, 442). But to be comprehensive, an analysis of the content of parliamentary debate would need to include all aspects of debate by all parliamentarians. The scale of such an analysis has the potential be prohibitively immense.

To analyze the millions of parliamentary speeches that would need to be examined to address comprehensively the question of whether elected women have an impact on parliamentary debate, this book leverages recent methodological advancements and data availability. Computational text analysis and machine learning tools, together with a massive dataset of digitized parliamentary debate transcripts (Beelen et al. 2017), make it possible to analyze the content of parliamentary speeches and the substantive representation of women therein on a previously unimaginable scale. I use these tools to analyze the content of nearly fifty years of parliamentary debate. But this large-scale analysis only tells part of the story about women's substantive representation, which, as noted above, must be understood to include advocacy and outcomes in addition to patterns of speech and debate. The large-scale analysis, in addition to establishing which MPs represent women and patterns of issue attention in parliamentary debate over time, also facilitates the identification of cases for closer qualitative investigation. This book therefore pairs the large-scale analysis of parliamentary debate with qualitative analysis of specific instances of legislative policymaking. These qualitative case studies generate a more granular understanding of how the substantive representation of women through advocacy and policymaking occurs. Used together, these two methodological approaches make it possible to understand all dimensions of the substantive representation of women more holistically.

Finally, it is difficult to assess the impact of elected women in Canada because there is a tendency in Canadian political science to overlook the potential role and influence of individual MPs. The strength of party discipline and executive dominance of the legislative process discussed above mean that legislator independence and opportunity for influence are typically seen as relatively minor features of Canadian parliamentary politics. Party affiliation tends to be treated as the key explanatory variable that accounts for patterns of legislator behaviour. Other aspects of an MP's identity, such as gender, tend to be overlooked or treated as less relevant in terms of what they bring to their parliamentary role. This tendency is beginning to change as research has begun to probe the ways in which individual MPs represent constituents and attempt to shape policy beyond the confines of partisan constraints (Blidook 2010, 2012; Russell and Cowley 2016;

Russell et al. 2017). But this renewed focus on parliamentary institutions and behaviour has not yet included an exploration of the role and impact of women MPs in Canada.

Building on this renewed focus, this book takes up the empirical question of whether and how women MPs navigate institutional contexts and constraints to exert influence and represent women. It focuses on the opportunities – however minor – that exist for women MPs in Canada to have an impact on politics. These opportunities for influence have tended to be seen as marginal to the legislative policymaking process in Westminster systems. But this project takes seriously the possibility that even within an institutional context in which cabinets set policy direction and political parties constrain MP behaviour, there are still opportunities for MPs to act as representatives of something other than their political party and to have an impact on the legislative policymaking process. By focusing on the ways in which women MPs navigate an institution in which they remain numerically underrepresented to influence politics, we can better understand how parliamentary composition matters for the issues that are addressed and the decisions that are made by one of our core democratic institutions. This focus also helps build a clearer understanding of how Canadian parliamentary institutions operate and the opportunities for legislator influence within them.

OVERVIEW OF THE ARGUMENT

This book advances three related arguments, grounded in a new typology of the substantive representation of women. In chapter 1, I present the theoretical framework that provides the foundation for the empirical analysis that follows. Building upon this framework, I argue first that women's presence in the House of Commons changes the content of parliamentary debate. Focusing on the substantive representation of women as parliamentary speech and leveraging a massive dataset of digitized parliamentary debate transcripts and computational text analysis tools, I show in chapter 2 that women MPs are dramatically more likely than are their male colleagues to make parliamentary speeches about women, regardless of partisan stripe. When it comes to this first dimension of the substantive representation of women, gender actually matters more than party in determining legislator behaviour – an unexpected pattern given the constraints created by the Canadian parliamentary context. Chapter 3 digs deeper into the issue content of parliamentary speeches about women using machine learning techniques and shows that parliamentary speeches about women tend to focus almost entirely on issues relating to women's equality and autonomy, reinforcing feminist views of the content of the substantive representation of women.

In the second part of the book, I argue that periods of sharp increases in attention to women's equality issues in parliamentary debate are a response to government initiatives that threaten to roll back previous equality gains. These spikes in attention are not the result of dramatic shifts in parliamentary composition but, instead, reflect women parliamentarians' efforts to push back against hostile policy initiatives through a range of advocacy strategies. Chapter 4 identifies the factors that contributed to spikes in the number of speeches about women in two parliaments and identifies two policy cases for further investigation – the Mulroney government's attempt to recriminalize abortion in the 34th Parliament and the Harper government's attempt to cut funding and weaken the mandate of Status of Women Canada in the 39th Parliament. Case studies in chapters 5 and 6 examine whether and how women MPs acted as substantive representatives of women in these two parliaments and show that women led the charge in resisting government initiatives that undermined women's equality. Building upon these case studies, I argue finally that, in these moments of resistance, the strategies MPs deployed to advocate for women – and their chances of achieving their desired outcomes – can be explained by the institutional roles they occupy and the political context in which they operate.

Drawing these threads together, I argue that the presence of women in parliament does indeed matter for the substantive representation of women's interests, but it matters in different ways than we might expect. Women's presence is important not only for driving progress towards equality – it is an important factor in guarding against regress. Despite operating within an institutional context in which it is challenging for individual MPs to act independently and influence policy, elected women nonetheless manage to navigate this context in order to have an impact on Canadian politics, particularly during moments of threat. This suggests that there may be more scope for individual MP behaviour and impact than is typically assumed, and the presence of more diverse legislators has the potential to shift and have an impact on the issues that get discussed in parliament and the policy decisions that get made.

1

Explaining the Impact of Elected Women

Does the presence of elected women have an impact on parliamentary debate and policymaking in Canada? To be able to answer the central question motivating this study, we need clear conceptual parameters around what is meant by "impact." As Celis and Childs (2020, 67) rightly point out, the "question as to 'what difference women make' can often hide a great deal more than it reveals." The potential for this question to obfuscate comes down at least in part to a lack of clarity around what is meant by "making a difference." What kind of difference or impact are we actually looking for? And how would we know if we found evidence of it? Additionally, who are the women who might be engaged in making a difference, and what mechanisms might they leverage to do so?

In this chapter, I outline a theoretical framework that aims to make it easier to answer the question of whether the presence of women has an impact on politics. This framework conceives of impact in terms of the substantive representation of women, clarifies what is meant by this concept, and outlines a process through which substantive representation occurs in the Canadian parliamentary context. Grounded in Pitkin's (1967) conception of political representation, it distinguishes between descriptive representation (who a representative is) and substantive representation (what a representative does) and considers whether and under what conditions these dimensions might be linked. The framework conceives of elected women's potential impact in terms of improved substantive representation of women's interests and proposes additional specificity in terms of what that substantive representation consists of.

The tendency among gender and politics scholars to disaggregate concept of political representation as I propose to do has come under recent scrutiny. Celis and Childs (2020, 73) argue that a focus on *either* descriptive *or* substantive representation alone leads to an incomplete understanding of the quality of women's political representation. The disaggregated conceptual framework presented in this chapter, however, facilitates – indeed, I contend is necessary for the possibility of – effective empirical analysis of whether, when, and how representation occurs. It focuses on and disaggregates substantive representation in order to clarify how impact might be measured. But it also recognizes that each dimension of substantive representation operates in relation to the others. The framework also foregrounds the role elected women (i.e., descriptive representatives) might play in the substantive representation of women's interests and presents each dimension of the substantive representation of women as part of a larger representational whole.

A NEW TYPOLOGY OF THE SUBSTANTIVE REPRESENTATION OF WOMEN

To facilitate empirical analysis and clarify several key distinctions about the ways in which the substantive representation of women can be realized in practice, I propose several refinements to the foundational concept of the substantive representation of women. Recall from the introduction that substantive representation refers to the actions a representative takes on behalf of those they represent – in this case, actions on behalf of women as a group. However, the details of what "acting for women" consists of is the source of debate within the literature on women's representation – both in terms of what actions are covered by "acting for" and in terms of what it means for those actions to be "for women." The substantive representation of women is understood to include a range of activities – from legislative speeches, to voting, to bill introduction, to policy outputs – depending on the study. There is also disagreement over how to determine whether an action is in fact "for women" or aligned with women's interests. Are we concerned with actions that address certain women's policy issues, promote gender equality, or align with women's movement objectives? On what basis can it be claimed that these actions are in fact reflective of women's interests – particularly given the internal diversity of women as a group?

The disaggregated typology of the substantive representation presented below aims to bring order to some of this confusion. It allows for a more specific understanding of what representatives actually do when they act for women, the likelihood of each of those actions leading to concrete impacts, and the aims towards which these actions are oriented. I identify two dimensions of the substantive representation of women that must be disentangled in order to facilitate a clearer understanding of what the substantive representation of women is and how it occurs: (1) the type of action that representatives take on behalf of women – that is, the form or mechanism through which representatives act for women; and (2) the content of that representation or the direction or aims towards which those actions are oriented. These refinements account for the fact that the substantive representation of women can occur through a variety of activities and interventions (e.g., parliamentary speech in official debates, policy advocacy, and the achievement of policy outcomes). It also recognizes that each of these actions might be oriented not only in terms of pro-equality feminist aims but also in non-feminist terms, oriented around the preservation of traditional values and gender roles. The disaggregated typology is summarized in figure 1.1. The details of the typology and the literature they build on are outlined below.

Representational Forms

Building on Franceschet and Piscopo's (2008) crucial distinction between process- and outcome-oriented forms of substantive representation, I identify three forms the substantive representation of women might take: (1) speaking for women in parliamentary debate, (2) advocating for women in the policymaking process, and (3) winning for women through the achievement of policy outcomes. As I explain below, speaking, advocating, and winning for women are distinct but related forms of substantive representation.

The first representational form in the disaggregated typology, speaking for women in parliamentary debate, is a process-oriented instance of substantive representation. Parliamentary speeches are an instance of position-taking, political communication, and agenda-setting that allows parliamentarians to signal their own policy priorities and attempt to influence government agendas. The independent ability of parliamentary speeches to change policy outcomes is limited – speeches alone are unlikely to lead to concrete policy

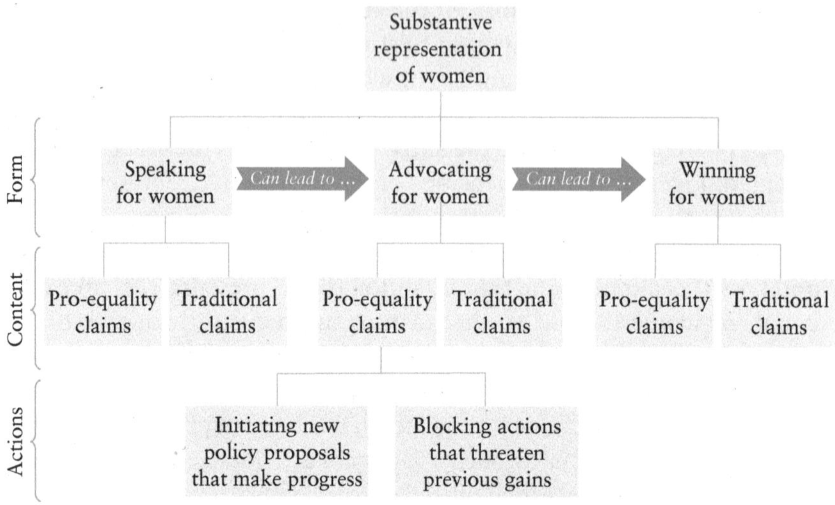

Figure 1.1 Disaggregated typology of the substantive representation of women.

results. Parliamentary speechmaking is nonetheless an important part of the process of substantive representation.

Speaking for women in parliamentary debate ensures that women's perspectives are heard as part of the legislative process. Parliamentary speech is often dismissed as "cheap talk with limited effects on decision-making" (Proksch and Slapin 2015, 18), but speech is important for political representation. Proksch and Slapin argue that parliamentary speech enables MPs to "communicate policy positions to other members within their own party, to members of other parties, and, most important, to their voters" (1). By signalling their positions on issues publicly and officially in a venue covered by media, "MPs demonstrate that they listen and are responsive" to the citizens they represent (3). Parliamentary speech is thus an important means through which elected officials signal their policy positions and priorities in a public forum.

Parliamentary speech-making is also connected to the policymaking process. Opposition MPs use their speeches to hold governments to account, to critique, and to propose alternatives. Speech also provides a venue through which backbench MPs can register their disagreement with an official government position without going so far as to vote against their party. In parliamentary systems that are characterized by strong partisan control over MPs' voting, speech can thus be a better indicator of MPs' policy positions and preferences than roll-call voting. Moreover, it can signal the issues that MPs might advocate for outside the legislative chamber in venues that are less publicly visible but that are nonetheless important sites of policy debate – for example, in caucus or cabinet deliberations and in communications with extra-parliamentary actors.

In addition to serving as an important tool for public communication and position-taking that signals an MP's policy positions and priorities, parliamentary speech also matters insofar as it tries to shift public and parliamentary attention. Patterns of parliamentary speech serve an important agenda-setting role through which MPs attempt to put issues on the political agenda and create policy windows or opportunities for action (see, for example, Howlett 1998). This understanding of the role of parliamentary speech is grounded in work on agenda-setting that emphasizes the importance of issue attention as a necessary precursor to policy action. Insofar as issue attention is finite, parliamentary attention to an issue (i.e., bringing up an issue in parliamentary debate) signals a preference for policy action on that issue (Baumgartner and Jones 2002; Kingdon 1995). Parliamentary debate thus serves a potential agenda-setting function in the policy process. By raising issues on the official record of House of Commons debate, MPs can direct government attention to issues that require action or can highlight public concerns with or objections to government action.

An examination of patterns of parliamentary speech therefore offers insight into two dimensions of parliamentary politics. First, speech is an important act of democratic representation through which constituent views and concerns are formally heard and MPs' policy positions are publicly signalled. Second, it is a tool through which MPs attempt to influence policy and government agendas. It is thus a procedurally important aspect of representation that increases the democratic legitimacy of political processes by providing a space in which diverse views and opinions are heard even if they are not acted upon. Parliamentary speech may, to a certain extent, be performative, but it is nonetheless connected to the process of policymaking and change.

The second representational form, advocating for women in policymaking, is also a process-oriented instance of substantive representation. Policy advocacy includes a range of actions through which parliamentarians might attempt to influence policymaking, from the introduction of or support for motions or bills in the House of Commons, to advocacy behind the scenes in caucus deliberations, to collaboration with extra-parliamentary women's organizations. Policy advocacy requires somewhat more effort or initiative from the representative than simply speaking about women in parliamentary debate. Activities that fall under this category are typically more concrete and directly oriented towards influencing policy outcomes.

Focusing on advocacy in addition to speech provides a more complete picture of how the process of the substantive representation of women occurs. Speaking in parliamentary debate is a form of advocacy insofar as parliamentarians use their time in debate to draw attention to an issue through oral questions or motions. But advocating for women requires more than just speaking in parliamentary debate. Not only is speech important beyond its advocacy function, it also does not exhaust the full range of advocacy tools an MP might use. As noted above, advocating for women includes a range of activities – introducing bills and motions, lobbying for women in caucus or cabinet discussions, and working with women's groups outside parliament to bring their perspectives onto the parliamentary agenda. The strategies MPs use to advocate for women give clues about where the opportunities to influence policymaking might exist within a particular institutional context.

Looking at advocacy and speech together – and at the relationship between the two – is particularly useful. If a parliamentarian is frequently making speeches about women in parliamentary debate, this may be a signal that they are advocating for women through other means. Their patterns of parliamentary speechmaking are likely to reflect advocacy for women in other venues, like caucus deliberations or in discussions with extra-parliamentary actors. Looking to parliamentary speech as a potential indicator of advocacy is helpful given that some of the strategies MPs use to advocate for women will be more difficult to observe than others. For example, asking questions, introducing motions, or proposing legislation are forms of advocacy that are part of the formal parliamentary record and thus readily observable. Advocating for women in caucus or cabinet deliberations, however, is more difficult to observe. This advocacy is nonetheless an important strategy that MPs might use to act for women – especially in the Canadian and other Westminster parliaments, where public defection from the official party line is discouraged. There is evidence to suggest that caucus meetings are an important venue in which MPs can raise concerns (Marland 2020), and behind-the-scenes advocacy efforts are an important strategy through which MPs can influence policymaking (Russell and Cowley 2016). An examination of MPs' efforts to advocate for women using a range of strategies facilitates the development of a clearer understanding of how speech and policy change might be connected.

The third representational form in the typology, winning for women through the achievement of policy change, is an outcome-oriented instance of substantive representation. Policy wins for women are achieved when policy outputs or decisions reflect women's interests. When women are substantively represented in policy decisions, this is a concrete political output that reflects the interests and political preferences of women as a group. Representation through policy outcomes therefore constitutes a tangible manifestation of the inclusion of women's interests and concerns in policy decision making. Assessing the extent to which these outputs are achieved – separate from but in relation to whether individual actors pushed for them – is thus worthwhile insofar as it allows us to determine whether and to what extent the process-oriented forms of substantive representation were successful.

Whereas speaking or advocating for women can be undertaken by individual legislators, winning for women is an end state that results from multiple inputs in a complex policymaking process. Speaking and advocating for women can contribute to winning for women, but speech and advocacy may also fail to yield policy results since these are not the only factors that contribute to outcomes. Although the representation of women in parliamentary speechmaking and advocacy has the potential to precipitate policy action related to women's issues, it does not, independent of other factors, lead to these concrete changes. On its own, process-oriented representation through parliamentary speech and advocacy does not bring about outcome-oriented representation through policy change, but it has the potential to be a contributing factor.

Policy outcomes that promote women's equality are achieved as the result of a broad set of factors much larger than the efforts or interventions of any one political representative or policy actor. Studies of the process by which policy action to promote women's equality is implemented have tended to focus on the macro-level conditions that facilitate or constrain the achievement of feminist policy goals more than on the interventions of individual political actors (e.g., Bashevkin 1998; Mazur 2002; Collier 2006). The process through which these policy outcomes are achieved is complex and multi-causal, but the literature tends to agree that "the interplay between institutional factors, left-wing governments, and the role of women and women's movements and organizations" are key factors that contribute to the achievement of feminist policies (Mazur 2002, 39). At the level of individual actors, strategic partnerships between women's movement activists, women in public office, and feminist bureaucrats may also be important for the successful implementation of policy action to promote women's equality (see Vargas and Wieringa 1998; Holli 2008). Close examination of the specific role of parliamentarians in bringing about women's equality policy changes, however, has tended to attract less attention (see Childs and Withey 2006 for an exception).

The three forms of the substantive representation of women identified in the disaggregated typology – parliamentary speech, advocacy, and policy outputs – are potentially linked insofar as the issues raised in parliament can reflect or precede policy advocacy, and speech and advocacy can contribute to policy outputs. But any such connection is far from assured. By examining these three aspects of the substantive representation as distinct but interrelated manifestations of the same concept we can identify the connections and relationship between parliamentary speech, policy advocacy, and policy change. The analysis in this study focuses on the ways in which individual actors engage in speech and advocacy for women and the ways in which these actions contribute to policy outcomes. This focus on process- and outcome-oriented forms of substantive representation provides a clearer indication of the tangible impacts the presence of elected women might have for the representation of women's interests.

Representational Content

Distinguishing the different forms the substantive representation of women can take is an important part of establishing a clearer understanding of the concept. In addition to form, we must also consider the issue content of that representation. What does it mean, in concrete policy terms, to act for or defend the interests of women in speech, policy advocacy, or outcomes? As noted in the introduction, the answer to this question is contested within the literature.

On one side is an approach that conceives of the representation of women's interests in terms of a predetermined set of policy issues. Studies approach the question of which issues "count" as women's issues using a range of strategies. Some define the parameters of so-called women's issues in terms of issues that distinctively affect women or that fall under women's traditional areas of interest or responsibility given the gendered division of labour and women's role as caregivers (e.g., Thomas 1994; Carroll 1994; Osborn and Mendez 2010). This typically includes policy issues relating to women's health, children, families, and education. Another approach conceives of women's issues in terms of policies that recognize and address women's social inequality or gender-based discrimination and that align with feminist or women's movement policy aims (e.g., Wängnerud 2000; Bratton 2002; Mazur 2002; Beckwith and Cowell-Meyers 2007; Kittilson 2008). This approach tends to include issues such as pay equity, employment discrimination, childcare, reproductive rights, family law, political equality, and so on. Some studies incorporate multiple approaches to define what counts as a women's issue – for example, focusing both on issues that fall under women's traditional areas of interest and on issues that address gender-based inequality (e.g. Tremblay 1998; Swers 2002).

Despite the variation in terms of how to set the boundaries of what counts as a women's issue, consistent across approaches is a recognition that women occupy a social position that is distinct from and unequal to that occupied by men. The literature tends to agree on the policy areas that are central to the advancement of women's equality. These include policies relating to women's constitutional equality and equal rights, political representation, employment equality, maternity and parental leave, childcare, family law, violence against women, and reproductive rights (see Bashevkin 1998; Mazur 2002; Htun and Weldon 2018). Within this approach, the substantive representation of women is broadly equated with the representation of feminist concerns.

These approaches that pre-define what counts as a women's issue, however, draw criticism for misconceiving of women as an undifferentiated group with uniform interests and policy priorities (e.g., Trimble 2006; Smooth 2011; Schwindt-Bayer and Taylor-Robison 2011; Celis et al. 2014). Women do not exist as an undifferentiated social category – gender is intersected by other social identities such as race, class, religion, sexual and gender identity, and so on. Approaches to the substantive representation of women that predefine the issue content of women's interests risk essentializing women as a homogenous group in which the interests of privileged white, middle-class, heterosexual women are foregrounded and the interests and concerns of marginalized women are overlooked. Smooth (2011, 437) argues for an intersectional approach that conceives of "women's interests as complex, fluid, and varied," while still making space for the possibility that shared interests might exist and that women's group mobilization remains possible.

An alternate approach that takes up this imperative to account for the diversity of women conceives of the representation of women in more iterative, inductive terms. Rather than defining the specific policy content of what constitutes women's interests a priori, this approach conceives of the substantive representation of women in terms of representative claims made by legislators about women (e.g. Celis 2006; Celis and Childs 2012; Erzeel 2012; Celis et al. 2014). In this view, the content of women's interests is constructed through the act of making claims about women. This approach recognizes disagreement and debate "over what constitutes 'women's issues' and 'women's interests'" (Celis and Childs 2012, 216) and makes space for greater diversity in terms of which women and whose interests count as manifestations of the representation of women and who the representatives of women might be. This claims-making approach is agnostic on the question of who the substantive representatives of women are and what the policy content of women's interests consists of. By adopting this agnostic stance, this approach is better equipped to account for the diversity of perspectives, needs, and preferences held by women. In this view, the substantive representation of women can thus include a range of perspectives and claims about issues that affect women and policy interventions that are in women's interests. Studies that apply a claims-making approach have nonetheless found that the policy issues raised in the context of claims about women tend to overlap with the policy issues identified as important for the promotion of women's equality. For example, Celis (2006) and Erzeel (2012) both find that representational claims about women in the Belgian parliament tend to focus on women's substantive social equality and autonomy, women's employment, women's political representation, reproduction, and balancing the demands of work and family.

In this study I adopt the claims-making approach in order to make space for the diversity of women's perspectives that may be articulated and defended by political actors. This approach treats the specific issue content of representative claims about women as a question for empirical investigation. Within each of the three forms of the substantive representation of women – speaking, advocating, and winning for women – we can therefore think of the content of the substantive representation of women as being oriented in two broad directions: (1) focusing on issues that would promote women's social and economic equality, consistent with feminist aims, and (2) focusing on gendered concerns and women's distinctive needs but in a non-feminist direction concerned with the promotion or preservation of traditional values and gender roles. This traditional view of gender roles might include an emphasis on natural differences between men and women, women's role in the private sphere, and mothering and caring roles (see Celis and Childs 2018).

The inclusion of non-feminist perspectives within this conception of the substantive representation of women might give some readers pause. There is a tendency to think of the substantive representation of women in terms of feminist representation, oriented towards increasing women's equality. One could reasonably argue that non-feminist initiatives or initiatives that would limit women's rights should not be considered an instance of the substantive representation of women. And while such initiatives certainly would not count as instances of pro-equality feminist substantive representation, the ideological diversity among women requires that the substantive representation of women be conceived of in broader terms (Celis and Childs 2012). To the extent that there are women in the population who hold non-feminist views and perspectives, the responsive representation of women would require that these perspectives be brought forward by representatives in political debate. Representation must be responsive to and inclusive of the full diversity of perspectives of women in the population – even those that do not align with feminist aims (Celis and Childs 2018). Failure to account for these perspectives within the concept of the substantive representation of women will lead to "both a blind spot and a bias in our empirical research" (Celis and Childs 2012, 214).

The inclusion of non-feminist perspectives within the concept of the substantive representation of women, however, does not mean that all representative claims have the same value or are desirable. Representation oriented towards increasing women's equality is qualitatively different from the representation of more regressive perspectives. We of course can and should make normative assessments about the quality of competing representative claims – for example, evaluating the extent to which the representative claims reflect the perspectives of women in the population and align with representatives' actions and other claims (Celis and Childs 2012, 2018) or the extent to which they are responsive to and deemed acceptable by the affected women on whose behalf the claims are made (Celis and Childs 2020). This normative task is important but separate from the question of whether something should be included as an instance of the substantive representation of women for the purpose of empirical analysis.

The framework applied here conceives of women's substantive representation in broad terms, encompassing both pro-equality and more traditional non-feminist perspectives, but allows us to distinguish between – and make normative assessments about – instances of substantive representation in each of those directions. This accounts for the diversity of views among women, both within the population and as political actors, and acknowledges the reality that there is disagreement over the policy content of what counts as women's interests.

The disaggregated typology of the substantive representation of women outlined above allows for greater conceptual clarity and specificity in terms of the actions and orientations the substantive representation of women implies. It provides a structure for being precise about the types of actions and the issue content we are referring to when we discuss the substantive representation of women. But perhaps more important, distinguishing among the different manifestations of the substantive representation of women can increase analytical leverage. The identification of distinct categories – in terms of form and content – within the larger concept can help explain divergent or theoretically unexpected patterns of representative behaviour. For example, empirical research may find that the presence of women does not improve the substantive representation of women under all conditions or that the actors involved in women's substantive representation are not the ones we might expect. But by distinguishing between the substantive representation of women through speech, or advocacy, or policy outcomes, and allowing for the possibility of both feminist and non-feminist perspectives within each of those forms, we are equipped with a conceptual framework that can help us to understand these theoretically unexpected findings more clearly and account for the different factors that facilitate or constrain the realization of each. By disentangling the different dimensions across which the substantive representation of women can occur, the disaggregated typology outlined above can support a clearer understanding of complex patterns of representative behaviour.

CONNECTING PRESENCE AND IMPACT

The Politics of Presence

With the details of what the concept of the substantive representation of women consists of clarified, we can now turn our attention to whether and under what conditions the presence of women in politics will have an impact on women's substantive representation. Although descriptive and substantive representation need not be linked, feminist political science has theorized the importance of women's presence for the substantive representation of women's interests in politics (Phillips 1995; Mansbridge 1999). Theories of the politics of presence posit that women politicians are "best equipped to represent the interests of women" by virtue of a shared lived experience that gives rise to a shared perspective (Wängnerud 2009, 52).

Theories of the politics of presence are grounded in an understanding of gender as a socially and politically relevant group identity. Women exist in the world as members of what Young (2002) calls a structural social group. The fact of existing and being perceived as a woman by others positions women in relation to others in a way that "condition[s] their opportunities and life prospects" (94). The social location that women occupy gives shape to what women's lived experience of the world will look like insofar as membership in the social group "women" "implies predictable status in law, educational possibility, occupation, access to resources, political power, and prestige" (95). Women are of course not a homogenous group and there will be variations in terms of how the various aspects of their positionality will be experienced. But the point is that this lived experience of moving through the world *as a woman* – even as one might be a member of other structural social groups – gives rise to some degree of shared experience.

This shared experience provides the basis for the possibility of identifying shared concerns in need of political representation (Phillips 1995). Phillips argues that increasing the presence of women in politics is a necessary but not sufficient precondition for the effective representation of women's interests. Increasing women's descriptive representation is "one minimal condition for transforming the political agenda" – but this condition does not constitute a guarantee for women's substantive representation (82). Instead, the presence of women in politics increases the chances that women's interests will be well represented – it is "a shot in the dark: far more likely to reach its target than when those shooting are predominantly male, but still open to all kinds of accident" (83). Improved descriptive representation of women can thus help to improve substantive representation, but presence alone is not enough to ensure impact.

Mansbridge (1999) argues that the descriptive characteristics of the representative are particularly important for facilitating substantive representation when there is mutual distrust between historically excluded groups and their representatives, and when the political interests of a group have not yet been fully crystallized into a coherent set of policy demands. Under these conditions, representatives who share ascriptive characteristics with those they represent will be better representatives because they can draw on their own experiences and perspectives to inform their decision making and bring this background to bear in political debate and deliberation (Mansbridge 1999). Shared experience thus provides direction in terms of what the effective substantive representation would consist of. These contexts of uncrystallized interests are particularly relevant for the substantive representation of women, who may have a shared experience of existing in the world as women but who do not necessarily have a clearly delineated and universal set of interests that emerge on the basis of that shared experience. Particularly on issues relating to gender equality, in which institutionalized political representational arrangements that are centred around party or geography are less instructive (Campbell et al. 2010), the presence of women in politics will be especially important.

Competing Representational Obligations

Although there is a strong theoretical basis for expecting that parliamentarians' gender will matter for whether they act as substantive representatives of women, MPs' representational responsibilities are of course much broader and more complex than representation on the basis of gender. As elected representatives, women MPs act on behalf of a range of constituencies. They are representatives of their political parties and of their geographical constituencies in addition to acting as representatives of communities of interest that can be based on many other ascriptive characteristics such as gender, race, class, and so on.

In the Canadian parliamentary system, MPs are elected as representatives of a political party: they run for election under a party banner with the expectation that, if elected, they will act to advance their party's policy platform. Once elected, the requirement for the executive to maintain the confidence of the legislature within the framework of responsible government, alongside the power of party leaders over candidate nomination and career advancement, means that party discipline exerts a strong influence over MP behaviour in the Canadian House of Commons (Franks 1987; Docherty 1997; Kam 2001, 2009). Additionally, the single-member plurality electoral system creates strong representational ties between the representative and her geographical constituency. These partisan and geographical pressures limit the scope for MPs to engage in representation on the basis of interests that are not clearly aligned with partisan policy agendas or that cut across geographical boundaries, including issues of importance to women (Tremblay 2007; Rayment and McCallion 2023).

In the face of these competing representational pressures, the concept of surrogate representation – that is, "representation by a representative with whom one has no electoral relationship" – offers a useful framework for thinking about the link between the descriptive representation and the substantive representation of women (Mansbridge 2003, 522). While "there is no relation of accountability between the representative and the surrogate constituent," surrogate representatives nonetheless feel a sense of responsibility to represent constituents based on shared experiences or perspectives (523). Evidence from elite interview-based studies tends to confirm that women legislators across institutional contexts feel this sense of responsibility to represent women from beyond the boundaries of their geographic constituencies (see Carroll 2002; Tremblay 2003, 2007; Dittmar et al. 2018). In Canada, historical research suggests that even the earliest women MPs felt compelled to act on behalf of women as a group, albeit reluctantly (Bashevkin 1993). Agnes Macphail, the first woman elected to the House of Commons in 1921, did not come to the position as a feminist or with any formal involvement in the women's suffrage movement – she cut her political teeth on farm issues and co-operatives (Stewart and French 1959). Once elected, however, she saw that "few policy concerns raised by Canadian feminists received serious attention" and took it upon herself to "work diligently on family allowance, equal pay, and women's prison issues" (Bashevkin 1993, 12–13). In her memoir, Liberal MP Judy LaMarsh, who served in the Pearson cabinet from 1963 to 1968, articulated a similar reluctance to act "as spokesman and watchdog for women" but was forced to take on the role due to circumstances and the unwillingness of her colleagues to pay attention to women or their policy concerns (LaMarsh 1969, 292–307).

As discussed in the introduction, empirical research has established that elected women are indeed more likely than are elected men to support gender-equality policies (Campbell et al. 2010; Lovenduski and Norris 2003), to address women's interests in legislative debate (Bird 2005; Catalano 2009; Erzeel 2012; Blaxill and Beelen 2016), and to advocate for women through other legislative mechanisms (Childs and Withey 2004). Also, the presence of more elected women is likely to have an impact on policy outcomes (Bratton and Ray 2002; Kittilson 2008; Clayton and Zetterberg 2018). The relationship between the descriptive representation and the substantive representation of women is nonetheless contingent and probabilistic rather than deterministic (Childs and Krook 2006; Mackay 2008; Wängnerud 2009). While there may be good reasons to expect that women representatives are more likely to act for women than are their male colleagues, the presence of women does not translate automatically into improved substantive representation of women's interests. Women's ability and willingness to represent women is conditioned by a range of competing individual and political factors. As Mackay (2008, 127) puts it, "there are no guarantees: shifting identities, differences amongst women, partisan loyalties and institutional factors are all seen to play a part in shaping and constraining their inclination and capacity to 'act for women.'"

How, then, can we account for whether and when the presence of women will have an impact on how politics gets done? On the one hand, there are good reasons to expect that there is a connection between women's presence and impact, that elected women will behave differently from men, and that this will somehow change politics. On the other hand, that connection is conditioned and limited by contextual factors, and the presence of more women is no guarantee that politics will look any different.

To understand whether and how women's presence might translate into impact in practice, we must consider women's *inclination* and *ability* to act on behalf of women. A critical actors framework can help make sense of women's *inclination* to act for women. Feminist institutionalism and a clear understanding of the specific institutional constraints that operate within the Canadian parliamentary context help to explain women's *ability* to act for women and for these actions to have an impact on outcomes in Canada. Each of these considerations is explored in greater detail below. Ultimately, it is the interplay between the two – the agency of individual actors and the institutional structures in which they operate – that determines whether and when women will have an impact.

Critical Actors and the Inclination to Act for Women

Whereas earlier research suggested that the presence of a critical mass of female legislators was necessary for elected women to have an impact on policy action, more recent scholarship has questioned this expectation. The focus on numerical thresholds, these critiques argue, neglects the mechanisms and dynamics through which women might influence policymaking as well as the political and institutional context in which policymaking occurs (Childs and Krook 2006; 2009; Beckwith and Cowell-Meyers 2007). Instead, the presence of women matters for policy action not through the presence of a critical mass of elected women but, rather, through the challenging actions of key representatives known as critical actors, who are inclined and motivated to act for women (Childs and Krook 2009).

The critical actors framework sees policy action that promotes women's interests as potentially resulting from the efforts of a few pivotal individuals. Childs and Krook (2009, 138) define critical actors as "legislators who initiate policy proposals on their own and/or embolden others to take steps to promote policies for women." The defining characteristic of critical actors is their willingness at a relatively low threshold to take action to advance women's issues in policymaking, regardless of how many women are present in the legislature. Their actions on behalf of women may in turn create space for and mobilize others to act for women as well. These actors prioritize the surrogate representation of women above other representational obligations to party or geographical constituents.

Critical actors do not need to be women – indeed, "men may play a crucial role in advancing women's policy concerns" (Childs and Krook 2009, 138). Given the logic of the politics of presence and women's own reported sense of obligation to act for women (e.g., Tremblay 2007; Dittmar et al. 2018), there are nonetheless good reasons to expect that women will be more likely than men to step into this role. Focusing on the efforts and actions of these critical actors rather than on the impacts of women writ large recognizes that not all elected women will be uniformly inclined to act for women. Creating space to account for this variation among women allows for a clearer understanding of the process through which the substantive representation of women occurs.

The above definition of critical actors and the framework for analysis it implies foreground the importance of initiating new policy proposals or initiatives that make active progress towards increased women's equality. Although the introduction of new policy proposals that address women's interests is an important aspect of the substantive representation of women, an exclusive focus on this aspect provides an incomplete understanding of how the substantive representation of women occurs. Critical actors do not operate exclusively under conditions in which policy action pertaining to women moves in a unidirectional trajectory towards progress and increased gender equality. Governments can and do initiate policy proposals that would undermine women's substantive equality interests (Bashevkin 1998). And in some instances – including the cases explored in chapters 5 and 6 – pro-equality women's interests are substantively represented in contexts in which government policy agendas work against previous gains by legislators who push back against these policy efforts.

To account for instances of action under this wider range of political contexts, I refine the critical actors framework to more explicitly include both pro-active and defensive manifestations of the substantive representation of women. I argue that critical actors must be more clearly understood to include not only those who work to initiate new policy proposals that promote women's interests but also those who work to defend against hostile initiatives that would roll back previous gains. These defensive actions are just as important as are actions that make progress for women, but they might be overlooked if our definition of critical actors focuses exclusively on the initiation of new policies. I therefore propose a theoretical refinement that emphasizes the contributions of critical actors who push back against hostile government interventions that threaten women's equality or undermine previous gains. This refinement expands the scope of who we might consider a critical actor and the types of actions in which they engage. It reveals the important efforts of MPs who are willing to step up to defend women's interests when circumstances require it, but who, otherwise, might not be inclined to push for new policy initiatives on behalf of women. The case studies in chapters 5 and 6 show how this expanded definition of critical actors plays out in practice.

Institutions and the Ability to Act for Women

Critical actors do not operate without constraints. Even the efforts of the most committed advocate or defender of women's interests may be stymied by the formal rules and informal norms of the institutional context in which they operate. Those who might be *inclined* to act for women must navigate the pressures and opportunities for action within their institutional context in order to be *able* to do so. The critical actors framework calls on researchers to consider the legislative context in which actors operate and to consider the ways in which these contexts might "affect the behaviour of individual representatives and legislative outcomes" (Childs and Krook 2009, 144). Situating the efforts of critical actors within their institutional context permits a clearer understanding of the mechanisms through which descriptive and substantive representation might be linked.

Feminist institutionalism provides a useful framework for thinking about the way in which institutional context facilitates and constrains critical actors' ability to speak and advocate for women and their chances of success. This approach emphasizes the role played by institutions – understood to include both formal structures and informal norms – in shaping legislative behaviour and outcomes (Mackay et al. 2010; Kenny 2014). Formal institutions, such as the rules of legislative-executive relations or the committee system, will shape the types of activities legislators can engage in to act for women. For example, an institutional context in which the executive has strong legislative agenda-setting powers will have limited opportunities for individual legislators to act for women through the introduction of women's rights bills (Franceschet 2011). Alternatively, the presence of a formal committee tasked with addressing women's issues creates a venue within which the substantive representation of women can occur (Grace 2016). Informal norms, such as those that govern internal party dynamics and collaboration, can also condition behaviour within those formal structures (Francheschet 2011). Identifying and accounting for these formal and informal institutions facilitates a clearer understanding of how women's presence in politics might translate into impact.

Although some women MPs may be inclined to act as surrogate representatives of women, institutional pressures are such that they may not be able to do so. Actors must balance any potential representational obligation to women with competing obligations to act on behalf of their political parties and their geographical constituents. In the Canadian context, the structure of political institutions tends to minimize opportunities and incentives for women to operate as representatives of women.

The single-member plurality electoral system creates strong institutional ties between MPs and the voters in their ridings, resulting in an electoral incentive to act on behalf of geographical constituents. If MPs want to be re-elected, they must act in a way that is consistent with – or, at a minimum, not at odds with – their constituents' interests. Despite this electoral incentive, geographical representation tends to be overshadowed by partisan representation. There is nonetheless evidence to suggest that geographical representation occurs. For example, MPs use question period and private members' business to draw attention to the issues of their geographical constituents in parliament, motivated in large part by re-election considerations (Soroka et al. 2009; Blidook 2012). They also build connections with and give voice to the priorities and concerns of their ridings in Ottawa "in part to enhance their own re-election prospects" (Koop et al. 2018, 204).

In the Canadian context, the primary competing representational obligation MPs face is to their political party. There are powerful incentives and pressures for MPs to act as representatives of their political parties. As discussed in the introduction, party discipline is not a strict institutional requirement of Westminster parliamentary systems, but it results from one of the central tenets of responsible government – namely, that the government must maintain the confidence of the majority of members in order to remain the government (Smith 2003). In Canada, researchers have documented high levels of voting cohesion and rare defections from the party line (Kam 2009; Godbout 2020). Parties have also been shown to exert a high degree of message control in parliamentary and public communications (Marland 2020). These patterns contribute to the widespread view that the majority of MPs simply toe the party line and are little more than "trained seals." The power of party whips and leaders to secure cohesive voting among internally diverse party caucuses (Malloy 2003) is thus significant.

To maintain the confidence of the House and to avoid the constant threat of defeat, the government must, at a minimum, be able to rely on the votes and support of its own caucus. Caucus solidarity and support for a government's program are maintained through the promise of career advancement and sanctions (or the threat thereof) wielded by party leaders and whips. Acts of dissent or defection from the party line can be punished by the party leader through the expulsion of members from caucus or their removal from key committee positions (Docherty 1997). Party whips also wield subtler means of persuasion by awarding or withholding desirable office space, or controlling access to participation in question period or debate (Franks 1987). For government MPs who have already obtained cabinet positions, the norm of cabinet solidarity requires cabinet ministers to support the government's decisions publicly or to resign their positions (Sutherland 1991). The incentive structure of parliamentary careers and the ability of MPs to advance to positions of greater influence are thus organized around the maintenance of caucus solidarity. Those MPs who toe the party line are more likely to be rewarded, while those who defy the party leadership or whip are likely to remain in or be demoted to positions of relative insignificance.

Party whips' control over access to speaking time in parliamentary debate as one of the tools at their disposal for ensuring party cohesion means that MPs' ability to speak for women may be limited by party gatekeepers. While there is no formal mechanism through which political parties control who speaks in debate, in practice, party whips develop lists of which MPs will speak during debate and these are given to the speaker (Cochrane et al. 2021). While the speaker is not required to follow the speaking lists provided by the party whips, it is standard practice to do so. An MP who is inclined to speak for women during parliamentary debate therefore may have limited opportunity to do so if their party's whip is unwilling to place them on the speaking list. MPs who refuse to toe the party line may have a harder time gaining access to speaking time in parliament than do their colleagues who consistently support the party position. The content of parliamentary speech is thus an important indicator of MPs' policy positions and preferences and is less constrained by partisanship than voting, but speech is not entirely unconstrained since access to speaking time is in practice managed by party whips.

Partisan representational obligations will also shape the direction in which an MP engages in the substantive representation of women. Conservative parties are often seen as less sympathetic to feminist women's equality claims than are centrist or left-leaning formations. This is largely because the promotion of feminist interests is generally more compatible with the ideological orientation of leftist political parties (Celis and Childs 2012). Comparative research finds a positive relationship between the strength of left-of-centre parties and the presence of pro-equality policy measures on issues such as parental leave, childcare, and reproductive rights (Kittilson 2008; Htun and Weldon 2018). Through an analysis of twenty-seven cases of feminist policy adoption across thirteen post-industrial democracies, Mazur (2002) concludes that the presence of a left-wing government is one of the key factors that contributes to the adoption of feminist policy. Put another way, conservative governments are less likely to implement feminist policies.

There is evidence of this tension between feminist policy goals and conservative governments in Canada. In an analysis of Canada, the United States, and the United Kingdom, Bashevkin (1998) shows how conservative governments in the 1980s were, with varying degrees of success, active opponents of the pro-equality claims of women's movements (see also Bashevkin 1994). Within Canada, Collier (2006) finds that left-wing parties at the provincial level were more likely to implement feminist policies than were parties of the right – although she does recognize that conservative governments can be compelled to act if a strong and electorally powerful women's movement can exert enough pressure. Similarly, Young (2000) finds that conservative parties at the federal level in Canada were the least responsive to the demands of organized feminism. Opposition and hostility to these demands, however, was more typical of the harder-right populist Reform Party, which emerged in 1993, than of the older more brokerage-oriented Progressive Conservatives. On feminist issues, the Reform Party was characterized by (1) a refusal to recognize women as a politically relevant group or to acknowledge the existence of "women's issues"; (2) opposition to policies such as "state-funded childcare, affirmative action, abortion on demand, and public financing for feminist organizations" that address women's systemic inequality; and (3) a connection to organized anti-feminism, including endorsements by REAL Women of Canada (180–1). This refusal to "engage with women as a political category" or with feminist policy aims has continued under the Conservative Party, which emerged in the early 2000s following the unification of the Reform/Canadian Alliance and Progressive Conservative parties (Thomas 2017, 130).

The disinclination of right-wing parties to implement feminist policies is underpinned by weak support for women's equality claims among conservative party elites. In Canada, for example, one study of the attitudes of parliamentary candidates on a range of issues relating to gender equality – including appropriate gender roles and openness to initiatives to increase women's political representation – finds that members of conservative parties are less supportive of pro-equality policies and positions than are members of left and centrist parties (Erickson 1997). Similarly, Tremblay and Pelletier (2000) find that parliamentary candidates for right-wing parties are less likely to be concerned about gender inequality, are less supportive of interventions designed to increase women's equality, and have lower levels of feminist consciousness.

Partisan variation in support for feminist policy issues suggests that if MPs must act as representatives of their political parties, then party affiliation will shape whether and how they act for women. MPs who are members of parties that reject feminist policy positions or that do not conceive of women as a relevant political category will face more constraints on their ability to act for women should they be inclined to do so. Recall, however, that the content of the substantive representation of women does not need to consist exclusively of support for feminist policy issues. Party affiliation therefore would not prevent an MP from acting for women, but it might shape the direction in which they do so.

The incompatibility between conservatism and feminism, however, may not be as firmly entrenched as is typically assumed. In Germany, Och (2018) finds that the conservative Christian Democratic Union (CDU) adopted feminist policies relating to parental leave and corporate board quotas with the support of CDU members who justified their support for these policies in explicitly feminist terms. Even in this context, the adoption of pro-equality feminist policies by conservative governments is seen as an anomalous occurrence undertaken at least in part to appeal to voters and to increase electoral support. Through an analysis of the attitudes of grassroots Conservative Party members in the United Kingdom, Webb and Childs (2012) find support "for what might be considered liberal feminist positions on questions of gender," with support for feminist policy issues such as pay equity, childcare, and abortion typically stronger among women and younger cohorts than it was among the overall party membership (21). But despite this compatibility on certain issues, Conservative Party members tend not to support interventions to increase women's political representation. Erzeel et al. (2014) find that, although Belgian voters with a high degree of feminist awareness are less likely to support conservative parties, at least one-fifth of voters combine feminist attitudes with support for conservative parties – but this compatibility tends only to hold among those who support centre-right conservative parties. O'Brien (2018) also draws attention to the differences among conservative parties and their respective inclination to substantively represent women. She finds that, although conservative parties as a whole tend to make fewer references to women in their platforms than do other parties, more moderate centre-right Christian Democrats make as many references as do more left-leaning social democratic parties – although these claims tend to focus on women's traditional roles.

It is against this backdrop of competing pressures to represent partisan and geographical constituent interests that MPs who might be inclined to act as surrogate representatives of women must find opportunities to do so. Among MPs who find ways to speak and advocate for women, their ability to influence policy outcomes – the third dimension of substantive representation – will be constrained by the limited opportunities for individual policy influence that exist in the Canadian parliamentary context and in Westminster parliaments more broadly. Executive control over the legislative agenda means that individual MPs have limited sway over the policy issues that are addressed in parliament. Government policy results from cabinet decision making, and the introduction of legislation with fiscal implications is the exclusive purview of cabinet ministers. There are nonetheless opportunities for individual MPs to influence policymaking – for example, through committees (Docherty 1997; Franks 1987), private members' business (Blidook 2012), question period (Soroka et al. 2009), or through caucus and cabinet deliberations (Russell and Cowley 2016) – but these opportunities for policy influence are relatively minor when compared with the control the executive wields over the legislative policymaking process. Those who would act for women are thus constrained in their ability to influence outcomes by the limited scope for individual policy influence within the Westminster parliamentary structure.

SYNTHESIZING THE THEORETICAL EXPECTATIONS

The question of whether and under what conditions the presence of women will translate into action and impact in politics must be considered in relation to the factors outlined above. Women must be inclined to act for women, they must be able to act for women given the constraints created by competing representational obligations, and they must be able to identify opportunities for their actions to influence outcomes within the institutional context in which they operate. What, then, do the prospects for women to influence politics look like in the Canadian parliamentary context? Drawing together the proposed typology of substantive representation, the logic of the politics of presence, and the interplay between critical actors and institutional constraints, I outline below a framework for thinking about how women's presence might translate into impact in Canadian politics. This framework pays particular attention to actions that are oriented around the defence of women's interests in response to government proposals that threaten to undermine them – a dimension of women's substantive representation that is relatively underexplored. This framework considers: (1) whether MPs choose to act for women, (2) the means through which they act for women and the mechanisms they leverage to influence government policymaking, and (3) whether their actions have an impact on outcomes (i.e., whether they win for women).

For an MP to choose to act for women, they must at the outset feel compelled to do so – either through some internally motivated sense of conviction or because in the absence of other champions they feel compelled to fill a void. This initial inclination will then be conditioned by the constraints and incentives created by their own policy preferences and their primary representational obligations – to their political party, their geographical constituents, and women in general. Following the logic of the politics of presence, women MPs will be more likely to be inclined to act for women than will their male colleagues by virtue of their lived experience and perspective as women (Phillips 1995; Mansbridge 1999; Young 2002).

When acting for women takes the form of parliamentary speech (speaking for women) the effect of women's presence should be reasonably straightforward. Because parliamentary speech is a relatively low-stakes venue through which MPs can engage in substantive representation, constraints generated by competing representational obligations should be more limited. However, the reality of Canadian parliamentary politics is such that parties exert significant control over how MPs behave, and political parties are not all equally concerned about or interested in issues relating to women. We can therefore expect the connection between an MP's gender and inclination to prioritize the perspectives of women in parliamentary speeches to hold as long as this inclination is not constrained or overridden by other representational obligations, such as partisanship or constituents' wishes.

Following logically from this expectation, the presence of a growing number of elected women should translate into increased representation of women in parliamentary speeches overall. By speaking about women in parliamentary debate, women MPs signal to their parliamentary colleagues and to the public their interest in and attentiveness to women's concerns. This, in turn, puts women's concerns on parliamentary agendas and creates pressure on other parliamentarians to engage with these issues (the content and direction of which is left as a matter for empirical investigation). As their presence increases, elected women thus have the capacity to shift parliamentary and public attention towards previously ignored issues and perspectives. Patterns of parliamentary speech and policymaking are thus at least potentially connected. Speaking for women in parliamentary debate may be part of a broader attempt to advocate for women or it might reflect parliamentarians' advocacy efforts in other venues.

When it comes to the representation of women through policy advocacy and outcomes, the effect of women's presence will be more complex. For clarity, the focus here and throughout the empirical analysis in the chapters that follow is on pro-equality advocacy and outcomes, even though it is conceptually possible within the framework proposed here to consider advocacy and outcomes for non-feminist women's policy issues. Policy outcomes result from the input and influence of multiple actors within an institutional context rather than from the simple aggregation of legislators' priorities and preferences. A would-be critical actor who is inclined to advocate for women will need to balance this inclination with the policy positions and preferences of the other constituencies to whom they have obligations. For example, a woman MP who is inclined to advocate for women by virtue of her lived experience, and who is a member of a party that opposes a government initiative that is at odds with women's equality interests, would have strong incentives to speak or advocate for women's equality. By contrast, a woman MP who by virtue of her own policy preferences feels compelled to advocate for women, but who is a member of a party whose government has initiated policy action that undermines women's equality interests, and who represents a constituency that supports the government measure, will be more constrained in her ability to act on behalf of women in a feminist direction.

These representational obligations, however, will not on their own determine whether and how an MP acts on behalf of women.

Opportunities for action will be conditioned by an MP's institutional role. The means through which critical actors attempt to influence government action will depend upon their position in parliament. Critical actors will work to advance women's policy interests using the tools available to them based on where they are situated within the institution. Opposition members will seek to influence the government's agenda and decisions by scrutinizing and focusing public attention on the potential harms of government action through oral questions and private members' business (Blidook 2010; Soroka et al. 2009). They will also leverage the support of extra-parliamentary actors, such as women's movement organizations and leaders, to amplify public opposition to proposed government actions (Vargas and Wieringa 1998; Holli 2008). For opposition MPs, their institutional role essentially requires them to speak out against government policy.

For backbench government MPs, the pressure of party discipline is such that they will be more constrained in their ability to speak out publicly or to vote against their party's policy proposals than will opposition MPs, but backbenchers will be less constrained in their ability to speak out against government policy than will cabinet ministers. These constraints, however, do not rule out entirely the possibility that members of a government caucus might defect from the party line either through speech or voting (Kam 2009; Proksch and Slapin 2015). Their willingness to defy the party whip will be conditioned by the strength of their other representational obligations and their willingness to incur the costs of partisan disloyalty (Docherty 1997; Kam 2009). In addition to these more costly (and potentially less effective) acts of resistance to government initiatives that would undermine women's equality, government backbenchers also have the opportunity to articulate their opposition to government initiatives and to convince colleagues to modify or abandon a proposed policy through other, less visible, means – namely, through caucus meeting discussions and through lobbying of caucus colleagues and cabinet ministers (Franks 1987; Erzeel 2015).

For cabinet ministers, the more institutionalized requirement of cabinet solidarity is such that they will be even less likely than government backbenchers to defect publicly from the party position. Cabinet solidarity demands "that all cabinet members must take the same line" when a policy issue has been deemed an instance "of cabinet policy" (Sutherland 1991, 95). If a minister does not agree with a policy of the government and is unwilling to support it, there is an expectation that she must resign from cabinet. By virtue of their institutional position in closer proximity to the locus of decision-making power, however, cabinet ministers may have greater opportunities to influence government action through behind-the-scenes lobbying in cabinet and caucus meetings (Franks 1987). If they are compelled to act for women, cabinet ministers can speak out in defence of women's equality in less publicly visible but potentially more powerful ways.

Differently situated parliamentarians thus have divergent opportunities to influence policy outcomes. On the one hand, opposition MPs are institutionally positioned such that there are virtually no partisan constraints on their ability to oppose government policy initiatives, but their efforts to influence policy are likely to have a limited impact on government decision making. They may speak and advocate in defence of women's interests, but they do so from positions outside and far removed from the centre of decision-making power, able only to influence government policymaking indirectly. On the other hand, cabinet ministers are positioned much closer to the centre of government decision making. But the constraints of the institution are such that they must confine any defence of women's interests that opposes the government's policy direction to discussions and debates behind closed doors. When they advocate for women, cabinet ministers have a much better chance than do opposition MPs of directly influencing government decision making and action, but they may lack the ability to articulate their defence of women's equality publicly. Government backbenchers are also positioned within the government party and constrained in their ability to publicly advocate for women against the government's position (although they have greater latitude for dissent than do cabinet ministers). But they lack the proximity to the centre of government decision making that would allow their efforts to have a direct impact.

The ability of each of these differently situated critical actors to effectively influence government agendas and policy outcomes – that is, their ability to win for women – will be shaped by the political context in which they operate. Critical actors will succeed in blocking or mitigating the impact of government initiatives that would undermine women's interests when the internal or external pressure they exert on cabinet reaches a tipping point for action to which the government must respond. The location of that tipping point will depend upon two key factors, each of which will make the critical actors' chances of success more or less likely: (1) the strength of the government's commitment to the policy initiative and (2) the government's perception that opposition to its proposed policy action poses a political threat. Critical actors in government caucuses will aim to influence the former and will focus on weakening the government's commitment to its proposed initiative by demonstrating internal resistance. Critical actors on the opposition benches will aim to influence the latter and will focus on raising the public profile of the anticipated harms of the government's proposal to roll back previous equality gains, thus making it more politically and electorally challenging for the government to proceed with its intended proposal. Each of these pressures will of course be shaped by a range of other contextual factors beyond the interventions of critical actors, such as the ideological position and campaign commitments of the governing party as well as its share of seats in the House, public perceptions of other government policy initiatives, and government approval ratings across party lines. Nonetheless, the interventions of critical actors have the potential to influence government action. If the government's commitment to the policy can be weakened enough, or the threat of political damage or electoral loss strengthened enough, it might be willing to modify or even reverse its policy proposal.

SUMMARY

The conceptual and theoretical framework outlined in this chapter clarifies what the substantive representation of women consists of, how it occurs, and the role elected women might play in this process. Foundationally, the framework disaggregates the core concept of substantive representation along dimensions of form and content. This conceptual disaggregation is intended to facilitate clearer empirical analysis. In terms of form, the substantive representation of women can consist of parliamentary speech, policy advocacy, and policy outcomes. When it comes to the content of substantive representation, each of these three forms can be oriented either in a pro-equality direction towards feminist aims, or in a more traditional direction towards non-feminist aims. While the framework proposes a conceptual disaggregation, it also recognizes that each component exists in relation to the others, with speech reflecting advocacy and advocacy influencing outcomes.

With the core concept of substantive representation clarified, the chapter also proposes a framework for thinking about how the presence of women might have an impact on politics in the Canadian context. Recognizing that the connection between descriptive representation and substantive representation is contingent and context dependent rather than guaranteed, the framework accounts for both the inclination of critical actors to act for women and their ability to do so given the institutional context in which they operate. Strong party discipline, ideological pressures, and executive dominance of the legislative agenda all have the potential to constrain the extent to which women might speak, advocate, and win for women. There are nonetheless ways in which actors might navigate this context.

The chapters that follow explore a series of empirical questions that build on this theoretical foundation. Who speaks for women in parliament and how have patterns of speeches about women changed over time? What policy issues do parliamentary speeches about women address? What factors contribute to heightened levels of attention to women in parliamentary debate and how is this connected to policy advocacy and outcomes? And, finally, what role do elected women play in advocating and winning for women on specific policy issues? The framework presented here ensures that there is clarity around what each of these empirical investigations can tell us about substantive representation and women's impact.

2

Gender, Party, and Parliamentary Speeches about Women

Who represents women in parliamentary debate? And does the presence of more women in parliament shift the content of what gets discussed on the floor of the House of Commons? Chapter 1 presents a framework for thinking about the substantive representation of women that distinguishes between speaking for women in parliamentary debate, advocating for women in policy deliberations and decision making, and achieving policy outcomes for women. This chapter applies that framework and begins to address the empirical question of whether and under what conditions women parliamentarians might have an impact on politics by speaking for women in parliamentary debate.

Recall that the logic of the politics of presence expects that women representatives will be more inclined to represent women's interests in politics by virtue of their shared experience and perspective (Phillips 1995; Mansbridge 1999). Based on this theoretical starting point, we would expect women MPs to be more likely than men MPs to represent women in debate. But presence does not translate automatically or directly into improved substantive representation. Women may be more inclined than men to speak for women, but their ability to do so will be constrained by the institutional context in which they operate. Key features of the Canadian parliamentary system, in particular strong party discipline, may limit the extent to which we might expect to see a clear connection between women's presence and impact on the substantive representation of women in parliamentary debate. If MPs are expected to toe the party line, their ability to speak for women may be constrained. If patterns of parliamentary speech are driven more by party affiliation than by MPs' ascriptive characteristics, such as gender, then we might instead find that party affiliation and the partisan composition of the House of Commons will matter more in shaping patterns of the substantive representation of women in parliamentary debate, with left-leaning political parties more likely to represent women's interests than are their right-leaning counterparts (e.g., Young 2000; Tremblay and Pelletier 2000; Thomas 2017).

This chapter tests the expectation that women parliamentarians are more likely to speak for women and investigates the extent to which women's presence in Canadian politics has had an impact on the representation of women in parliamentary debate. Did the representation of women in parliamentary speech increase as the proportion of women MPs increased? In particular, were there spikes in parliamentary attention to women following significant increases in the number of elected women? Which groups of MPs made the most speeches about women? And were women MPs, regardless of party or institutional position, more likely than other groups of MPs to represent women in parliamentary debate?

CASES, DATA, AND MEASUREMENT

To investigate the relationship between the presence of women MPs and the substantive representation of women in legislative speech, this chapter analyzes the content of nearly fifty years of parliamentary debate from the Canadian House of Commons, from 1968 to 2015. This period includes fourteen parliaments, from the 28th Parliament to the 41st Parliament, and provides adequate breadth to establish a comprehensive picture of variation over time in the representation of women in parliamentary speech. The fourteen parliaments included in the analysis capture variation in the proportion of elected women in the House of Commons. Women's share of parliamentary seats steadily increased from one woman, or less than 1 per cent of seats, following the 1968 election to 76 women, or 26 per cent of seats, following the 2011 election. Prior to 1968, there were very few women MPs – never more than 2 per cent of House of Commons seats – so the inclusion of earlier parliaments would add little to the analysis. The fourteen parliaments included in the study also capture useful variation in terms of the party in power as well as majority and minority governments. Seven of the parliaments were led by Liberal governments (two of them minorities – in 1972 and 2004), while six were led by Progressive Conservative or Conservative governments (three of them minorities – in 1979, 2006, and 2008). Table 2.1 summarizes the key characteristics of each parliament included in the analysis.

Table 2.1
Key characteristics of each parliament, 1968–2015

Parliament	Years	Party in power	Majority/ minority	Elected women	
28	1968–72	Liberal	Majority	1/264	(0.4%)
29	1972–74	Liberal	Minority	5/264	(2%)
30	1974–79	Liberal	Majority	9/264	(3%)
31	1979	Progressive Conservative	Minority	10/282	(4%)
32	1980–84	Liberal	Majority	14/282	(5%)
33	1984–88	Progressive Conservative	Majority	27/282	(10%)
34	1988–93	Progressive Conservative	Majority	39/295	(13%)
35	1993–97	Liberal	Majority	53/295	(18%)
36	1997–2000	Liberal	Majority	62/301	(21%)
37	2000–04	Liberal	Majority	62/301	(21%)
38	2004–05	Liberal	Minority	65/308	(21%)
39	2006–08	Conservative	Minority	64/308	(21%)
40	2008–10	Conservative	Minority	69/308	(22%)
41	2011–15	Conservative	Majority	76/308	(25%)

To examine patterns of discursive attention to women in parliamentary debate over the nearly fifty-year period from 1968 to 2015, this chapter uses the recently digitized and annotated Canadian Hansard made available through the Linked Parliamentary Data Project, or Lipad dataset (Beelen et al. 2017). Hansard is the official record of Canadian parliamentary proceedings dating back to 1880. Although it is not a strictly verbatim transcript, it offers an accurate and reliable account of everything that is said in parliament. The Lipad dataset makes available the complete official record of parliamentary proceedings dating back to 1901 in a digital, machine-readable, and searchable format.

The dataset is based on the complete English language version of Hansard. Canadian MPs can speak in either English or French on the floor of the House of Commons and the Hansard office creates a complete English language and a complete French language record of every speech made in the House of Commons, regardless of the language in which a speech was originally made. The English language version of Hansard therefore includes speeches originally made in English and English translations of speeches originally made in French. The Lipad dataset compiles this Hansard content as a series of speeches, wherein each speech is an uninterrupted intervention by a single MP. Within this dataset, a speech can be as short as a single sentence or as long as several paragraphs. The dataset includes millions of speeches that cover all aspects of parliamentary debate – from question period, to statements by members, to petitions and debate on proposed legislation. The length of speeches included in the dataset varies considerably, from interventions of fewer than one hundred words in question period to interventions of several hundreds of words during sustained debate on a bill.

The corpus of parliamentary speeches used for this study includes every speech made in parliament from the first day of the 28th Parliament in 1968 to the last day of the 41st Parliament in 2015. The corpus excludes interventions made by the speaker of the House because the analysis addresses substantive issues that are raised and discussed in parliament. Interventions by the speaker tend to be procedural in nature, focused on keeping the business of the House moving forward and adjudicating procedural matters rather than engaging with the content of parliamentary debate. The corpus of speeches used for this study thus includes 1.347 million speeches, accounting for 285 million words. Of those, 149,510 speeches, or approximately 11 per cent of the total, were made by women MPs.

Each speech in the dataset is linked to the MP who made the speech as well as to several biographical data points about the MP, including their name, party affiliation, the riding they represent, and any government roles they occupy (e.g., minister, parliamentary secretary). Using data from the Parliament of Canada website and publicly available biographical information, I also link the parliamentary speech data with additional information about each MP, including their gender, whether they identify as Indigenous, and whether they are racialized. Speeches are linked to MPs' gender to assess the central expectation that women parliamentarians are more likely to speak for women. But gender does not operate uniformly or in isolation from other identity factors. Following decades of intersectionality research there is, as Collins (2015, 2) notes, a general consensus that "race, class, gender, sexuality, ethnicity, nation, ability, and age operate not as unitary, mutually exclusive entities, but as reciprocally constructing phenomena that in turn shape complex social inequalities." Race and Indigeneity are therefore tracked in the dataset and included in the analysis to offer initial insight into the ways in which intersecting identities might influence MPs' inclination and ability to speak for women in parliamentary debate. Race and Indigeneity are recorded because they are the identities for which data are available and for which MPs are present in large enough numbers to make quantitative analysis possible. Additionally, these are identities that previous research identifies as politically relevant but understudied in Canadian political science (e.g., Thompson 2008; Tolley 2019; Ladner 2017). The inclusion of race and Indigeneity in the dataset alongside gender makes possible a very preliminary analysis of intersectional patterns of the substantive representation of women in parliamentary debate, but the primary focus remains on the effect of gender writ large.

To track the representation of women in parliamentary debate over time and to identify which MPs are more likely to represent women in parliamentary speech, I use computational text analysis tools to review and filter the content of millions of speeches in the Lipad dataset. I develop a metric for identifying parliamentary speeches about women and, using this metric, determine the frequency with which women are represented in parliamentary debate over time, by gender, and by party. I then use multivariate analysis to identify which groups of MPs are likely to make more speeches about women in parliamentary debate.

The analysis in this chapter is focused on the substantive representation of women in parliamentary speech. In chapter 1, I argue that, conceptually, the substantive representation of women must be understood to include a range of activities and outcomes – parliamentary speech, policy advocacy, and the achievement of policy outcomes – any of which can be oriented in either a pro-equality or non-feminist direction. To operationalize the concept of the substantive representation of women in parliamentary speech, I adopt a content-neutral approach that treats parliamentary speeches about women as representative claims. This approach does not make any predeterminations pertaining to (1) the policy or issue content of these speeches about women or (2) who might make these claims on women's behalf. Using this approach, speeches about women could include speeches that support feminist policy goals and increased equality and autonomy, but they might also include speeches that defend a more traditional approach to gender roles and relations.

But how can we determine which speeches include representative claims about women and thus count as a parliamentary speech about women? Previous research on the substantive representation of women in legislative debate has typically adopted one of two approaches. First are studies that classify speeches that address a predetermined list of so-called women's issues as speeches about women. For example, in her study of the 35th Canadian Parliament, Tremblay (1998, 439–40) classifies speeches that address policy issues that directly affect women's equality (e.g., "pay equity, violence against women" and reproductive health) or that deal with "women's traditional areas of interests" (e.g., "family and children, education, health and welfare") as speeches about women. In their analysis of floor speeches in the US Senate, Osborn and Mendez (2010, 7) treat speeches about "women's traditional policy" (e.g., healthcare, family, education, social issues) and "issues of direct relevance to women" (e.g., abortion, women's health, "women's crime issues") as instances of the substantive representation of women. Although the parameters and rationales are somewhat different in these two examples, the end result in terms of the issues and topics that are included as women's issues, and instances of the representation of women are broadly the same.

A second approach focuses on speeches that make representative claims about women. These studies do not predetermine women's issues but instead leave space for political actors to identify which issues are relevant to women by scoping in speeches that mention women. For example, Pearson and Dancey (2011) treat the one-minute speeches by US members of Congress as being about women if they mention women at least once. Dietrich et al. (2019) use a similar approach that counts any speech that refers to women at least once as being about women. They also test several other operationalizations, including one that measures the proportion of words that refer to women in a speech and one that uses a structural topic model, but they find no major differences in the results across these operationalizations. In their analysis of parliamentary speeches at Westminster, Blaxill and Beelen (2016) identify any speech of any length that mentions women at least three times as a speech about women. Researchers differ in terms of the specific words they treat as a mention of women and the frequency with which those words must appear in a legislative speech but, otherwise, use the same principles to identify what counts as a speech about women.

In this chapter and throughout this book I use this second approach. A speech (the key unit of analysis in the Lipad dataset) is determined to be about women if it contains a minimum number of references to women – specifically, mentions of the words "woman" or "women" (or any variations of either of these words – e.g., "women's" or "businesswoman") relative to the total length of the speech.[1] Mentions of women as part of the phrase "men and women" or "women and men" are not counted as a mention of women since this phrase is essentially equivalent to referring to "people" and thus does not indicate attention to women specifically. This approach is a simplified but domain-specific dictionary method that classifies documents (in this case, parliamentary speeches) as being either about women or not about women based on the presence or absence of key words in those documents (Grimmer and Stewart 2013, 274).

By focusing on speeches that mention women – regardless of the context in which these speeches are made – this metric captures instances of the substantive representation of women in parliamentary debate across a range of policy issues, including on topics that might not be considered women's issues. This approach helps to ensure that the empirical results about individual MPs' patterns of behaviour are meaningful despite the gatekeeping constraints placed on them by political parties. While party whips may decide to put certain MPs on speaking lists for debate on women's policy issues, these are not the only issues in which the substantive representation of women might occur. This measure allows us to capture a more complete picture of the substantive representation of women in parliamentary speech. Moreover, it makes space for MPs who might not be inclined (or assigned) to speak during debate on so-called women's issues to nonetheless emerge as substantive representatives of women.

To ensure that this operationalization captures primarily those speeches that are substantially about women (rather than speeches that simply mention women in passing), I measure the relative frequency with which words referring to women appear in a speech and set a minimum threshold of the proportion of words in a speech that must refer to women for a speech to qualify as being substantially about women. The threshold I use for this analysis includes speeches that mention women at least once every 330 words (i.e., at least 0.3 per cent of words in the speech are mentions of women). To meet this threshold, a 250-word speech would have to mention women at least once, a 500-word speech would have to mention women at least twice, a 2,000-word speech would have to mention women at least six times, and so on.

There are trade-offs associated with setting higher or lower thresholds. One can claim with greater certainty, for example, that a speech is substantially about women if the proportion of words referring to women in that speech is higher. For example, we can be quite confident that a 250-word speech that mentions women twice (i.e., 0.8 per cent of words in the speech are mentions of women) is substantially about women. A lower threshold, by contrast, would capture a larger number and a broader range of speeches on topics that might be relevant to women, but it would also capture more speeches in which women are not the primary focus. For example, a 1,500-word speech that mentions women only once (i.e., 0.03 per cent of words in the speech are mentions of women) might include a brief discussion of issues that are relevant to women, but this discussion is unlikely to be the central focus of the speech.

The threshold used here – one mention of women for every 330 words in a speech – was selected because it is high enough to ensure that the speeches that are captured are likely to be meaningfully about women but low enough to ensure that a wide variety of different types and lengths of speeches is still captured. A higher threshold would include relatively more short speeches that only mention women once – for example, interventions made during question period. This threshold would only include longer speeches if they mentioned women numerous times – for example, speeches made during debate on a bill whose primary focus or impact was on women, such as women's health, employment equity, and so on. A lower threshold would include all the same short speeches included at the higher threshold, but it would also include more long speeches whose main focus might not be on women – for example, speeches made during debate on a bill that is not primarily focused on women, such as a budget bill. Appendix 1 shows the parliament-to-parliament variation in the number of speeches about women using three different thresholds – one mention of women for every 500, 330, and 250 words. A larger number of speeches is captured at the lower threshold of once every 500 words, and a smaller number of speeches is captured at the higher threshold of once every 250 words, but the directional trend in the pattern of variation from one parliament to the next remains consistent. This consistency means we can be confident that the threshold selected does not systematically include or exclude any subset of potential speeches about women.

The relative count threshold approach used here differs slightly from those discussed above and offers some advantages. Pearson and Dancey (2011) as well as Dietrich et al. (2019) use a single mention of women as the threshold for what counts as a speech about women. Depending on the length of the speech, this approach has the potential to include a large number of speeches that are not substantively about women. Blaxill and Beelen (2016) use a minimum threshold of three mentions per speech as the criterion for determining whether a speech is about women. This has the potential to systematically exclude shorter speeches while also including longer speeches about a topic unrelated to women but that mentions women in passing enough to meet the threshold. By using a relative count (at least one mention of women every 330 words) rather than an absolute count (at least one or three mentions regardless of the length of the speech), the approach used here is better equipped to capture shorter speeches (e.g., speeches from question period) that are substantially about women but might only mention women once or twice, while also including longer speeches. It is also better equipped to include only those longer speeches that are in fact substantively about women by ensuring that women are mentioned frequently enough relative to the total length of the speech to qualify as being about women.

To confirm the validity of the metric I inspected a random sample of two hundred speeches about women, stratified by parliament. Ninety-seven per cent of speeches were confirmed to be substantially about women. There will inevitably be instances at the margins of speeches that make substantial references to women but that do so in the context of a longer speech and, therefore, are not included, or speeches that meet the criteria for inclusion as a speech about women but make no substantial claims about women. Given the massive scale of the analysis, however, marginal errors of categorization are unlikely to skew overall results.

The Lipad dataset and the metric for identifying speeches about women discussed above make it possible (1) to identify changes in the number of parliamentary speeches about women over time and (2) to determine which parliamentarians are most likely to represent women in parliamentary debate. To understand patterns of change over time, I analyze the proportion of parliamentary speeches about women in each parliament from 1968 to 2015, broken down by gender and by party. To determine with greater precision which groups of MPs make the most speeches about women, I use multivariate regression to isolate the independent effect of gender and party affiliation on an MP's propensity to make speeches about women.

TRACKING SPEECHES ABOUT WOMEN OVER TIME

Before making an assessment about which MPs are most likely to engage in the substantive representation of women in parliamentary debate, it is helpful to understand how the frequency of parliamentary speeches about women has changed over time. Figure 2.1 shows the percentage of all parliamentary speeches about women in each parliament from 1968 to 2015 overlaid with the share of parliamentary seats held by women in each parliament. I report speeches about women as a proportion of total speeches since the overall total number of speeches in each parliament varies significantly – from just over ten thousand speeches in the short-lived 31st Parliament (1979) to more than 170,000 speeches in the 30th Parliament (1974–79). Focusing on proportions allows for clearer more consistent comparisons across parliaments.

Looking at figure 2.1, two things stand out. First is that the proportion of speeches about women is consistently low. Parliamentarians have never spent more than 1.6 per cent of debate time making speeches about women, and, in some cases, less than half a per cent of parliamentary speeches were about women. This is consistent with earlier research from Canada, which found that the representation of women was an infrequent object of focus in parliamentary debate (Tremblay 1998). The representation of women is thus a minor component of debate in the House of Commons. The second thing to notice is that the proportion of parliamentary speeches about women and women's share of seats in the House of Commons have both tended towards a gradual increase over time. This shared directional trend is evident from a visual inspection of figure 2.1 and is confirmed by a high Pearson correlation coefficient (0.84) between women's share of seats and the percentage of speeches about women in each parliament. Attention to women in parliamentary debate has increased as women's presence in the House of Commons has grown.

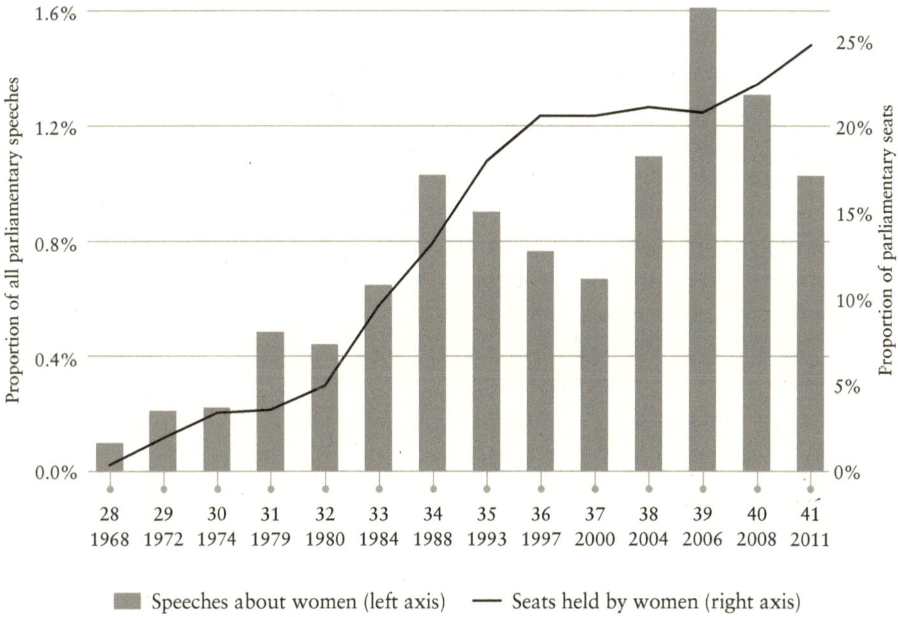

Figure 2.1 Percentage of parliamentary speeches about women and women's share of parliamentary seats, 1968–2015.

This raises the question of whether and how the increase in attention to women in parliamentary debate is linked with the increase in women's share of parliamentary seats. If the proportion of speeches about women were driven exclusively by the presence of women, we would expect the largest increases in speeches to follow the largest increases in women's seats. This does not appear to be the case. Although there is a general upward trend in the proportion of speeches about women over time, the pattern is not uniform – there are periods of increase and backsliding – and the peaks in speeches about women did not occur in the same parliaments in which the proportion of elected women increased dramatically. For example, there are spikes in the proportion of speeches about women in the 34th Parliament (1988–93) and again in the 39th Parliament (2006–08). These were both parliaments in which the number of elected women either increased modestly (from 10 to 13 per cent in the 34th Parliament) or not at all (holding steady at 21 per cent for the fourth election in a row in the 39th Parliament). The most significant increases in the proportion of women in the House of Commons were in 1984 and 1993. The number of elected women doubled after the 1984 election from 5 to 10 per cent, and it rose from 13 to 18 per cent after the 1993 election. There was no spike in the proportion of speeches about women in the parliaments following these two elections. In fact, the increases were either modest (as in the 33rd Parliament after the 1984 election) or declined relative to the previous parliament (as in the 35th Parliament after the 1993 election). Increases in the number of elected women are thus not the only factor driving changes in the proportion of speeches about women.

The timing of the peaks in the proportion of speeches about women suggests that these increases were shaped by factors other than the share of seats held by women. Policy initiatives and external events may have contributed to increased attention to women in parliamentary speech in the 34th and 39th Parliaments. Chapter 4 examines the political context and patterns of issue attention in these two parliaments to better understand what factors contributed to the spike in the proportion of parliamentary speeches about women.

Even though increases in the proportion of speeches about women in parliamentary debate were not driven exclusively by the presence of women in parliament, there nonetheless appears to be a connection between women's presence in parliament and the proportion of speeches about women that warrants further investigation. To what extent were women MPs responsible for driving changes in the share of speeches about women over time? An examination of the distribution of speeches about women by gender over time allows us to probe further on this question and offers a preliminary test of the hypothesis that women MPs will represent women in parliamentary speech more than men MPs.

Figure 2.2 shows the distribution of speeches about women by gender, as a percentage of all parliamentary speeches. Again, I report each group's share of speeches about women as a proportion of all parliamentary speeches to facilitate parliament-to-parliament comparison. This figure suggests that women MPs did the bulk of the heavy lifting when it came to representing women in parliamentary debate. Two key features of this figure should be noted in support of this assessment. First, beginning in the 33rd Parliament (1984–88), women MPs made more speeches about women than did men *in absolute terms*. Women MPs continued to make more speeches about women than did men MPs in every subsequent parliament. This pattern is

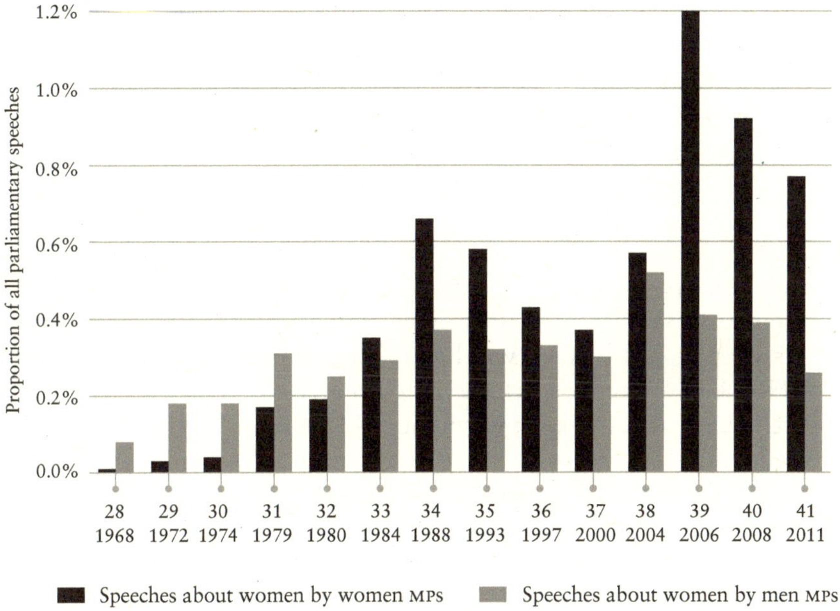

Figure 2.2 Speeches about women by men and women MPs as a percentage of all parliamentary speeches, 1968–2015.

notable when we consider that women have consistently held fewer than 30 per cent of parliamentary seats and held only 10 per cent of seats in the 33rd Parliament when they first overtook men in terms of the number of speeches they made about women.

The second thing to note is that patterns of change in the overall frequency of speeches about women reported in figure 2.1 move in tandem with variation in women MPs' proportion of speeches about women reported in figure 2.2. Variation in the proportion of speeches about women made by men MPs over the fourteen parliaments was relatively modest. But the share of speeches about women made by women MPs fluctuated considerably from one parliament to another. The parliaments in which the overall representation of women in parliamentary speech peaked were also the parliaments in which women's share of speeches about women spiked and the gap between men's and women's share of parliamentary speeches about women widened. This suggests that, over time, variation in the representation of women in parliamentary debate was driven more by women MPs than by men MPs.

That women MPs tended to outperform men in parliamentary speeches about women in absolute terms is especially notable when we consider that, to begin with, women MPs had fewer opportunities to speak in parliament than did their male colleagues. Figure 2.3 shows the percentage of all parliamentary seats held by women and the percentage of all parliamentary speeches made by women MPs in each parliament from 1968 to 2015. In all but the 39th and 41st Parliaments, women's share of all parliamentary speeches was lower than their share of seats. Women MPs' larger share of speeches about women, despite their smaller share of parliamentary speeches overall, suggests that, even though women MPs had fewer opportunities to participate in House of Commons debate than did men MPs, they spent more time talking about women when they did have the floor. Put another way, women MPs prioritized the representation of women in parliamentary debate more than did their male colleagues.

Figure 2.4 confirms this interpretation, showing the number of speeches about women by gender as a percentage of each group's total number of speeches. Speeches about women account for a much larger share of women MPs' speeches than of men's. For example, 5.84 per cent of women MPs' speeches were about women in the short-lived 31st Parliament (1979). In the same parliament, only 0.32 per cent of men MPs' speeches were about women. The gap between men and women MPs' tendency to prioritize the representation of women in parliamentary debate is sizeable. Whereas women MPs consistently dedicated more than 2 per cent of their parliamentary speeches to making representative claims about women, less than half a per cent of men's speeches were about women in all but two parliaments (the 38th and 39th).[2]

These findings suggest that variation in the overall level of attention to women in parliamentary debate was driven by women MPs. In absolute terms and as a share of MPs' speeches, women MPs made significantly more speeches about women than did their male colleagues. And the parliaments in which the level of representation of women spiked and dropped mirror the parliaments in which the representation of women by women MPs spiked and dropped. By contrast, speeches about women by men MPs tended to increase gradually and steadily over time, though still remaining a much smaller share of male MPs' parliamentary speeches. This trend suggests that women MPs' patterns of speech were responsible for driving patterns of speech overall, even if those overall patterns did not happen in direct relation to the changing proportion of House of Commons seats held by women.

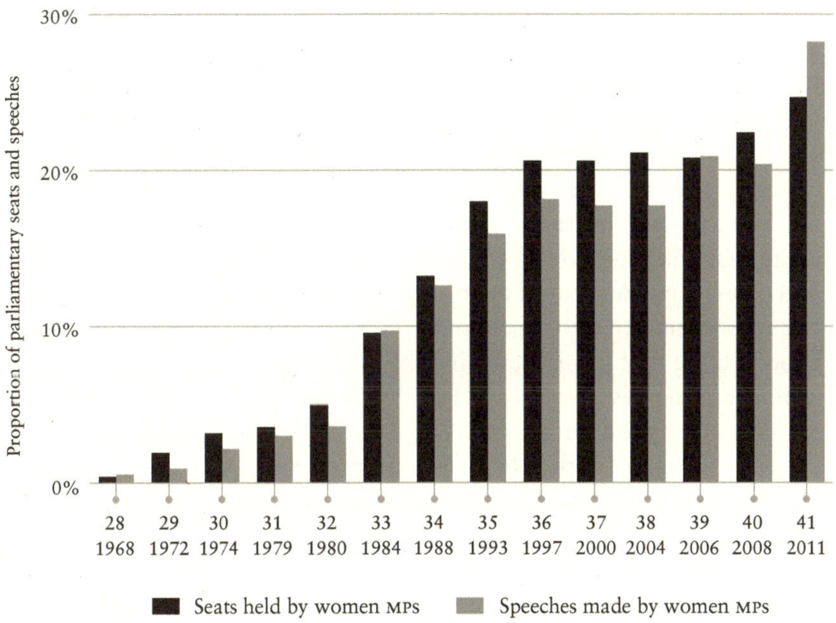

Figure 2.3 Women's share of parliamentary seats and speeches, 1968–2015.

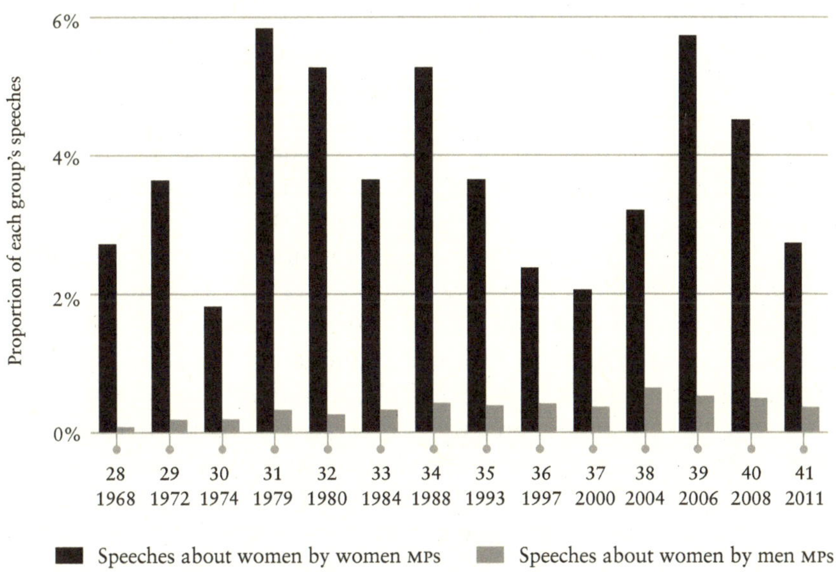

Figure 2.4 Speeches about women by men and women MPs as a percentage of each group's total number of speeches, 1968–2015.

But what about the role of the political parties? To what extent might the partisan composition of the House of Commons have contributed to changes in the proportion of speeches about women made in each parliament? Political parties are a key building block around which Canadian parliamentary politics is organized, and previous research suggests that parties on the political left and centre will represent women more than will parties on the political right. If this is the case, then we would expect to see evidence that MPs from left and centrist parties would be more inclined to prioritize the substantive representation of women in parliamentary debate. We might also expect to see that parliaments in which more seats were held by left-leaning and centrist MPs would feature a higher proportion of speeches about women than would parliaments with fewer of these MPs.

Is the expectation that left and centrist parties will prioritize the representation of women in parliamentary debate reflected in changes in the frequency of speeches about women over time? Consider first whether left-leaning MPs do in fact prioritize the substantive representation of women in parliamentary debate. Figure 2.5 shows the percentage of speeches about women by party as a share of each party's total number of speeches in each parliament. The results from this figure are nowhere near as striking as the breakdown by gender. They nonetheless offer partial support for the expectation that left and centrist MPs are more likely to represent women in parliamentary speech. In virtually every parliament, MPs from the left-leaning New Democratic Party (NDP) devoted a larger share of their party's parliamentary speeches to the substantive representation of women than did any other party. MPs from the sovereigntist, social democratic Bloc Québécois (BQ) devoted a similarly high proportion of their parliamentary speeches to the representation of women. MPs from the centre-right Progressive Conservative (PC) and harder right Reform/Canadian Alliance (REF/CA) parties tended to have the lowest share of speeches about women. Among centrist Liberal Party (LPC) MPs, the share of speeches about women was somewhere between the NDP and Progressive Conservatives. Counter to expectations, MPs from the right-leaning Conservative Party (CPC), which was created following the unification of the Progressive Conservative and Reform/Canadian Alliance parties in 2003, made more speeches about women than did its predecessor parties. In fact, Conservative MPs had a higher share of speeches about women than did centrist

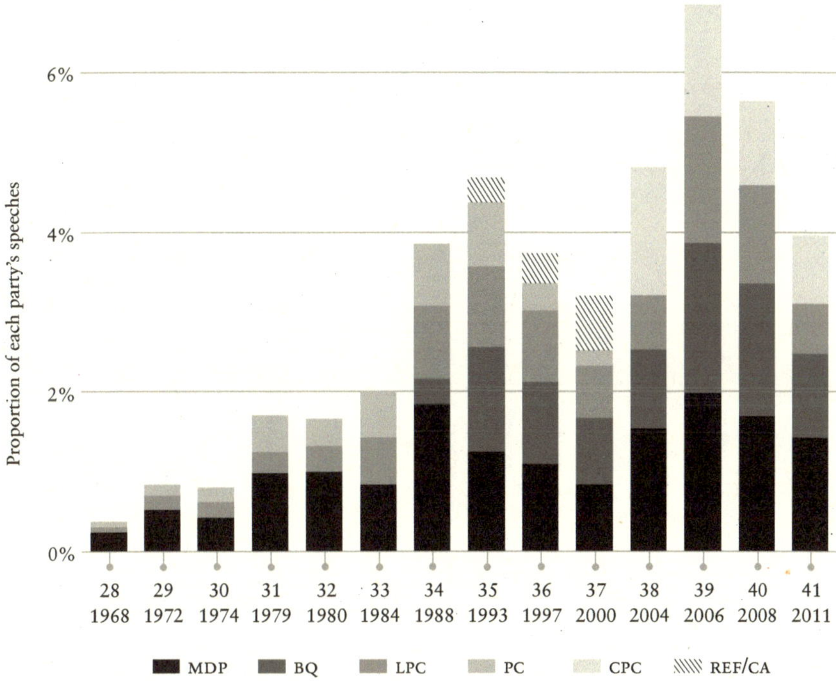

Figure 2.5 Speeches about women by party as a percentage of each party's total number of speeches, 1968–2015.

and left-leaning parties in the 38th Parliament. These findings are preliminary, but the multivariate analysis below offers greater clarity about the extent to which party affiliation shapes an MP's inclination to make speeches about women with greater precision.

Given this preliminary evidence that some left-leaning parties did prioritize making speeches about women, we can now consider whether parliaments that included more left-leaning MPs paid more attention to women in parliamentary debate overall. Figure 2.6 shows the percentage of all parliamentary speeches about women overlaid with the proportion of parliamentary seats held by left and centrist MPs (Liberals, New Democrats, and members of the Bloc Québécois). What stands out in this figure is the absence of any clear relationship between the frequency of legislative speeches about women and the proportion of parliamentary seats held by left and centrist MPs. The lack of relationship suggested by visual inspection is confirmed by a very

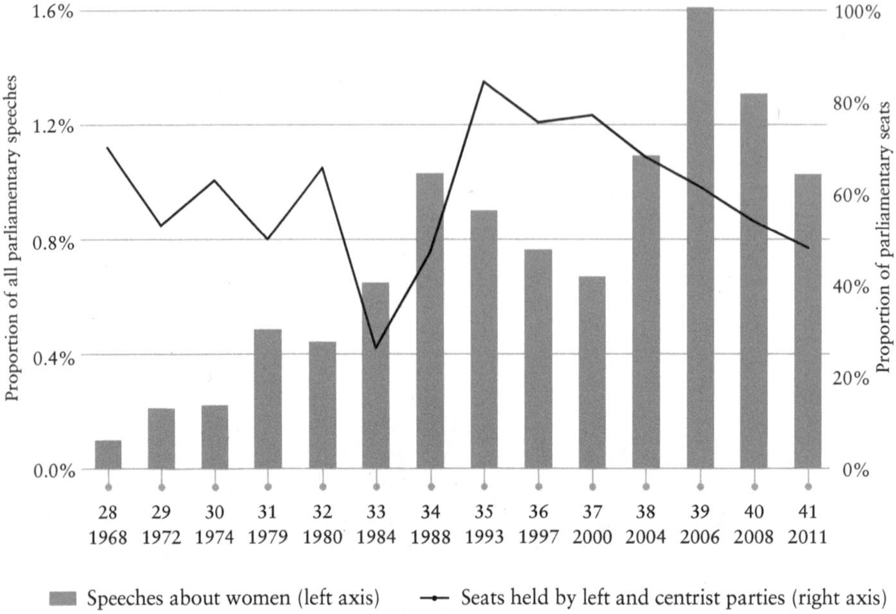

Figure 2.6 Percentage of parliamentary speeches about women and share of parliamentary seats held by left and centrist political parties, 1968–2015.

low Pearson correlation coefficient (-0.04). There is no indication that parliaments with a larger share of left-leaning MPs had more frequent representation of women in parliamentary debate.[3] This suggests that factors other than the partisan composition of the House of Commons cause fluctuations in the level of discursive attention to women in parliamentary debate.

The influence of party on the overall patterns of variation in the share of parliamentary speeches about women over time is not as clear cut as is the influence of gender. Women MPs made more speeches about women than did their male colleagues in absolute terms and as a proportion of their total number of speeches. Despite their small numbers in the House of Commons, the extent to which women MPs prioritized the representation of women in parliamentary debate had an impact on patterns of speech overall. By contrast, while there is evidence that some left-leaning MPs prioritized the representation of women in parliamentary debate, their speeches about women did not contribute to overall patterns of change over time in the same way as did speeches by women.

WHICH MPS REPRESENT WOMEN?

With the broad patterns of change over time established, we can now take a closer look at which groups of MPs made the most speeches about women. Recall that the theoretical expectation driving the analysis is that women and MPs from left-of-centre political parties will be more likely to speak for women in parliamentary debate. The preliminary results in the section above offer initial confirmation of these expectations – women MPs seem to be more likely than men MPs to make speeches about women, and left-leaning MPs from the NDP appear to prioritize making speeches about women more than do MPs from other parties, although the partisan differences are less clear cut. Multivariate analysis allows us to determine with greater precision which groups of MPs make the most speeches about women.

To estimate the predicted count of speeches about women in each parliament, I reorganized the original dataset described above so that observations are organized by MP rather than by speech. The reorganized dataset captures the total number of speeches made by each MP in each parliament and the total number of speeches made about women. Each observation in this dataset is for one MP, as a member of a political party, in one parliament. Each observation indicates the number of speeches about women and the total number of speeches an MP made in a parliament. In some cases, there is more than one observation for an individual MP in one parliament, typically in cases in which an MP has crossed the floor. For example, there are two observations for Belinda Stronach in the 38th Parliament because she was elected as a Conservative MP in 2004 but crossed the floor to join the Liberals in 2005. For this reason, the total number of observations in the dataset (4,152) is slightly larger than the sum of the number of parliamentary seats in the fourteen parliaments included in the analysis (4,062).

A quick look at which MPs spoke most frequently about women in this reorganized dataset offers a helpful starting point for understanding the factors that might contribute to an MP's inclination and ability to speak for women in parliamentary debate. It also provides a helpful snapshot of which MPs are doing the heavy lifting of speaking for women in parliamentary debate. Table 2.2 lists the twenty-five MPs who made the most speeches about women. The speech counts shown in the table are for each MP, as a member of a political party, in one parliament. As a result, there are some MPs who appear in

Table 2.2
MPs who made the most speeches about women

Name	*Gender*	*Party*	*Number of speeches about women*	*Parliament*	*Status of Women parliamentary role*
Dawn Black	Woman	NDP	153	34 (1988–93)	Critic
Niki Ashton	Woman	NDP	102	41 (2011–15)	Critic
Mary Clancy	Woman	LPC	100	34 (1988–93)	Critic
Margaret Mitchell	Woman	NDP	95	33 (1984–88)	Critic
Bev Oda	Woman	CPC	94	39 (2006–08)	Minister
Lucie Pépin	Woman	LPC	89	33 (1984–88)	Critic
Irene Mathyssen	Woman	NDP	85	40 (2008–11)	Critic
Susan Truppe	Woman	CPC	82	41 (2011–15)	Parl. Sec.
Christiane Gagnon	Woman	BQ	77	35 (1993–97)	Critic
Margaret Mitchell	Woman	NDP	75	32 (1980–84)	Critic
Flora MacDonald	Woman	PC	73	32 (1980–84)	Critic
Maria Minna	Woman	LPC	65	39 (2006–08)	Critic
Irene Mathyssen	Woman	NDP	65	39 (2006–08)	Critic
Nicole Demers	Woman	BQ	62	39 (2006–08)	Critic
Mary Collins	Woman	PC	61	34 (1988–93)	Minister
Barbara McDougall	Woman	PC	61	33 (1984–88)	Minister
Mylène Freeman	Woman	NDP	57	41 (2011–15)	Critic
Nicole Demers	Woman	BQ	55	40 (2008–11)	Critic
Pauline Jewett	Woman	NDP	49	32 (1980–84)	Critic
Sheila Copps	Woman	LPC	47	33 (1984–88)	N/A
Anita Neville	Woman	LPC	46	40 (2008–11)	Critic
Joy Langan	Woman	NDP	46	34 (1988–93)	N/A
Audrey McLaughlin	Woman	NDP	46	34 (1988–93)	N/A
Marlene Catterall	Woman	LPC	44	34 (1988–93)	Assistant Critic
Marion Dewar	Woman	NDP	43	33 (1984–88)	Critic

the list more than once – for example, Margaret Mitchell, with ninety-five speeches about women in the 33rd Parliament and seventy-five speeches about women in the 32nd Parliament.

There are several things to note about which MPs appear (and do not appear) on this list. First and foremost is that all twenty-five of the MPs who made the most speeches about women were women.[4] Second, all but three of the MPs who made the most speeches about women occupied parliamentary roles explicitly tasked with addressing women's issues – either the minister responsible for the status of women, parliamentary secretary, or opposition critic. MPs in these roles can reasonably be expected to speak about women more often than the average MP, and these roles are occupied almost entirely by women. Third, the NDP is overrepresented among the top performers relative to their parliamentary presence. The list includes MPs from all political parties except Reform/Canadian Alliance, but eleven of them were New Democrats even though the NDP was consistently the third-place party with a relatively small share of parliamentary seats. Finally, party leaders are all but absent, even though they typically speak more frequently in parliamentary debate than any other MPs (see Cochrane et al. 2021) and thus would have more opportunity to make speeches about women than would other MPs. The exception is Audrey McLaughlin, who served as NDP leader from 1989 to 1995 and appears at the twenty-third position on the list. As the woman leader of a left-leaning party, it is consistent with what we have seen so far that she would be among the MPs who made the most speeches about women. But the other two women to have served as federal party leaders – Alexa McDonough, McLaughlin's successor as NDP leader, and Progressive Conservative prime minister Kim Campbell – were not among the top makers of speeches about women, so there is more at play than just gender and party leadership.

Taken together, these patterns reinforce the findings from the analysis above – namely, that women and, to a lesser extent, New Democrats tend to prioritize speaking about women in parliamentary debate more than do other groups of MPs. The absence of party leaders from the list of top performers reconfirms that the representation of women in debate is a relatively minor component of debate and that attention to these issues is not a top priority. Notably, MPs who made the most speeches about women tended to serve in parliamentary roles related to the status of women portfolio, but MPs in these roles are not necessarily the only ones representing women in parliamentary debate.

Multivariate analysis allows us to identify more precisely which MPs made the most speeches about women by isolating the extent to which the key factors of interest – gender and party affiliation – contribute to an MP's propensity to represent women in parliamentary debate. The outcome variable of interest here is the number of speeches about women an MP makes in each parliament. I therefore fit a negative binomial regression model of the count of speeches about women an MP makes in a single parliament.[5] Using this model, I then calculate the predicted number of speeches about women an MP with a particular set of characteristics is expected to make in a single parliament. By providing estimates in terms of the number of speeches about women an MP will make, this model provides results that are easily interpretable in concrete terms. I estimate the total number of speeches about women an MP is predicted to make in a single parliament (rather than, for example, in a single parliamentary session, month, or day) because the total number of speeches about women made by all MPs is already quite low. Focusing on the number speeches within a parliament allows for the calculation of predicted count values that are slightly larger and thus easier to interpret.

Three models measure the effect of gender and party on the number of speeches about women an MP will make, with controls added incrementally. The first model includes only gender and party affiliation, using a dummy variable for each of the parties, with the Liberal Party as the reference category.[6] The second model adds controls for several individual-level factors that might influence the frequency with which an MP makes speeches about women. These controls include whether the MP is a member of the government or opposition, whether the MP occupies a formal parliamentary role related to the status of women, and whether the MP is Indigenous or racialized. Opposition members can be expected to have more latitude to represent women than can members of a government party whose agenda may or may not include attention to women's issues and interests. By holding a formal parliamentary role that is explicitly tasked with addressing women's issues and interests, a minister responsible for the status of women, parliamentary secretary, or critic from one of the opposition parties would be expected to make more speeches about women than would the average MP. Racialized and Indigenous MPs might be more inclined to speak about women, particularly about racialized and Indigenous women, more frequently than would white MPs.

Conversely, as surrogate representatives of other identity groups, it might also be the case that racialized and Indigenous MPs lack opportunities to take on the responsibility of representing women. The third model adds interaction terms between gender and party, between gender and being racialized, and between gender and being Indigenous. These interaction terms help to assess whether the effect of gender is contingent upon party affiliation, race, or indigeneity – that is, whether women from certain political parties or identity groups tend to make more speeches about women than do others.

All three models include parliament-fixed effects to account for contextual factors that changed over time, such as the share of parliamentary seats held by women, the percentage of speeches about women in each parliament, and any other unobserved changes from one parliament to the next. All three models also include an offset for the total number of speeches made by each MP. This offset accounts for the fact that the total number of speeches about women made by individual MPs will be linked to the total number of speeches they make – an MP who spoke only a few times in a parliament will have had fewer opportunities to make speeches about women than would an MP who spoke multiple times every parliamentary sitting day. This offset is important since MPs' access to speaking time is unevenly distributed – party leaders and cabinet ministers have been shown to speak far more frequently than government backbenchers (Cochrane et al. 2021). By accounting for the total number of speeches an MP makes, the results from the models and the predicted number of speeches about women an MP will make are not skewed by the fact that some MPs speak more frequently than do others.

The full results of the models are reported in table 2.3. To facilitate interpretation of these results, we can also calculate the predicted count of speeches about women different MPs will make using the final model. Overall, gender quite clearly appears to be the most important factor in determining whether an MP will represent women in parliamentary debate, even when controlling for other relevant factors. The size and significance of the key covariates of interest – gender and party affiliation – are relatively stable across all three models, which suggests that these effects are robust. The effect of gender is significant at the 99.9 per cent confidence level across all three models and is larger than the effect of any other variable. The effect of party affiliation is significant for NDP and Conservative

Party MPs. The effects of race and Indigeneity are also statistically significant, suggesting that gender and party are not the only factors that might matter for how often an MP makes speeches about women. This suggests, at least in a preliminary way, that the gender composition of the House of Commons is not the only dimension of parliamentary diversity that might matter for patterns of representation. Being in government or opposition appears to have no bearing on the frequency with which an MP will speak about women, but the effect of holding a formal parliamentary role related to the status of women is positive and is significant at the 99.9 per cent confidence level. Serving as minister, parliamentary assistant, or critic for the status of women increases the number of speeches about women an MP will make – a reasonable finding given that an MP in one of these roles is specifically tasked with addressing issues related to women and therefore likely to spend more time in parliamentary debate speaking about women than is the average MP. Several of the interactive effects between gender and party, between gender and race, and gender and Indigeneity are also significant. These are best understood with the help of predicted counts of speeches about women.

Looking at predicted counts, on the key variable of interest, the model predicts that women MPs will make about seven speeches about women in a single parliament, while men MPs will only make one, holding all other variables at their mean. Women MPs are predicted to make about seven times as many speeches about women as their male colleagues. For context, we can compare the scale of this gender gap with differences across parties. Figure 2.7 shows the predicted count of speeches about women made by gender and by party. Compared with the sevenfold difference between men and women MPs, differences across parties are modest. Cross-party variation in the predicted count of speeches about women ranges from a low of 1.14 expected speeches about women by Reform and Alliance MPs to 2.03 expected speeches about women by Conservative MPs. Quite unexpectedly, right-leaning Conservative MPs are predicted to make more speeches about women than any other partisan group, although the left-leaning NDP is not far behind. Differences in the predicted count of speeches across parties barely register when compared with the gap between men and women MPs overall. This suggests that an MP's gender is much more important than their party affiliation in determining the frequency with which they mention women in parliamentary speech.

Table 2.3
Correlates of MPs' count of speeches about women

	Predicted count of speeches about women		
	(1)	*(2)*	*(3)*
Gender (woman = 1)	2.21***	1.86***	2.03***
	(0.06)	(0.06)	(0.10)
NDP (Base = Liberal)	0.42***	0.44***	0.48***
	(0.08)	(0.09)	(0.10)
Bloc Québécois (Base = Liberal)	-0.02	-0.08	0.01
	(0.10)	(0.11)	(0.13)
Progressive Conservative (Base = Liberal)	0.0003	0.02	-0.01
	(0.08)	(0.08)	(0.09)
Conservative (Base = Liberal)	0.50***	0.44***	0.52***
	(0.10)	(0.09)	(0.10)
Reform/Alliance (Base = Liberal)	-0.12	-0.09	0.06
	(0.13)	(0.13)	(0.14)
Racialized		0.22	0.41**
		(0.11)	(0.15)
Indigenous		0.56**	0.83***
		(0.19)	(0.24)
Opposition		-0.07	-0.06
		(0.07)	(0.07)
Status of Women Parliamentary Role		1.64***	1.70***
		(0.13)	(0.13)
Gender * NDP (Base = Liberal)			-0.25
			(0.16)
Gender * Bloc Quebecois (Base = Liberal)			-0.30
			(0.19)
Gender * Progressive Conservative (Base = Liberal)			0.34+
			(0.20)
Gender * Conservative (Base = Liberal)			-0.36*
			(0.17)
Gender * Reform/Alliance (Base = Liberal)			-1.20***
			(0.32)
Gender * Racialized			-0.42+
			(0.23)
Gender * Indigenous			-0.91*
			(0.39)
Parliament FEs	yes	yes	yes
Observations	4,152	4,152	4,152
2*Log Likelihood	-11,612	-11,406	-11,373

+p<0.1, *p<0.05, **p<0.01, ***p<0.001

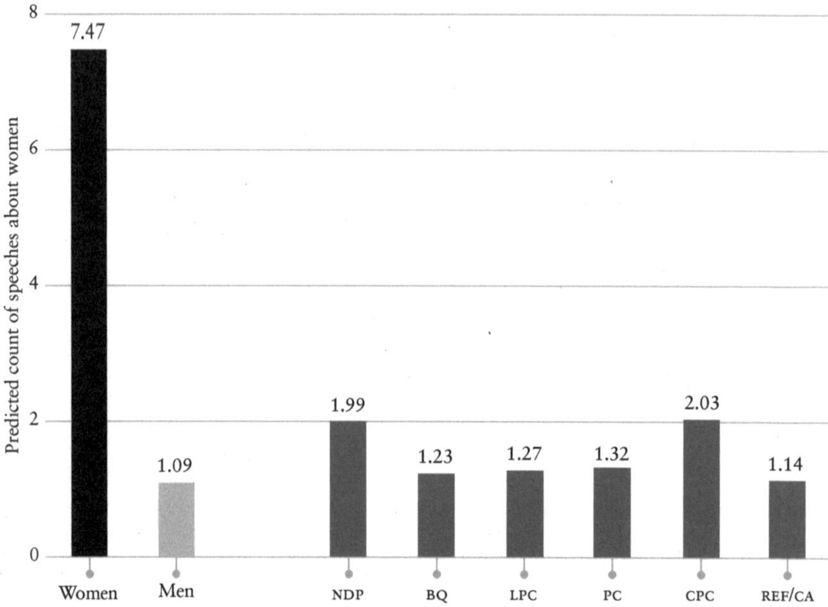

Figure 2.7 Predicted count of speeches about women by gender and by party.

The limited cross-party differences in the number of speeches about women make sense when we consider that (1) men tended not to make many speeches about women and (2) men were a majority in all the parties examined here. It is therefore useful to look at the interactive effect between gender and party through an examination of gender differences *within* political parties to understand the extent to which gender gaps might be contingent upon partisanship. Put another way, is it the case that only women in certain parties are more inclined to represent women in parliamentary debate? Figure 2.8 summarizes the interactive effect between gender and political party and shows the predicted count of speeches about women by men and women MPs within each party. There are two main things to notice in this figure. First and most important is that, for the most part, women MPs regardless of party are likely to make dramatically more speeches about women than are their male co-partisans. The sevenfold difference in the count of speeches about women observed among men and women MPs in general appears to hold more or less consistently across virtually all parties. The one exception to this is among Reform/ Canadian Alliance MPs, where the gender gap in speeches about

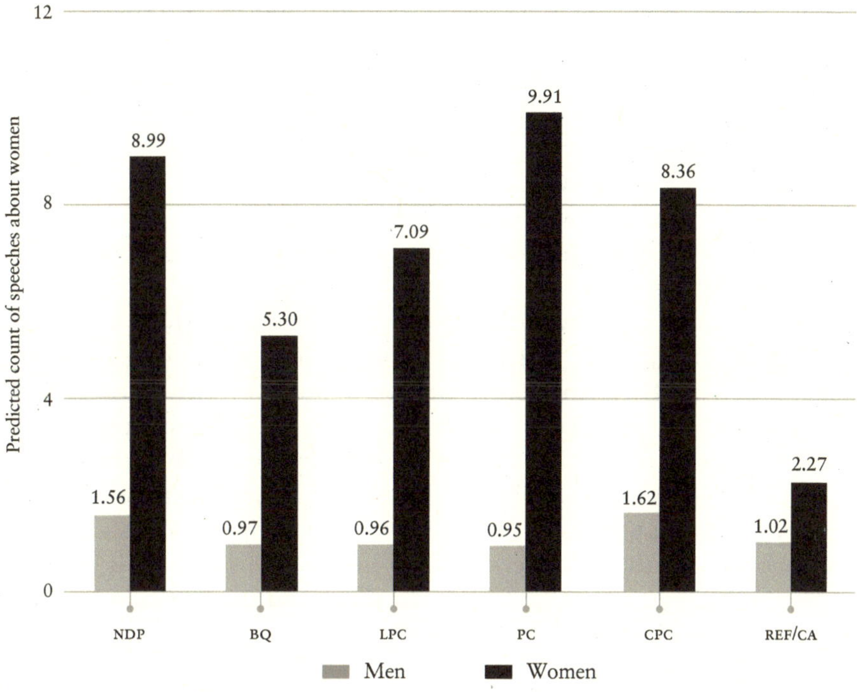

Figure 2.8 Predicted count of speeches about women by gender within each party.

women is dramatically smaller. Reform/Canadian Alliance men are predicted to make about one speech about women per parliament, on par with men from other parties. But Reform/Canadian Alliance women are predicted to make only two speeches about women per parliament. This gender gap is dramatically smaller than is the gap for all other parties. This suggests that, although women from most parties were likely to represent women in parliamentary speech much more frequently than their male colleagues, Reform/Canadian Alliance women were uniquely disinclined to do so.

The second thing to notice is that, although Conservative MPs overall had the highest predicted count of speeches about women, Conservative women were not the top performers when we disaggregate by gender and party. They were outpaced by women in the now defunct Progressive Conservative Party and the NDP. Progressive Conservative women were predicted to make the most speeches about women, at 9.91 speeches per parliament. This strong performance is partly accounted for by the fact that the majority of Progressive Conservative MPs who served as minister or critic for the status of women were men, whereas the MPs serving in these roles in other parties were almost entirely women. As a result, the effect of gender is absorbed by the effect of parliamentary role more for other parties than for Progressive Conservatives. This means that Progressive Conservative women who made a lot of speeches about women were more likely to be making them as regular MPs than as minister or critic for the status of women.

Left-leaning NDP women are predicted to make 8.99 speeches about women per parliament, but Conservative women are not far behind with 8.36 speeches about women. Notably, however, Conservative men are predicted to make more speeches about women than are men in any other party. The tendency for Conservative MPs overall to outperform all the other parties thus appears to be driven at least in part by the fact that Conservative men make more speeches about women than do men in other parties. This finding is again unexpected and warrants further investigation, which I discuss in greater detail below.

As the results in table 2.3 suggest, race and Indigeneity also matter for the number of speeches about women an MP will make, and the effect of gender is contingent upon these identity factors. Figure 2.9 shows the predicted count of speeches about women made by racialized, Indigenous, and white women and men. This figure clarifies an important intersectional insight: namely, that the inclination to represent women in parliamentary speech is not equally shared – either by all women or by all men. There are some minor differences in the predicted count of speeches about women among racialized, Indigenous, and white women, but gender differences across these three groups are more pronounced among men. Indigenous and racialized women are predicted to make slightly fewer speeches about women than are white women, but racialized and Indigenous men are much more inclined to represent women in parliamentary speech than are their white male colleagues. Indigenous men are predicted to make more than twice as many speeches about women as are white men. The effect of gender is thus contingent upon race and Indigeneity largely through racialized and Indigenous men's tendency to make more speeches about women than do their white male colleagues.

Racialized and Indigenous women's slightly lower predicted count of speeches about women suggests that, as descriptive representatives

Figure 2.9 Predicted count of speeches about women by gender among racialized, Indigenous, and white MPs.

of multiple groups with only so many opportunities to speak in parliament, these women may simply have less bandwidth to speak for women since they are also speaking for other underrepresented communities. For racialized and Indigenous men, the findings suggest that, as members of politically marginalized communities, they may be more attuned to the perspectives of other underrepresented groups – in this case, women – than are their white male colleagues. These findings are preliminary, however, and further research into the ways in which gender interacts with other identities to shape patterns of legislator behaviour is needed to understand the full complexity of the patterns observed here. The observed variation in the inclination to represent women in parliamentary speech among the full diversity of elected men and women nonetheless offers a useful reminder that, despite the increased tendency among women MPs as a group to represent women in parliamentary debate, this willingness and inclination is not a uniform phenomenon across all elected women. Moreover, it is not just women who will be more inclined to speak for women.

The results from the multivariate analysis show that an MP's gender is the key determinant of whether and how frequently they will make speeches about women. The effect of gender is statistically significant and is larger than the effect of all other variables across all three models. These findings offer strong confirmation of the expectation that women MPs are more likely to make speeches about women than are their male colleagues. Predicted counts based on the final model, however, show that the inclination to represent women is not evenly shared by all women MPs. The results also show that the effect of party affiliation is much less decisive for the number of speeches about women an MP will make. Differences in the predicted count of speeches about women across parties are decidedly more modest than are gender differences. And although party differences are small, right-leaning Conservative MPs are predicted to make more speeches about women than are MPs in any other party. This calls into question the expectation that the relationship between party affiliation and the representation of women in parliamentary debate is based primarily on left-right ideological differences, with left-leaning MPs more likely to represent women.

ASSESSING THE FINDINGS

The results presented above show that women MPs are significantly more likely than are men MPs to make speeches about women, regardless of party affiliation. This offers a strong confirmation of the logic of the politics of presence when it comes to the substantive representation of women in parliamentary debate. The impact of partisan differences on patterns of the representation of women in parliamentary speech are much less decisive. The anticipated constraints on individual MPs' behaviour created by party discipline within the Canadian parliamentary context and the expectation that left-leaning political parties would be more likely to represent women than right leaning parties are not clearly borne out by these findings.

The results presented in this chapter confirm the importance of the presence of women for the substantive representation of women in parliamentary debate. However, there are two unexpected findings that raise important questions that warrant further investigation. First, the presence of more women parliamentarians appears to be linked to increased speeches about women over time, but women's presence is not the full story. Big increases in the proportion of speeches about women do not simply follow big increases in the number of elected women. For example, even as the number of women in the House of Commons increased significantly following the 1993 election and held steady under Liberal governments throughout the 1990s and early 2000s, the share of speeches about women in parliamentary debate actually declined over this period, as did the extent to which women MPs prioritized the representation of women in parliamentary speech. Instead, the number of speeches about women peaked during parliaments in which the increase in the proportion of elected women from the preceding parliament was modest or non-existent – the 34th Parliament (1988–93) and the 39th Parliament (2006–08).

The partisan composition of the House of Commons during these two parliaments fails to offer a compelling alternate explanation for what might have been causing these spikes in parliamentary attention to women. The 34th Parliament was led by a majority Progressive Conservative government in which the majority of sitting MPs were from a more right-leaning party. The 39th Parliament featured a Conservative minority government, in which Liberal and NDP MPs combined held more seats than did Conservatives. The spike in parliamentary speeches about women in these two parliaments thus appears to be unrelated to the ideological bent of the majority of MPs in the House.

Why, then, did we see spikes in the proportion of speeches about women in these two parliaments? What other factors might have contributed to the overall level of discursive attention to women in parliamentary debate? One potential explanation is that these spikes are driven by patterns of issue attention. Increases in the frequency of speeches about women may be the result of certain policy issues with particular relevance for women making their way onto the parliamentary agenda – either through external events or through the efforts of individual parliamentarians to draw attention to them. To investigate this possibility, chapter 3 identifies the issue content of parliamentary speeches about women and chapter 4 identifies the patterns of issue attention that contributed to the spike in the frequency of speeches about women in the 34th and 39th Parliaments specifically. These chapters help to identify the ways in which the emergence of and attention to certain policy issues might contribute to changes in the frequency of speeches about women over time.

The second unexpected finding is the tendency for right-leaning Conservative MPs to make so many speeches about women. Much of the literature on the substantive representation of women suggests that conservative political parties are typically seen as less sympathetic to women's equality claims than are their left-leaning counterparts (Celis and Childs 2012, 2018). But right-leaning Conservative MPs are predicted to make more speeches about women than are MPs from all other parties, although left-leaning NDP MPs are a close second.

This finding runs counter to expectations that members of right-leaning parties will be less likely to represent women, but it is consistent with research from Europe and the United Kingdom that suggests the incompatibility between conservatism and the representation of women's interests may not be as firmly entrenched as is typically assumed (Och 2018; Webb and Childs 2012; Erzeel et al. 2014; O'Brien 2018). Regardless, the finding warrants further investigation.

We might be tempted to attribute the surprising frequency of Conservative MPs' speeches about women to the fact that this party only held seats in the four most recent parliaments examined here – a period that coincides with a greater proportion of parliamentary speeches about women overall. However, the parliament fixed-effect controls in the multivariate analysis would account for these over-time differences. A more compelling potential explanation for this unexpected finding is that Conservative MPs might address a different set of issues or introduce a different perspective about women than MPs from other parties. For example, the propensity for Conservative MPs to make speeches about women might result from an emphasis on traditional family values and gender roles, consistent with the broader ideological orientation of the party. While this kind of issue attention would not count as feminist or pro-equality representation, speeches on these topics would nonetheless constitute representative claims about women, consistent with the broadly conceived, content-neutral operationalization of the substantive representation of women that I use here. Chapter 3 investigates the possibility that Conservative MPs address a distinctive set of policy issues when speaking about women by unpacking the issue content of speeches about women and exploring partisan differences in patterns of issue attention.

IMPLICATIONS

Taken together, this chapter offers strong evidence that women MPs as a group, regardless of party, are more likely than men MPs to represent women in parliamentary debate in the Canadian House of Commons. Women MPs consistently prioritized the representation of women as a proportion of their speeches far more than did their male colleagues. Logically, then, as women's share of seats increased, so, too, did the representation of women in parliamentary speech overall. Women MPs were the driving force behind patterns of discursive attention to women in parliamentary debate over time. The multivariate analysis confirms that women MPs are consistently more likely to make speeches about women than are their male colleagues and shows that the effect of gender is stronger than is the effect of all other variables. By comparison, the impact of party is less decisive. The multivariate analysis confirms that differences across parties are modest but that, rather unexpectedly, right-leaning Conservative MPs emerge as the party group with the highest predicted count of speeches about women, although the NDP are close behind. Overall, this chapter confirms that gender matters for the substantive representation of women in parliamentary speech – even in an institutional context in which party affiliation exerts a strong influence over legislator behaviour.

Some might suggest that there is nothing surprising about these findings – that of course women MPs are going to make more speeches about women. But the empirical confirmation of this perhaps intuitively compelling pattern is important in and of itself. Before now, there has been no rigorous empirical assessment of whether women MPs do in fact engage more frequently than do their male colleagues in the substantive representation of women in parliamentary debate. The massive scale of the data used here to make this assessment means we can be confident about these findings. Moreover, in the Canadian institutional context, finding that women MPs have consistently different patterns of behaviour than do their male colleagues, regardless of party affiliation, actually *is* somewhat surprising given the strength of party discipline in Canadian politics. The identities of individual MPs are typically seen as less important than party affiliation for determining patterns of behaviour. The fact that gender matters more than party when it comes to the representation of women in parliamentary speech is therefore notable.

There are two important implications that follow from these findings. First is that electing more women makes a difference with regard to what gets discussed in parliament. More than any other factor, an MP's gender is what matters when it comes to whether they will make speeches about women, and women MPs drive patterns of attention to women in parliamentary debate. Having more women in parliament can thus change the issues that get addressed in this key institution of democratic representation. Second, and related to the first point, is that the constraints on MP behaviour created by partisanship might not be as all-encompassing as is typically assumed, at least when it comes to patterns of parliamentary speech. This chapter provides clear empirical evidence that an MP's gender matters more than partisan affiliation in shaping the inclination to represent women in parliamentary debate. In the Canadian parliamentary system – and indeed in Westminster systems more broadly – politics is organized around political parties, and there is often an expectation that relevant political differences will break along party lines. This chapter's finding that key differences are happening along gender lines and that party affiliation is less important in determining patterns of attention to women in parliament runs counter to this widely held expectation that relevant political differences will all be accounted for by partisanship. These findings suggest that the scope for MPs to deviate from the party line might be broader than is typically assumed and opens up space to begin to consider the ways in which individual parliamentarians, rather than partisan blocs of MPs, behave and influence parliamentary activity.

Clearly gender is a decisive factor in determining an MP's inclination to represent women in parliamentary debate – and it matters more than any of the other factors explored. There remains, however, much more to unpack when it comes to understanding the issue content of parliamentary speeches about women, the connection between parliamentary speech and policy action, the process by which women's equality policy change occurs, and the role that women parliamentarians play in bringing about these policy changes. The chapters that follow address these questions.

3

Policy Issues in Parliamentary Speeches about Women

We now know that women MPs are more likely than are men MPs to speak about women in parliamentary debate, regardless of party affiliation. Women's presence in the House of Commons shifts discursive attention towards women. But even though we have established that women will make more parliamentary speeches about women than men, we still don't know what those speeches are actually about. What policy issues were MPs talking about when they spoke about women in parliamentary debate? The operationalization of the substantive representation of women in chapter 2 relies on a content-neutral approach to what counts as an instance of the substantive representation of women in parliamentary debate. Any speech that contained a minimum number of references to women relative to the total speech length – regardless of what else was discussed in that speech – was counted as a speech about women. To develop a more comprehensive understanding of the substantive representation of women in parliamentary debate, this chapter digs into the content of these speeches about women to identify the policy issues MPs raised when they spoke about women in parliamentary debate.

Unpacking the issue content of parliamentary speeches about women provides additional clarity about what the substantive representation of women in parliamentary speech consists of and what it means for women MPs to be more inclined than their male colleagues to speak about women in parliamentary debate. It also provides the foundation for thinking about the connection between parliamentary speech and policy action and, by assessing whether these MPs focused on a distinctive set of policy issues, allows us to probe further into the unexpected finding from chapter 2 that right-leaning Conservative

MPs are predicted to make the most speeches about women. Guided by these objectives, this chapter examines the issue content and patterns of issue attention in parliamentary speeches about women. What substantive policy issues are addressed when parliamentarians discuss women in parliamentary debate? How do these patterns of issue attention shift over time? Do women MPs prioritize certain topics more than men MPs? And do patterns of issue attention vary by party – in particular, do right-leaning MPs focus on a distinctive set of issues when speaking about women in parliamentary debate?

DATA AND METHODS

The analysis in this chapter focuses on the content of parliamentary speeches about women. The corpus of speeches about women is derived from the original Lipad dataset of parliamentary speeches from 1968 to 2015 that was the basis for analysis in chapter 2. Recall that speeches were determined to be about women if they included at least one mention of the words "woman" or "women" for every 330 words in a parliamentary speech. Using this metric, the corpus of speeches about women includes 8,922 speeches in total. The text of these speeches was preprocessed to facilitate analysis of speech content. Preprocessing steps included the removal of standard English-language stop words – frequently used words such as "the," "a," "an," or "in" – as well as Canadian parliament-specific stop words that are used frequently by all parliamentarians by virtue of the institutional context in which they operate – for example, "speaker," "member," "house."[1] These words are removed from the corpus because their wide usage means they are not useful for differentiating between categories of speeches. Speeches in the corpus are linked to the key biographical details about the MP who made each speech (gender, party) as well as the parliament in which each speech was made.

To identify the major policy issues that were addressed in these 8,922 speeches about women, I use unsupervised machine learning to analyze speech content. Unsupervised machine learning models make it possible to classify textual documents into relevant categories based on the words contained in the documents without knowing anything in advance about the categories into which the documents will be classified. This technique groups together documents (in this case, individual speeches about women) based on observed similarities in the presence and distribution of words in each of the documents in a corpus. The primary task for the researcher when constructing these types of models – and "one of the most difficult questions in unsupervised learning" – is to specify the number of categories into which the documents in a corpus should be divided (Grimmer and Stewart 2013, 285). The analysis here relies on a non-negative matrix factorization, or NMF, model that divides the corpus into twelve topics.[2] These model specifications were selected based on a balanced assessment of three factors: (1) the coherence of the topics generated by the model measured using the approach described by Mimno et al. (2011), (2) the intuitive quality of the topics generated by each model, and (3) the goodness of fit of the models.[3]

Using the twelve-topic NMF model, each speech in the corpus is assigned to a topic category generated by the model. For each topic, I then extract the top words that best define each topic – that is, the words that are most important for determining whether a speech is associated with that topic. The words that best define the topics provide a high-level indication of the substantive issues that are addressed in speeches assigned to each topic. This provides an initial picture of the types of issues and policies that MPs associate with women in parliamentary speech.

The unsupervised machine learning approach to the categorization of speeches by topics results in broadly accurate assignments of speeches to appropriate topics. While there may be some errors of categorization at the margins – for example, there may be nuances in the use of language that the model does not detect, the number of topics to be included in the model may not be optimal for organizing speeches into internally coherent and distinct categories, or some speeches may not fit neatly within any of the automatically generated topics – these errors are unlikely to be consequential. When using textual datasets as large as the corpus of speeches about women, this method provides valuable insight into the broad patterns of issue attention among speeches in the corpus, even if every speech assigned to a topic is not precisely related to that topic's substantive focus.

The alternative to this automated approach to categorizing speeches about women comes with its own limitations. Manually reviewing the content of all parliamentary speeches about women, developing criteria according to which these speeches should be categorized, establishing topics and assigning each speech in the corpus to a topic would be extraordinarily time consuming given the volume of text to be analyzed – nearly nine thousand speeches and 1.7 million words. Even if these time constraints could be overcome, manual approaches to the categorization of speeches are also subject to the same risks present in the machine learning method. Manual as well as automated approaches risk creating incorrect categories or assigning speeches to an incorrect grouping.

The automated approach thus allows for a previously unimaginable volume of parliamentary debate to be systematically analyzed and offers significant advantages over manual analysis and hand coding. In addition to facilitating the analysis and categorization of nearly fifty years of parliamentary debate transcripts, the machine learning approach identifies the issues raised in speeches about women according to systematic and rigorous criteria that are not subject to potential variations in interpretation by human coders. Moreover, the automated method of analysis can identify ways of organizing and partitioning documents that manual review and human analysis alone might not pick up on (Grimmer and Stewart 2013). Given the quantity of text to be analyzed and the inductive nature of the research task at hand – namely, identifying the issue content of representative claims about women – the unsupervised machine learning techniques offer a more practical and appropriate methodological solution than does manual coding. Moreover, by unpacking and disaggregating the content of such a vast quantity of textual data, the approach can uncover previously unobserved patterns that can generate new research questions and lines of inquiry.

With the speeches about women automatically categorized into twelve distinct topics, it is then possible to examine speech content and patterns of issue attention in greater detail. I confirm that the issue focus of speeches in each topic is in fact consistent with the topics implied by the features from the machine learning model through a qualitative manual review of a sample of speeches assigned to each topic. I track the over-time variation in attention to each issue in relation to government policy action and outside events as an additional check on the validity of the automatically generated topics and to gain initial insight into how patterns of parliamentary speech and policy action might be linked. I then examine patterns of attention to each of the twelve topics by gender and by party to determine whether the tendency for Conservative MPs to make frequent speeches about women, as identified in chapter 2, is driven by a particular issue focus among these MPs.

ISSUE CONTENT OF SPEECHES ABOUT WOMEN

What specific policy issues were addressed in parliamentary speeches about women? Table 3.1 lists the topics created by the twelve-topic NMF model. It shows the top fifteen words or features that are most important for determining whether a speech is associated with each topic and the number of speeches assigned to each topic. The topic names were generated based on a qualitative review of the most important features of each topic. These features suggest attention to a reasonably clear set of issues: abortion, childcare, employment, Indigenous women, International Women's Day, marriage, pay equity, program funding, rights, status, violence against women, and women's health. But an examination of the words that best characterize each topic only gets us so far. To understand in a more robust way the issues that were discussed when MPs spoke about women in parliament and the ways in which these issues were addressed further analysis is required.

I manually review a random sample of 5 per cent of the speeches assigned to each topic to more clearly identify the issues addressed by speeches in each topic and to assess the extent to which the issue content implied by the automatically generated topics was in fact reflected in the speeches assigned to each category. Based on this review, the topics generated by the model can be grouped into three categories: (1) topics that capture speeches that are thematically linked but that lack a singular or specific policy issue focus (rights, status of women, and International Women's Day); (2) topics in which the policy issue focus is broadly consistent with the topic implied by the model results, but the topic includes numerous speeches that are somewhat misaligned (abortion and childcare); and (3) topics in which the speeches clearly and consistently focus on the issues implied by the categories in table 3.1 (employment, Indigenous women, marriage, pay equity, program funding, violence against women, women's health).

In the first group of topics (those in which speeches were thematically linked but lack a clear issue focus), the substantive issue content of speeches about rights varies considerably. Of the thirty-three speeches examined in the random sample, three address women's rights in the workplace and the need to address workplace discrimination. Three discuss the inclusion of equality rights in section 28 of the Charter and the application and implications of this section. Three address abortion rights – one in the context of the debate on government legislation

Table 3.1
Topics automatically generated by the unsupervised machine learning model

Topic	*Number of speeches*	*Features*
Abortion	616	woman, abortion, right, court, man, supreme, pregnant, decision, young, life, person, case, quebec, years, justice
Childcare	833	child, children, care, poverty, women, tax, income, families, budget, need, single, housing, family, help, home
Employment	1,143	jobs, employment, cent, women, labour, insurance, benefits, unemployment, force, training, job, 000 [thousands], work, men, programs
Indigenous women	508	aboriginal, missing, murdered, inquiry, women, indigenous, girls, sisters, action, spirit, public, justice, issue, native, communities
International Women's Day	793	equality, women, day, international, world, march, week, persons, celebrate, work, society, economic, gender, history, role
Marriage	506	marriage, man, union, exclusion, petition, parliament, petitioners, woman, definition, institution, lifelong, petitions, present, law, recognize
Pay equity	423	pay, equity, equal, public, service, legislation, work, value, federal, right, years, equality, board, commission, proactive
Program funding	620	funding, program, groups, programs, centres, million, cut, secretary, state, organizations, cuts, budget, women, projects, money
Rights	658	rights, human, property, matrimonial, afghanistan, women, aboriginal, charter, indian, right, protection, reserve, protect, nations, equality
Status	1,325	women, status, responsible, committee, council, issues, advisory, colleague, action, cabinet, royal, standing, issue, comments, doing
Violence against women	1,023	violence, women, action, victims, end, girls, day, 14, sexual, young, december, polytechnique, remembrance, montreal, école
Women's health	404	health, breast, cancer, implants, research, disease, women, welfare, abortion, diagnosed, information, 000 [thousands], medical, die, awareness

during the 34th Parliament that would have recriminalized abortion, and two in the context of debate on Conservative private members' bills that sought to recriminalize abortion indirectly in the 40th and 41st Parliaments. In both cases, the speeches in the sample were made by NDP women who opposed Conservative initiatives. Four speeches focused on the rights of women in Afghanistan and Pakistan. Roughly a third of the speeches about rights (twelve in total) addressed Indigenous women in Canada – namely, discrimination against women under the Indian Act and matrimonial property rights for Indigenous women living on reserves. Many of these speeches likely could have been assigned to one of the other substantive policy topics (e.g., employment, abortion, Indigenous women). However, based on the language and framing of rights used in the speeches, they were assigned to the rights topic instead.

The status topic was even broader than the rights topic, capturing speeches that made explicit reference to the status of women and women's equality more generally on a wide range of issues. Speeches in the random sample referred to recommendations of the *Report of the Royal Commission on the Status of Women* (seven speeches), the status of Indigenous women under the Indian Act (three), and cuts to funding for Status of Women Canada (three). Speeches referring to women's social and economic status and equality more broadly focused on the appointment of women to senior positions in Crown corporations and corporate boards (seven speeches); the representation and participation of women in politics (five); the views and role of women's organizations on various policy issues (five); equality for women in the workforce (five); and the inclusion of equality rights in section 28 of the Charter (three). While held together by a shared focus on the status and equality of women, the range of issues covered in speeches assigned to this topic is somewhat muddled, and speeches share some overlap with those on rights. While the status topic is indeed characterized by a broad focus on the status of women, it lacks the issue specificity that emerged for most other categories generated by the unsupervised topic model.

Within the International Women's Day topic, the majority of speeches were made in response to International Women's Day, Persons Day, and the Persons Award. The latter, which recognizes contributions to improving the status of women in Canada, accounts for twenty-seven of the forty speeches in the random sample. Other speeches in this category mention the history of International Women's

Day or the *Persons* case, celebrate progress towards women's equality, recognize the contributions of individual women or organizations in promoting women's equality, or highlight the need for further action on gender equality in very general terms. Government MPs tended to trumpet their government's accomplishments in promoting women's equality while opposition MPs typically used International Women's Day or Persons Day as an opportunity to critique the government's record on women's equality issues, cite inadequate progress, or identify harmful policy actions. Similar to the rights and status topics, the speeches in this topic are thematically linked but do not share a specific policy issue focus.

In the second group of topics (those that include some misaligned speeches), the content of speeches in the abortion category is somewhat inconsistent with the issue focus implied by the characteristic features generated by the model. Only five of the thirty-one speeches in the random sample are about abortion and seventy-eight of the 616 speeches in the topic contain the word "abortion." Instead of an exclusive focus on the criminal status of abortion and other legal decisions and court cases as implied by the topic's distinctive features, the category includes speeches ranging from women in the armed forces, to the contributions of individual women in their communities or in politics, to the appointment of women to senior judicial roles. Speeches about abortion in the random sample were made in the context of the Progressive Conservative government's proposed legislation to recriminalize abortion in the 34th Parliament and, later on, in response to Conservative private members' bills that attempted to recriminalize abortion. Given the polarization of opinion on this issue, speeches that were substantively about abortion included articulations of both pro-choice and anti-abortion perspectives. Although it includes speeches about abortion, the categorization of speeches associated with this topic is somewhat muddled.

The childcare category also includes a wider range of speeches than anticipated. Among speeches about childcare, fifteen of the forty-two speeches in the random sample address childcare programs, tax credits, or child poverty. Seven are about pensions and income supports for older women living in poverty. The presence of speeches about pensions in this category was initially unexpected. However, federal government support for childcare and income security in old age have both been delivered as benefits or through tax credits. Therefore, the inclusion of speeches about pensions and other supports for low-income senior women within this category makes sense. The conceptual link holding together speeches about childcare and pensions is thus their shared role in providing income supports and addressing poverty among those who are outside of working age. The random sample of speeches assigned to this topic also includes seventeen speeches on a range of unrelated issues but mentions children in ways not related to childcare. Their inclusion in this category is understandable, but it highlights the imperfection of the automatically generated topic.

Finally, we can consider the third group of automatically generated topics – those in which speeches are clearly and consistently focused on the issues implied by the categories generated by the model. Almost every speech about employment addresses women's (un)employment, workforce participation, and access to employment-related benefits and training. Among the fifty-seven speeches in the random sample, only two are not explicitly about women's employment. Issues categorized under this topic include discrimination at the point of recruitment, women in the federal public service, employment equity, government programs to support women's workforce participation, access to employment benefits, and the impact of (un)employment insurance changes on women's ability to gain access to such provisions as maternity leave.

While employment equity and pay equity are closely related issues affecting women in the workplace, they have been treated as distinct policy challenges in Canadian politics (McDermott 1996). This distinction is reflected in the topics generated by the unsupervised model. Speeches assigned to the pay equity topic focus almost entirely on pay equity and the gender wage gap. Among the twenty-one speeches in the random sample, sixteen are explicitly about pay equity, while the remaining five are about women's employment in the federal public service more generally.

Within the program funding topic, virtually all speeches in the random sample are focused on funding for the federal Women's Program and women's equitable access to other government programs more generally. The Women's Program, administered by Status of Women Canada, funds organizations, projects, and services that promote women's equality (Brodie 2008). Speeches assigned to this topic were largely made during question period (seventeen of the thirty-one speeches in the random sample) when opposition MPs criticized funding cuts. Opposition questions were framed in increasingly combative partisan terms in later parliaments.

Virtually every speech in the random sample of speeches from the violence against women topic is substantively about violence against women. The issue entered parliamentary debate following the 1989 Montreal Massacre in which fourteen women engineering students were murdered at Montreal's École Polytechnique in a violent anti-feminist attack. Speeches tended to focus on calls for gun control, annual remembrance, and programs and initiatives to address violence against women. While many of the speeches in this category call on governments to take action to address violence against women, many also make commemorative acknowledgment of the tragedy without any substantive policy content or call to action. Speeches by Reform and Conservative MPs are distinctive in their focus on the need for tougher penalties for people who commit acts of violence.

The Indigenous women topic contains speeches on issues including Indigenous women's involvement in land claim negotiations and government consultations as well as the matrimonial property rights of Indigenous women living on reserve. However, the majority of speeches in the random sample (fourteen out of twenty-five) are explicitly and primarily about missing and murdered Indigenous women and girls, with opposition MPs, largely from the NDP, using oral questions and members' statements to call on the government to establish a public inquiry to address the crisis.

The women's health topic includes speeches relating to abortion, the health impacts of silicone breast implants, breast cancer and funding for research about it, and government funding for maternal and child health in developing countries. All but one of the twenty speeches in the random sample are substantively about a health issue that uniquely affects women.

Speeches categorized into the marriage topic are predominantly petitions calling on the government to define marriage as exclusively between one man and one woman. Manual inspection of the random sample reveals that the topic generated by the unsupervised model captures a small number of petitions on other issues, including calls for the government to remove the goods and services tax from feminine hygiene products and to criminalize sex work after existing Criminal Code provisions were struck down. While the topic includes speeches about issues other than the legal definition of marriage, the majority of speeches in the random sample (seventeen out of twenty-five) are explicitly focused on marriage, either through the presentation of petitions (fifteen speeches) or through motions proposing amendments to government legislation. All of the speeches in the random sample that focus on marriage call for a traditional approach to the institution, reflecting a socially conservative perspective. Although the issue of same-sex marriage is not exclusively about gender equality, the position expressed by the MPs making speeches on this topic (predominantly calling for the preservation of the definition of marriage as between one man and one woman) implies a traditional, socially conservative view of family structures and gender relations.

Overall, the categorization of speeches into the twelve automatically generated topics is accurate. With the exception of the abortion topic, there is a clear conceptual consistency among the vast majority of speeches included in each topic. All but three of the twelve topics include speeches that are focused on concrete policy issues on which legislative or other government action could be undertaken. These nine topics – abortion, childcare, employment, Indigenous women, marriage, pay equity, program funding, violence against women, and women's health – are all linked to women's social and economic inequality or initiatives to address it. The three topics that are not characterized by attention to a concrete policy issue include speeches that are nonetheless concerned with the status, rights, and equality of women as these considerations relate to a range of substantive issues (in the case of the rights and status topics) or to recognizing progress towards these goals (in the case of speeches about International Women's Day). In broad terms, the content of speeches about women is consistent with the topics that tend to be included as so-called women's issues by scholars who adopt a more content-specific approach to operationalizing the substantive representation of women – that is, issues that fall within women's traditional areas of interest or that have an impact on women's equality (e.g., Tremblay 1998; Osborn and Mendez 2010). These are also issues that are central to the advancement of women's equality that feminist policy scholars typically associate with the substantive representation of women (e.g., Mazur 2002; Htun and Weldon 2018).

While there is clear agreement about the issue content of speeches about women, MPs articulate diverse approaches to these issues. For the most part, MPs tend to agree that gender equality, stopping violence against women, ensuring women's equitable participation in the workforce, addressing the unique challenges faced by Indigenous women, and so on are all important and worthwhile goals. This is largely unsurprising. It would be difficult to imagine an MP or a political party explicitly adopting and articulating the position that women should have *less* social or economic explicitly equality. Nonetheless, what constitutes equality and the best way to achieve it remain contested. In the random sample of speeches, government MPs tend to present their government's initiatives – regardless of whether these initiatives aligned with women's movement objectives or feminist principles – as correct and appropriate actions to address women's issues, while opposition MPs criticize government action as either inadequate or counterproductive.

PATTERNS OF ISSUE ATTENTION OVER TIME

The above examination of the content of a random sample of speeches assigned to each topic provides a good indication of the substantive issue content addressed in speeches about women and confirms the validity of the topics implied by the features from the machine learning model. Looking at patterns of issue attention over time provides an additional check on the validity of the automatically generated topics. The twelve panels in figure 3.1 show the count of speeches about each topic and each topic's share of the total number of speeches in each parliament from 1968 to 2015. If we see that the frequency of speeches on a topic increases in parallel with government policy action or external events related to that topic, then we have even further reason to trust that the model's automatic categorization is good. Moreover, understanding the ways in which patterns of parliamentary speeches track with external events on the same topic offers initial insight into how patterns of parliamentary speech and policy action might be linked.

Changes in the frequency of speeches about status and International Women's Day appear not to be tied to moments of major policy activity (figures 3.1.x and 3.1.v). Peaks in the count of speeches about rights do appear to be tied to instances of concrete legislative policy action but across multiple issues (figure 3.1.ix). The peak in the count of speeches on rights in the 32nd Parliament likely reflects the passage of the Constitution Act in 1982 and the inclusion of women's equality rights in sections 15 and 28 of the Charter. The later peaks in the 39th and 41st Parliaments likely reflect the Harper government's attempts to pass legislation governing matrimonial property rights for Indigenous women living on reserves.

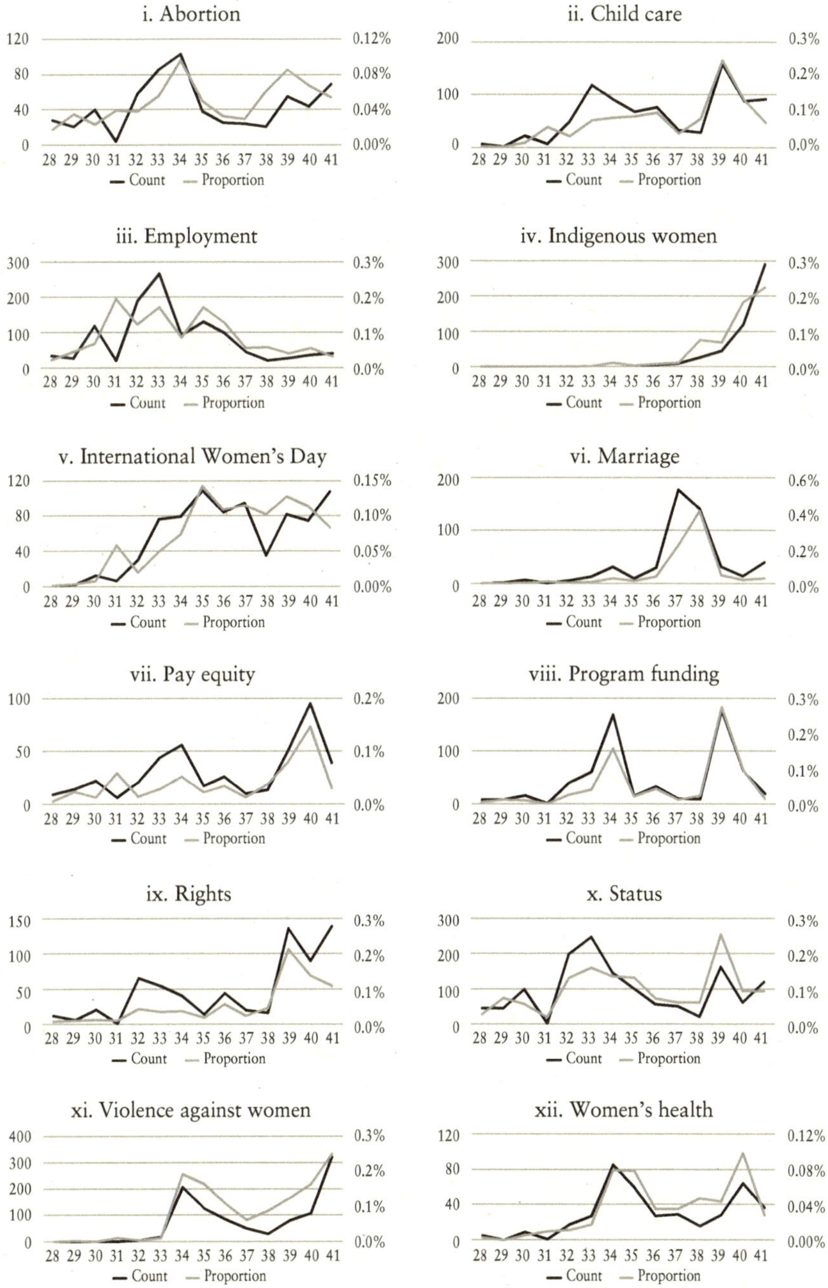

Figure 3.1 Speeches about each topic over time. Count of speeches (black) is measured on the left axis, percentage of all parliamentary speeches (grey) is measured on the right axis.

The number of speeches about abortion appears to have peaked in the 34th Parliament and in the three parliaments led by Conservative governments beginning in 2006 (figure 3.1.i). These spikes correspond to moments of concrete policy action pertaining to abortion, with the Progressive Conservative government's attempt to recriminalize abortion in the 34th Parliament (discussed in greater detail in chapter 5) and multiple attempts by Conservative Party backbenchers to introduce private members' bills that would serve indirectly to recriminalize abortion (Saurette and Gordon 2015). The peak in the number of speeches about abortion aligns with major moments of legislative policy action on abortion, suggesting that speeches assigned to the topic may not be as unfocused as the initial review of speech content implied.

Although the childcare topic includes speeches about income supports beyond an exclusive focus on childcare, the count of speeches assigned to this topic peaked in parliaments – the 33rd and 39th – when there was concerted government action pertaining to childcare (figure 3.1.ii). In the 33rd Parliament, the Mulroney Progressive Conservative government announced a national strategy that provided childcare tax credits to families and introduced, but failed to pass, the Canada Child Care Act, which would have allocated funding to the provinces to create and operate new childcare spaces (Philips 1989). In the 39th Parliament, the Harper Conservative government introduced the Universal Childcare Benefit, a taxable benefit of one hundred dollars per child per month, and rolled back a series of bilateral agreements that would have provided funding to the provinces to create additional childcare spaces negotiated by the previous Liberal government (Collier and Mahon 2008). Despite the inclusion of other issues in the category, the longitudinal pattern of attention to the childcare topic in relation to government policy action on childcare suggests the topic nonetheless serves as an accurate reflection of parliamentary attention to childcare policy.

Issues relating to women in the workforce garnered more attention in the earlier parliaments examined here, with the number of speeches assigned to the employment topic peaking in the 33rd Parliament and to a lesser extent in the 32nd and 35th Parliaments (figure 3.1.iii). These peaks in attention correspond to key moments of policy action relating to employment equity and employment insurance. In the 33rd Parliament, the Mulroney government, under the leadership of Employment Minister Flora MacDonald, introduced and passed the

Employment Equity Act. The act was introduced following the 1984 release of the report of the Royal Commission on Equality in Employment chaired by Judge Rosalie Abella. The legislation required federally regulated employers to remove barriers to employment for women, visible minorities, Indigenous people, and people with disabilities and to report annually on the representation of these groups to the federal government (Agocs 2014). The Abella Commission was established in the 32nd Parliament under the Liberal government of Pierre Trudeau. In the same parliament, the government made changes to human rights legislation to prohibit discrimination against employees based on pregnancy and added sexual harassment as an instance of workplace discrimination (Bashevkin 1998). In the 35th Parliament, the Liberal government of Jean Chrétien introduced amendments to the Employment Equity Act that expanded the scope of the legislation to include the federal public service, armed forces, and the Royal Canadian Mounted Police; increased reporting requirements; and implemented enforcement mechanisms for noncompliance with the legislation (Timpson 2001). In the same parliament, the government also introduced major changes to eligibility rules and benefits under the unemployment insurance program (Porter 2003; MacDonald 2009). Again, as with the abortion and childcare topics, peaks in the number of speeches categorized into the employment topic correspond to moments of major policy action on that issue.

On pay equity, the relationship between the frequency of speeches and major moments of policy action is slightly less clear than it is for other topics. Although the principle of equal pay for work of equal value was enshrined in the Canadian Human Rights Act in 1977, both the number and proportion of speeches about pay equity were relatively modest in the 30th Parliament when that legislation would have passed (figure 3.1.vii). Between 1984 and 1988 Manitoba, Ontario, Prince Edward Island, New Brunswick, and Nova Scotia introduced proactive pay equity legislation (McDermott 1996), but there was no major federal legislative action on pay equity. In 2009, the Harper government introduced the Public Sector Equitable Compensation Act, which would have created a separate pay equity regime for federal public sector employees that was seen by labour and women's organizations as harmful to the principle of pay equity and women's equality (National Association of Women and the Law 2009; Women's Legal Education Action Fund 2009; Public Service Alliance of Canada 2013). This moment of legislative action is reflected in the spike in the count and share of speeches about pay equity in the 40th Parliament.[4] The more modest spike in speeches about pay equity in the 34th Parliament seems unrelated to any legislative initiative by the federal government in that period but may have been driven by legislative activity in the provinces – an expectation that is supported by the tendency of speeches in this category to be made in question period or as members' statements.

Attention to program funding (figure 3.1.vii) peaked in the 34th and 39th Parliaments – both periods during which governments implemented major funding cuts and policy changes to the federal Women's Program (Brodie 2008; Rodgers and Knight 2011). The cuts and changes to the mandate of the Women's Program and Status of Women Canada in the 39th Parliament, including the role of women MPs in resisting these changes, are examined in greater detail in chapter 6.

Prior to the 34th Parliament, violence against women was hardly ever mentioned in parliamentary proceedings. Attention to the issue spiked dramatically in the 34th Parliament following the 1989 Montreal Massacre (figure 3.1.xi). During this parliament, the Subcommittee on the Status of Women held hearings focused on violence against women and submitted a report to parliament. Several of the recommendations outlined in the report were taken up by the Mulroney Progressive Conservative government, including the establishment of a task force on violence against women, changes to sexual assault provisions in the Criminal Code, and the incorporation of several of the committee's recommendations into the government's gun control legislation (Young 1997). While attention to violence against women dropped off somewhat after the 34th Parliament, it peaked again in the 41st Parliament. This spike appears to reflect, at least in part, the Harper government's law-and-order approach to violence against women and its problematic attempt to criminalize the already-illegal practices of polygamy, forced marriage, and so-called honour killings among immigrant communities through the Zero Tolerance for Barbaric Cultural Practices Act (Abji et al. 2019; Roach 2015).

Virtually no attention was paid to Indigenous women in parliamentary speech prior to the early 2000s, but speeches on this topic began to emerge in the 38th Parliament and increased dramatically in each subsequent parliament (figure 3.1.iv). The peak of attention in the 41st Parliament appears to be driven by repeated calls by NDP MPs for the government to take action on violence against Indigenous women by creating a national inquiry into missing and murdered Indigenous women and girls. Parliamentary attention appears to have been instigated by concerted efforts by the Native Women's Association of Canada to bring attention to systemic violence against Indigenous women and girls, and by the 2013 release of an RCMP report documenting 1,181 cases of missing or murdered Indigenous women and girls (Crown-Indigenous Relations and Northern Affairs Canada 2016). In addition to oral questions, NDP MP Niki Ashton introduced a private member's motion calling for the establishment of a national action plan on violence against women, including a national public inquiry into missing and murdered Indigenous women and girls (Ashton 2015). No legislative action was taken to address violence against Indigenous women in the 41st Parliament, but the Harper government passed legislation outlining the rights of spouses and common law partners to family homes held on First Nations reserves (after several unsuccessful attempts to pass similar legislation in the 39th and 40th Parliaments), which may have also contributed to the heightened number of speeches on this topic (Bill S-2 2013, Family Homes on Reserves and Matrimonial Interests or Rights Act; see also Bill S-4 2010, Bill C-8 2009, Bill C-47 2008, all with the same title).

Speeches about women's health spiked in the 34th and 40th Parliaments, reflecting two moments of heightened parliamentary attention and policy action (figure 3.1.xii). In the 34th Parliament, although no policy change or legislation was introduced, the Subcommittee on the Status of Women undertook a series of hearings and released a report on breast cancer (Young 1997). In the same parliament, the Mulroney government introduced and nearly passed legislation to recriminalize abortion (discussed in greater detail in chapter 5). During the 40th Parliament, as part of the 2010 G8 Summit that was held in Canada, the Conservative government introduced its Maternal, Newborn and Child Health initiative. The initiative was ostensibly designed to increase support for the Millennium Development Goal of improving maternal health but excluded support for abortion access and gender equality (Tiessen 2015).

Speeches about marriage emerged in response to federal legislative activity to recognize same-sex relationships. Speeches assigned to this topic spiked dramatically in the 37th and 38th Parliaments but were otherwise very rare during the period examined here (figure 3.1.vi). In the wake of the *M v. H* Supreme Court decision recognizing the equal legal standing of same-sex couples, the Liberal government of

Jean Chrétien introduced the Modernization of Benefits and Other Obligations Act in 2000, which modified sixty-eight legislative acts to recognize the rights of "common law partners" (Rayside 2008, 102–5). In 2003, following an Ontario Court of Appeal decision that immediately legalized same-sex marriage in that province, the Liberal government announced its intention to introduce legislation "formally defining marriage to include same-sex couples" (Rayside 2008, 110). Religious conservatives mobilized against marriage equality, and the Reform/Canadian Alliance Party became the primary legislative conduit for this counter-movement. In 2005, the Liberal minority government of Paul Martin introduced and narrowly passed the Spousal Relationships and Statue Law Amendment Act, which established a new definition of spouse to include same-sex couples (Rayside 2008).

In short, spikes in the number of speeches on each of the nine topics that deal with specific policy issues consistently reflect moments of concerted policy action on these issues. This provides additional confirmation that the issue foci implied by the automatically generated topics are accurate. It also provides an initial indication of how patterns of parliamentary speech and policy action might be connected. The patterns explored above suggest that increased attention to a topic in debate happens in one of two contexts: (1) instances of government policy action relating to that topic (as in the case of childcare, employment equity, program funding, and marriage equality) or (2) moments of concerted attention to an issue by MPs seeking to put that issue on the legislative or policy agenda to compel government action (as in the case of violence against women and Indigenous women).

Spikes during moments of government policy action reflect in part the logically necessary increase in the number of speeches on a topic that occurs following the introduction of and debate on a bill on that topic. Attention to an issue-driven legislative or policy action, however, is not merely a function of second and third reading of a bill. It also includes broader parliamentary engagement with and sometimes resistance to government initiatives through oral questions, members' statements, opposition motions, or committee work. When government legislative or policy initiatives constituted instances of regress for women's equality, spikes in the level of attention to these topics tended to reflect opposition and resistance to the government's approach – for example, with pro-feminist speeches opposing the Harper government's cuts to Women's Program funding or its

Public Sector Equitable Compensation Act. Conversely, speeches about marriage reflected a counter-movement backlash against feminist and LGBTQ+ interests; these perspectives expressed resistance to the Martin government's equality-promoting intention to legalize same-sex marriage.

Spikes during moments of attempted agenda-setting are typically driven by parliamentarians who seize upon current events to try to bring about government action, as occurred after the Montreal Massacre. In other cases, legislative attention to an issue builds upon and gives voice to extra-parliamentary efforts, as in the case of the Native Women's Association of Canada's work to highlight missing and murdered Indigenous women and girls. In each of these instances, MPs act as a conduit through which external concerns, events, or issues are brought to parliament for consideration and eventual policy action. In some cases, these efforts led to government action within the same parliament, as with the incorporation of some of the Subcommittee on the Status of Women's recommendations into the Mulroney government's gun control legislation in the 34th Parliament. In other cases, the spike in speeches did not lead to concrete policy action. For example, calls for the creation of a national inquiry into missing and murdered Indigenous women and girls were not taken up during any of the parliaments observed in this study. However, the Trudeau Liberal government responded to these calls early in its mandate, announcing in December 2015 the launch of a national inquiry into missing and murdered Indigenous women and girls (Indigenous and Northern Affairs Canada 2015).

GENDER AND PARTISAN DIFFERENCES IN PATTERNS OF ISSUE ATTENTION

With the issue content of parliamentary speeches about women more clearly identified, we can now consider whether different groups of MPs prioritized different policy issues in parliamentary debate. Did women and left-leaning MPs focus on different issues than did men and right-leaning MPs when speaking about women in parliament? An examination of gender differences in patterns of issue attention offer insight into whether women MPs' tendency to make more speeches about women is characterized by a particular issue focus. Closer attention to patterns of issue attention by party makes it possible to probe further into the unexpected finding from chapter 2 that Conservative MPs are predicted to make more speeches about women than are MPs in any other party group. Gender and party differences in attention to each of the twelve topics are examined below.

Table 3.2 shows the distribution of speeches for each topic by gender. Women MPs were responsible for the largest number of speeches on nine topics, six of which reflect a concrete policy issue focus: childcare, program funding, Indigenous women, pay equity, violence against women, and women's health. These six topics are concerned with women's social and economic equality. They reflect attention to issues and policy areas that are typically identified by feminist policy scholars as important for achieving women's equality.

Men MPs made more speeches than their female colleagues about employment (by a very small margin), abortion, and marriage. The employment topic is closely linked to broader questions about the state of the economy – workforce participation, unemployment rates, job losses, and so on. Economic issues are typically perceived to belong to the stereotypically masculine domain of the economy and the public sphere. The tendency for men MPs to focus on employment issues thus allows them to engage in the representation of women within the context of masculine coded policy issues.

The decriminalization of abortion and the legalization of same-sex marriage are both instances of liberalizing changes that increase equality. Positions on these issues are influenced by religious doctrine and tradition, such that changes are typically opposed by social conservatives (see Htun and Weldon 2018). As noted above, the content of speeches on abortion is somewhat muddled and included speeches that both defended and opposed abortion access, so it is difficult to draw firm conclusions. Nonetheless, men were responsible for more speeches about abortion than were women. The tendency for men to prioritize attention to marriage is noteworthy. Recall that speeches about marriage were almost entirely speeches that opposed the legalization of same-sex marriage and defended a traditional view of family structures and gender relations. Men were responsible for more speeches on this topic than were women by a significant margin – they made more than four times as many speeches as did women. These patterns suggest that men MPs tended to speak more about women in parliamentary debate on topics that are less explicitly concerned with redressing gender inequality or women's rights and that offer greater opportunity to advance a more traditional rather than equality-promoting position.

Table 3.2
Distribution of speeches by gender for each topic

	Women		*Men*	
	N	%	*N*	%
Abortion	275	45	**341**	**55**
Childcare	**564**	68	269	32
Employment	570	50	**573**	**50**
Indigenous women	**373**	**73**	135	27
International Women's Day	**562**	71	231	29
Marriage	93	18	**413**	**82**
Pay equity	**274**	**65**	149	35
Program funding	**426**	**69**	194	31
Rights	**392**	**60**	266	40
Status	**795**	**60**	530	40
Violence against women	**706**	**69**	317	31
Women's health	**273**	**68**	131	32

Note: The count of speeches and each group's share of speeches on that topic are both shown. The group responsible for the most speeches on each topic is shown in bold.

Table 3.3 shows the distribution of speeches for each topic by party. NDP and Liberal MPs are responsible for the largest share of speeches about most topics. New Democrats deliver the bulk of speeches about childcare, Indigenous women, and pay equity, while Liberals devote the most attention to abortion, employment, International Women's Day, program funding, rights, status, violence against women, and women's health. It should be noted, however, that the Liberal lead over the NDP is quite small, even though, for most parliaments considered, Liberals accounted for a much larger share of parliamentary seats and speeches than did NDP MPs. Some of these patterns may be a function of when attention to these issues spiked and the share of seats held by each party at the time. For example, the number of speeches about program funding (a topic about which Liberals made the most speeches) spiked in the 39th Parliament when the Liberals were the Official Opposition in a minority parliament. Similarly, the number of speeches about Indigenous women (a topic about which New Democrats made the most speeches) spiked in the 41st Parliament, when the NDP formed the Official Opposition. The tendency for parties to have made the most speeches about topics that also spiked during parliaments in which they formed the Official Opposition likely reflects the fact that opposition MPs use parliamentary speeches as a tool for bringing attention to issues that are a priority for them. Changes to the Canadian party system are also relevant to patterns of issue attention. For example, the Progressive Conservative Party made very few speeches about Indigenous women because the party had been dissolved by the time attention to this topic began to increase dramatically around the time of the 38th Parliament.

Beyond these particularities of timing, the topics each party focused on appear to reflect pre-existing partisan priorities. The NDP's focus on childcare and pay equity is consistent with the social democratic positioning of the party. Both issues require a high degree of government intervention, either through state provision (as in the case of funding for a public childcare system or state pensions) or through regulating the operations of private enterprise (as in the case of pay equity). Similarly, the Liberals' focus on rights, women's health, and violence against women reflects an issue focus that is compatible with the party's centrist orientation, which includes a preoccupation with formal equality of individuals in society. For Liberals, issues of rights, women's health, and violence against women are consistent with this outlook.

Although left and centrist MPs made the most speeches about nearly all topics, Conservative and Reform/Canadian Alliance MPs made the most speeches about marriage by a considerable margin. This is logical given the strong tendency for such speeches to defend a socially conservative view of family structures and gender relations. Parallel with this interpretation, Reform/Canadian Alliance MPs were responsible for a negligible share of speeches on the eleven other topics. This reflects a striking lack of interest in the representation of women by Reform/Canadian Alliance MPs except when representation meant defending traditional gender roles and family values.

Whereas chapter 2 finds that gender plays an important role in determining whether an MP will represent women, the analysis in this chapter shows how party affiliation shapes patterns of issue attention in parliamentary speech. On questions of women's social and economic inequality, left and centrist MPs in the NDP and Liberal parties made the most speeches, with MPs from these parties focusing on topics aligned with their broader ideological positions. The tendency for left and centrist MPs to take the lead on the representation of

Table 3.3
Distribution of speeches by party for each topic

	NDP		*BQ*		*LPC*		*PC*		*CPC*		*REF/CA*	
	N	%	N	%	N	%	N	%	N	%	N	%
Abortion	181	29	53	9	**185**	**30**	110	18	67	11	20	3
Childcare	**305**	**37**	81	10	251	30	81	10	104	12	11	1
Employment	337	29	144	13	**346**	**30**	282	25	28	2	6	1
Indigenous women	**229**	**45**	27	5	94	19	5	1	147	29	6	1
International Women's Day	151	19	85	11	**336**	**42**	108	14	100	13	13	2
Marriage	49	10	6	1	122	24	33	7	**165**	**33**	131	26
Pay equity	**174**	**41**	54	13	112	26	46	11	32	8	5	1
Program funding	153	25	64	10	**177**	**29**	101	16	121	20	4	1
Rights	171	26	56	9	**193**	**29**	62	9	155	24	21	3
Status	388	29	132	10	**390**	**29**	265	20	131	10	19	1
Violence against women	309	30	74	7	**324**	**32**	84	8	212	21	20	2
Women's health	115	28	43	11	**138**	**34**	53	13	40	10	15	4

Note: The count of speeches and each group's share of speeches on that topic are both shown. The group responsible for the most speeches on each topic is shown in bold.

women on issues relating to women's social and economic equality is consistent with the view that the promotion of feminist interests is generally more compatible with the ideological orientation of leftist political parties (Celis and Childs 2012).

Conservative MPs dominated on only one topic – marriage – and here their interventions defended a traditional view of family structures and gender roles. The tendency for Conservative and Reform/Canadian Alliance MPs to make the most speeches about women on an issue characterized by the defence of traditional family structures and gender roles suggests that MPs in these parties prioritize a traditional rather than a pro-equality approach to the substantive representation of women. This finding offers additional insight into, and valuable nuance to, the finding that Conservative MPs are predicted to make frequent speeches about women in parliamentary debate. Chapter 2 finds that Conservative MPs overall are predicted to make more speeches about women than are those from any other partisan group. The analysis from this chapter suggests that this tendency appears at least in part to be driven by frequent attention to issues in which MPs tended to adopt a more traditional view of gender roles rather than by a defence of a pro-equality feminist position. Right-leaning MPs therefore appear to be representing women, but in many cases they do so in a distinctively non-feminist way.

IMPLICATIONS

The results and analysis in this chapter provide valuable insight into the issue content of the substantive representation of women in parliamentary speech and help to account for the unexpected frequency of speeches about women among Conservative MPs. These findings provide greater clarity in terms of what it means for women MPs to be more inclined than their male colleagues to represent women in parliamentary debate. Topics generated by the unsupervised machine learning model together with a qualitative manual review of speeches assigned to each topic show that when MPs spoke about women in parliamentary debate they were typically speaking about issues that are clearly linked to women's social and economic equality and autonomy – abortion, childcare, employment, Indigenous women, marriage, pay equity, program funding, violence against women, and women's health. Broadly speaking, these are the same issues typically identified by feminist policy scholars as relevant to the substantive representation of women. Although there is a clear set of issues that constitutes the substantive representation of women in parliamentary speech, there are differences in terms of the issues MPs from different parties emphasize and the perspective from which they approach them. Women and left-leaning MPs made the most speeches on topics that were more clearly connected to issues relating to women's social and economic equality. Men and right-leaning MPs made the most speeches on topics that intersect with the stereotypically masculine sphere of the economy and on topics related to traditional family values and gender roles. Notably, the only topic for which Conservative MPs were responsible for the largest share of speeches was marriage, a topic in which speeches supported a socially conservative view of family structures and gender relations.

There are two key implications that follow from this chapter's findings. First is that there is consistency in terms of the issue content of the substantive representation of women across different approaches to operationalizing the concept. Even when a more content-neutral operationalization of the substantive representation of women in parliamentary speech is adopted, this chapter finds that speeches about women tend to be about issues or policies relating to women's equality and autonomy. Broadly speaking, these are the same policy issues identified by scholars who conceive of the substantive representation of women in more content-specific terms and are consistent with the issues identified by scholars who conceive of the substantive representation of women in feminist terms as issues related to the promotion of gender equality (e.g., Wängnerud 2000; Bratton 2002; Mazur 2002; Beckwith and Cowell-Meyers 2007; Kittilson 2008). These approaches have been criticized for being reductionist or essentializing insofar as they fail to account for the diversity of views held by women (e.g., Trimble 2006; Smooth 2011; Schwindt-Bayer and Taylor-Robison 2011; Celis et al. 2014). The evidence presented in this chapter suggests that the set of issues typically identified as women's issues by feminist scholars is largely accurate insofar as it aligns with the content of representative claims about women made by legislators.

This finding of course leaves open the possibility that the construction of women's issues in parliamentary debate merely reflects the perspectives of those who occupy seats in the House of Commons and who may differ in important and systematic ways from the full diversity of women in the population more broadly. Further research probing the extent to which the issues raised on behalf of women in parliament reflect the concerns of women in the population may thus be warranted. Methodologically, however, this finding provides reassurance that, regardless of the way in which the substantive representation of women in parliamentary speech is operationalized and measured – whether in terms of attention to a predetermined list of policy issues or in terms of representative claims about women – studies will capture broadly the same concepts.

The second implication is that, just as the election of women matters for *whether* parliamentarians will make speeches about women, party affiliation seems to have an impact on *how* they will speak about women. As we see in chapter 2, Conservative MPs are likely to be actively engaged in the substantive representation of women in parliamentary speech. But this pattern is at least partially attributable to the fact that a large portion of Conservative MPs' speeches about women reflected a more traditional, rather than equality-oriented, perspective on women and gender roles. While it is beyond the scope of this analysis, the quality of these claims and the extent to which they respond to and are deemed acceptable by the women on whose behalf they are made warrants further scrutiny. Conservative MPs represent women more than might typically be assumed, but this representation does not necessarily reflect engagement with feminist policy issues. If the objective is to increase attention to issues relating to women's social and economic equality, the election of women, left, and centrist MPs remains important.

Chapter 2 establishes that women MPs are more likely than are men MPs to speak about women in parliamentary debate; this chapter identifies the issue content of those speeches about women and shows that party affiliation matters for the types of issues parliamentarians raise in debate. The analysis in this chapter also provides preliminary insight into the connection between parliamentary debate and policy action. Periods of heightened attention to certain issues in parliamentary debate do appear to reflect moments of concerted policy action on these issues. This policy action came either in the form of government policy action or through attempts by MPs to place an issue on the political agenda. But we still need a more detailed understanding of the ways in which parliamentary debate and policy action on women's issues are connected and the ways in which policy action and change occur. In the chapters that follow, I explore in greater detail the connection between parliamentary issue attention and the role of women MPs in pushing for women's equality policy change.

4

Connecting Parliamentary Speeches and Policy Action

In November 1989, Progressive Conservative MP and cabinet minister Barbara McDougall spoke out on the floor of the House of Commons against a government bill that reinscribed abortion as an offence under the Criminal Code. In her remarks, she articulated her belief in the importance of women's ability to have access to safe and legal abortions, while also resigning herself to supporting legislation that placed restrictions on abortion access (McDougall 1989). In December 2006, New Democratic Party leader Jack Layton rose in question period and called on the Harper government to increase "core funding for the women's groups that advocate for equality" and condemned the government's cuts and policy changes to Status of Women Canada (Layton 2006a, 2006b). Both of these interventions were made during parliaments in which the proportion of parliamentary speeches about women increased dramatically. Speeches about women spiked in the 34th Parliament (1988–93) and in the 39th Parliament (2006–08). The interventions above speak to policy issues that contributed to the dramatic increase in the proportion of speeches about women during these two parliaments. This chapter examines the content of speeches about women and patterns of issue attention that contributed to the spikes in attention to women in parliamentary debate in the 34th and 39th Parliaments.

Unpacking the details of the patterns of issue attention that contributed to these spikes in speeches about women helps us to better understand the ways in which parliamentary debate and policy action on women's equality issues might be linked. Identifying the policy issues behind the spikes also allows for the identification of specific policy cases that can be investigated more closely through qualitative analysis. The substantive representation of women is multifaceted –

it encompasses parliamentary debate as well as policy advocacy and outcomes. These dimensions are distinct from one another but are nonetheless potentially connected. The analysis in this chapter and the chapters that follow is focused on figuring out whether and how patterns of speech, policy advocacy, and outcomes are connected. This investigation allows us to develop a more complete understanding of how the three forms of the substantive representation of women fit together to constitute a comprehensive whole.

Guided by these objectives, this chapter analyzes patterns of issue attention in parliamentary debate during the 34th and 39th Parliaments to understand the factors and context that drove the spikes in attention to women in these two cases. Why did the proportion of speeches about women increase dramatically in these two parliaments? What are the issues MPs were talking about the most when they made speeches about women in these two parliaments? Were the issues MPs were talking about in debate the same issues on which policy change was happening? And, if so, how did speech and policy action relate to one another?

CASES, DATA, AND METHODS

The analysis in this chapter focuses on patterns of issue attention among parliamentary speeches about women in the two parliaments that were characterized by heightened attention to women in parliamentary debate. The 34th and 39th Parliaments stand out as instances in which the proportion of parliamentary speeches about women was unusually high. As shown in figure 4.1, these cases are outliers from the overall trend line of gradual increase in the frequency of speeches about women in parliamentary debate. Consistent with the logic of nested analysis – an approach to mixed methods research through which a large-n analysis is used to guide case selection for more in-depth examination of a small number of cases (Lieberman 2005) – a closer examination of these "off-the-line" cases can generate new insights into the underlying processes and conditions that led to heightened attention to women in parliamentary debate. The patterns observed in these two parliaments can then be used to develop conceptual insights that can be assessed and refined in other contexts.

This chapter examines patterns of issue attention in the 34th and 39th Parliaments in order (1) to identify what contributed to the spikes in the substantive representation of women in parliamentary debate in these two parliaments and to better understand the connection between

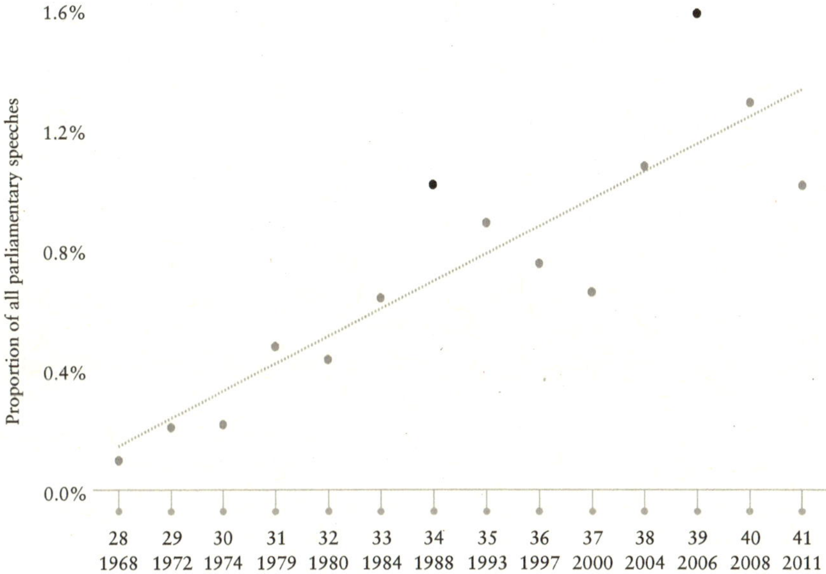

Figure 4.1 Percentage of parliamentary speeches about women by parliament, 1968–2015. Off-the-line cases are shown in black.

parliamentary speech and policy action, and (2) to identify specific policy cases for closer qualitative analysis. To do this, I manually examine the content of speeches about women in each parliament and, in each case, connect those patterns of issue attention with the broader women's equality policymaking context.

The corpora of speeches about women in the 34th and 39th Parliaments used for analysis is again derived from the original Lipad dataset of parliamentary speeches from 1968 to 2015 that is the basis for analysis in chapters 2 and 3. Recall that speeches about women are speeches that mention the words "woman" or "women" at least once every 330 words. Using this metric, the corpus of speeches about women in the 34th Parliament includes 1,108 speeches, and the corpus of speeches about women in the 39th Parliament includes 1,035 speeches. These corpora include interventions from all aspects of parliamentary debate, from oral questions and responses, to members' statements, to debates on proposed legislation.

To identify the patterns of issue attention that contributed to the spike in speeches about women in the 34th and 39th Parliaments, I use the two Hansard topic categorizations included in the Lipad database.

The Lipad dataset links every speech in the corpus to two different topic categorizations. One of the topic fields indicates the element of parliamentary proceedings in which the speech was made – for example, oral questions, routine proceedings, or government orders. This field reflects elements of parliamentary proceedings that are determined by the Standing Orders that govern the operations of parliament. The second topic field indicates the substantive issue or topic addressed in the speech – for example, violence against women, employment equity, and so on. These categories are generated by editors in the parliamentary Hansard office as topics emerge in debate and speeches are assigned to these categories as each day's Hansard is compiled (House of Commons 2019). Both layers of categorization are applied to the transcripts of parliamentary debate by the editors, and both tags in the Lipad dataset are drawn directly from the original Hansard source documents that were used to generate the digital dataset (Beelen et al. 2017). In this chapter, I refer to this second group of substantive issue topic categorizations as subtopics.

I use the Hansard topic categorizations rather than the automatically generated topics developed in chapter 3 to identify which issues contributed to the spike in speeches about women because they are better suited to the research task at hand. The Hansard subtopics are more granular and specific than are the automatically generated topics. The unsupervised machine learning model in chapter 3 sorted speeches about women into twelve categories that are useful for understanding overall patterns of issue attention and consistently comparing these patterns over time. Because there are only twelve categories, however, they are necessarily general and, as a result, are less instructive for understanding the specific issues that were raised in a specific parliament. By contrast, there are 241 Hansard subtopics among the 1,108 speeches about women in the 34th Parliament (125 of which only had one speech assigned to them, such as "impact on child care program" or "training programs – cuts in benefits for older women"). There are 160 Hansard subtopics among the 1,035 speeches about women in the 39th Parliament.

The Hansard topic categorizations offer a useful starting point for identifying the context and issue content of parliamentary speech, but they are admittedly imperfect. The Standing Orders are periodically updated and changed; as a result, there may be inconsistencies in references to the more minor categories of parliamentary proceedings. Since the topic categorizations that identify the subject of a speech are generated by Hansard editors on an ongoing basis, variation may occur over time in the specific wording used to refer to an issue or topic in Hansard. There may also be inconsistencies in how speeches are assigned to different topics.

Despite this potential for small discrepancies, the Hansard topic categorizations included in the Lipad dataset provide a useful tool for identifying at a high level the issues parliamentarians speak about in debate and the procedural context in which these issues are raised. The specificity of the Hansard subtopics means they are better suited to more detailed within-case analysis, in which the research goal is to understand which issues MPs spoke about most frequently and which issues might have contributed to the overall spike in the proportion of speeches about women in these two parliaments. The results based on the Hansard subtopics are more specific but are consistent with the analysis of patterns of issue attention based on the automatically generated topic categorizations in chapter 3, and parallels are noted throughout the analysis that follows.

To determine which issues contributed to the spike in the proportion of speeches about women in the 34th and 39th Parliaments, I identify the Hansard subtopics concerning which MPs made the most speeches about women. The subtopics with the most speeches indicate the issues that were raised most frequently when MPs made speeches about women in that parliament. If the issues addressed most frequently in speeches about women are related to women's equality policy initiatives that were undertaken in that parliament, then that is preliminary confirmation that the increased number of speeches about women is linked to action on women's equality. Below I examine the content of speeches about women under the relevant subtopics to develop a comprehensive understanding of the relationship between speech and action.

PATTERNS OF ISSUE ATTENTION IN THE 34TH PARLIAMENT

The proportion of parliamentary speeches about women spiked in the 34th Parliament, which sat from December 1988 to September 1993. Brian Mulroney's Progressive Conservatives were elected to their second majority mandate in 1988 with 169 out of 295 seats in the House of Commons. The Liberals formed the Official Opposition with 83 seats in the Commons and the NDP held 43 seats. Overall, women occupied 39 seats (13 per cent) in the House of Commons.[1]

Speech Content

Table 4.1 lists the five issues that were addressed most frequently in speeches about women in the 34th Parliament based on the Hansard subtopics from the Lipad dataset. The subtopic with the largest number of speeches about women in the 34th Parliament is violence against women. The prominence of this issue is notable, given that it did not appear as a subtopic under which speeches about women were categorized in any parliament prior to 1988. This pattern is also evident in patterns of issue attention measured using the topics generated by the unsupervised machine learning model in chapter 3. Figure 3.1.xi shows that there were virtually no speeches on this topic until the 34th Parliament, when the number of speeches on this topic spiked. Manual inspection of the content of these speeches reveals that well over half of the 115 speeches about violence against women were directly related to the antifeminist massacre of fourteen women engineering students at Montreal's École Polytechnique on 6 December 1989 – that is, they either made explicit reference to the Montreal Massacre, École Polytechnique, or were made on the anniversary of the tragedy. The Montreal Massacre therefore acted as a focusing event that put the issue of violence against women on the parliamentary agenda in a relatively stable way. In every parliament after the 34th, violence against women was one of the top ten most frequent Hansard subtopics into which speeches about women are categorized.

In the 34th Parliament, more than half the speeches about violence against women were oral questions asked during question period. Questions were often linked to the Montreal Massacre, but they also used the event to bring attention to the need for government action on related issues. For example, in a question asked on the second anniversary of the massacre, NDP leader Audrey McLaughlin called on the government to provide adequate core funding for women's shelters:

> Today, the entire country remembers the massacre in Montreal, but this day of remembrance can also be a day of action. Madam Speaker, the Minister of Finance says that he is preparing his budget. I would like to tell the minister that women are sick and tired of begging for shelters for battered women. We are sick and tired of organizing garage sales and bake sales so that our children can have a safe place to sleep. In Quebec alone,

> 12 shelters are threatening to close down. Will the minister tell women that in his next budget there will [be] enough money for these shelters? (McLaughlin 1991)

Many of the oral questions in this subtopic also called on the government to establish a royal commission on violence against women. On 19 June 1991, Justice Minister Kim Campbell confirmed that "a blue ribbon panel about violence against women was going to be established" (Campbell 1991). Campbell emphasized:

> the government's commitment to look at this issue very seriously and to identify it as a unique and particular issue of Canadian society, in other words, violence against women being a particular social phenomenon, is clear. We have every intention of following through not just with the study of violence against women, but with the appropriate actions to deal with its causes and its effects.

Despite the government's stated commitment to addressing the issue of violence against women, the panel was ultimately seen as a symbolic exercise that failed to gain the support of the National Action Committee on the Status of Women (Bashevkin 1996).

The tendency for speeches about violence against women to be made during question period suggests that MPs who raised the issue did so to put it on the government's agenda, to critique government inaction, or to compel the government to act. Oral questions are one of the key tools that opposition parties use to perform the scrutiny function that is central to parliamentary government accountability. Oral questions also allow opposition parties to put issues on to the parliamentary agenda. Question period has long been characterized by political theatrics. Yet it stands as the element of parliamentary proceedings that garners significant media attention and allows MPs to draw the attention of the government and the wider public to policy issues (Franks 1987; Docherty 2005; Soroka et al. 2009). In the case of calls for the establishment of a royal commission on violence against women, the government eventually responded. Of the forty-five questions that were asked, forty-three were posed by opposition NDP and Liberal MPs, and two came from government backbenchers. Although backbenchers may have been less inclined to criticize their own government, this distribution of speeches is a function of how questions are allocated to the parties, with

Table 4.1
Speeches about women in the 34th Parliament by Hansard subtopic

Subtopic	*Number of speeches*	*Proportion of speeches about women*
Violence against women	115	10.4%
Status of women	82	7.4%
Petitions	67	6.0%
Criminal Code	58	5.2%
Funding for women's centres	43	3.9%

government backbenchers receiving fewer opportunities to question the government than do opposition members.

The next largest share of speeches about women was about the status of women. Manual inspection of the eighty-two speeches in this subtopic reveals attention to a variety of substantive issues about women's equality, from funding for women's centres, to pay and employment equity, to childcare, to violence against women, to statements on International Women's Day. For example, in a member's statement categorized under this subtopic, Liberal MP Mary Clancy decried the government's failure to implement a national childcare program as a setback for women's equality:

> Yesterday's budget cuts put a roadblock on the highway to the advancement of women in Canada ... the government today announced that a national child care program is a dead issue. Canadian women who are in need of suitable affordable child care cannot find it and the increase in child care deductions will not create the needed spaces. Once again the government has backed down on its promise. (Clancy 1992)

In another member's statement categorized under this subtopic, NDP MP Margaret Mitchell highlighted the unique challenges racialized and immigrant women face in achieving equality:

> Madam Speaker, International Women's Week is over but double discrimination continues against women of colour and immigrant women. Domestic workers are locked into live-in

> jobs where they can be exploited and new policies will exclude many women of colour from coming to Canada as domestics. Lack of professional accreditation forces many immigrant women to remain in low-paying jobs. The Tory budget also has added another layer of hardship for these women. The $1 million cut to Canada Jobs Strategy training represents a 35 per cent cut to immigrant women who also lack child care ... This government has lost all respect for the rights of minorities, and especially for women of colour who are doubly jeopardized. (Mitchell 1992)

The status of women subtopic is thus not focused on a single policy issue or event, similar to the status topic generated by the machine learning model in chapter 3. Figure 3.1.x shows that the number of speeches in the automatically generated status topic did not reach its peak in the 34th Parliament, but was nonetheless quite high.

As with speeches about violence against women, the majority of speeches in the Hansard status of women subtopic (sixty-two out of eighty-two) were made during question period. Again, the use of question period and the content of the questions themselves suggest that these speeches were aimed at influencing policy agendas and holding the government to account for its policy actions, particularly on funding cuts to women's centres. For example, Liberal MP Shirley Maheu raised concerns about funding cuts and the government's decision to provide funding to the antifeminist organization, REAL Women of Canada:

> Two years ago, the government started cutting funding for women' programs while subsidizing the reactionary group REAL Women. Today, all women's groups are barely surviving as a result of these budget cuts. Can the minister give the House the assurance that this anti-equality group which still calls itself REAL Women will have no further grants from this government? (Maheu 1990)

Responses by government MPs typically downplayed the funding cuts and emphasized positive government actions related to women's equality. In response to an NDP question critical of the government's commitment to women's equality, the prime minister enumerated his government's record:

> We introduced employment equity legislation in 1986. We increased by 100 per cent the number of women in decision-making positions in commissions and agencies of the federal government. We introduced a family violence initiative of $40 million in June of 1988. We improved job training for women as part of the Canadian Jobs Strategy. We introduced a $25 million program for immigrant women, improved child tax credits for low-income families, a plan for equal pay for work of equal value in the federal Public Service and improved pension benefits for women. That is a partial list of the accomplishments of a government deeply committed to the notion of equality and fairness for women. (Mulroney 1990)

This response and others like it in this subtopic suggest that, despite policy decisions that undermined women's equality, the government was unwilling to be publicly portrayed as unconcerned about women or unsympathetic to women's issues.

Sixty-seven speeches about women were categorized as petitions. These were speeches that MPs made when presenting petitions from citizens to the House. Petition speeches focused on violence against women (twenty-four speeches), the removal of the goods and services tax from sanitary products (fourteen speeches), and the implementation of paid leave for pregnant women in hazardous workplaces (ten speeches). Because this subtopic is more procedurally focused, there is no parallel topic generated by the unsupervised machine learning model. Petitions signal the desire of signatories for government to respond to a specific grievance. When MPs present petitions to the House, they make a brief statement about the content of the petition; however, MPs who present a petition on behalf of their constituents are not required to agree with its content. Petitions typically have a limited impact on policy outcomes and tell us little about the issue priorities of MPs; instead, they offer insight into the issue priorities of reasonably well-organized and engaged citizens (Hough 2012).

The debate around the recriminalization of abortion attracted a significant share of speeches about women. Manual inspection of the fifty-eight speeches about the Criminal Code confirms that the vast majority (forty-five speeches) were about Bill C-43 – the Progressive Conservative government's proposed legislation to recriminalize abortion. The remaining speeches occurred as part of the debate on changes to the rape shield provisions of the Criminal Code that established rules around the use of a victim's sexual history as evidence. Not all speeches about women that were about abortion in the 34th Parliament were categorized under the Criminal Code subtopic. In addition to the forty-five speeches about abortion that were categorized under the Criminal Code subtopic, there were seven speeches about women categorized under a subtopic labelled "Bill C-43" and four speeches under a subtopic labelled "abortion." Speeches categorized under the Criminal Code subtopic were all made as part of second and third readings on a government bill, whereas speeches under the "Bill C-43" and "abortion" subtopics raised the issue of the recriminalization of abortion through oral questions and member's statements. The use of two different subtopic categories for speeches about abortion made during question period and members statements reflects the fact that the categories are generated by Hansard editors and are subject to imperfect or duplicative categorizations. The speeches about abortion in the Criminal Code subtopic are distinctive insofar as they signal focused and sustained attention to a specific instance of government legislative policymaking on a central women's equality issue. The large number of speeches about abortion in the 34th Parliament is again paralleled in the spike in the number of speeches about abortion using the automatically generated topic from the machine learning model in chapter 3 (figure 3.1.i).

Finally, the fifth most frequent issue addressed in the 34th Parliament was funding for women's centres. This is consistent with the spike in the number of speeches about program funding using the topic generated by the machine learning model in chapter 3 (figure 3.1.vii). All forty-three speeches about women in this subtopic were made as part of an opposition motion introduced by NDP MP Lynn Hunter, calling for the reinstatement of funding for women's centres following cuts to operating funding in the government's two preceding budgets. Hunter's motion stated: "That, in the opinion of this House, the government should reinstate core funding for women's centres, to enable those centres to continue to provide essential information, referral and support services to women" (Hunter 1990). Opposition motions do not directly influence policymaking but, like question period, provide an opportunity for opposition parties to draw attention to an issue and to force the government to account for its actions – in this case, the decision of the government to cut core operational funding to women's centres. Speeches in debate on this motion were longer than interventions in oral questions and wider ranging in their issue focus. Speeches in support of the motion tended to highlight the importance of the supports provided by women's centres and critiqued the government's decision to impose the cuts. As NDP MP Margaret Mitchell (1990) put it:

> There is so much that women's centres provide, and for such a small, piddling, little amount of money. The value that our society and women themselves have received for the very wonderful service that women's centres across the country provide is incredible. I want to repeat what everybody on this side of the House has been saying today, and the minister did not seem to hear this morning, that women's centres need core funding.

By contrast, government responses either disputed the basis of the motion itself or emphasized positive aspects of the government's record on women's equality. In her remarks, Progressive Conservative MP Pauline Browes highlighted that:

> There is $40 million in additional funds over the next four years to help the problem of family violence, $22 million for 500 new transition houses, and $18 million to help improve social and health services for Canadian women. Now that is a remarkable accomplishment. When looking at the total picture, these are remarkable initiatives that the government has pursued and we will continue to work with the women of Canada in order to provide that social justice that we believe is so important. (Browes 1990)

Again, the tendency for government responses to the motion to push back against the validity of the motion's critique suggests that, even though a government was actively engaged in implementing policy decisions that negatively affected women's organizations, it was unwilling to be seen as bad on women's equality.

Women's Equality Policymaking Context

To better understand the spike in the number of speeches about women in the 34th Parliament, it is also helpful to consider the broader policymaking context during this period. In addition to debates about abortion, violence against women, and funding for women's centres, the 34th Parliament was marked by the establishment of two cross-party women's groups: the Subcommittee on the Status of Women and the Association of Women Parliamentarians (Young 1997; Bashevkin 1996). The subcommittee was established under the Standing Committee on Health and Welfare, Social Affairs, Seniors and the Status of Women to study and focus on two main issues: violence against women and breast cancer (Young 1997). The subcommittee held hearings on violence against women, received testimony from key women's movement organizations, and produced a final report that "offered a holistic feminist analysis of the problem of violence against women" (95). Several of the report's recommendations were taken up by the Mulroney government. A government task force on violence against women was established, although its impact was seen as primarily symbolic (Young 1997; Bashevkin 1996). The government's legislation on gun control incorporated many of the subcommittee's recommendations, although the eventual legislation "did not go as far as the subcommittee report recommended" (Young 1997, 96). The subcommittee also tackled the issue of breast cancer, holding extensive hearings that heard from women and medical professionals. The subcommittee's report called for increased "public education aimed at early detection, more sensitive treatment of women with breast cancer, [and] greater priority for research on breast cancer" (ibid.). Within the year the report was released, the minister of health had announced a $25 million government commitment to support breast cancer research and funding "to assist in breast cancer screening, education, and developing national standards for treatment" (Sharpe 1994, 42).

The subcommittee was thus reasonably effective at forcing issues and policy ideas onto the political agenda. Moreover, the issues addressed by the subcommittee are reflected directly in the most frequent topics of speeches about women, suggesting that the women on the subcommittee who used that institutional structure to address women's equality issues in that venue also contributed to heightened attention to these issues in House of Commons debate.

The Association of Women Parliamentarians was a cross-party women's group established in 1991 in response to "negative aspects of parliamentary life experienced by women" (Young 1997, 92). Rather than engaging directly with questions of public policy, the Association of Women Parliamentarians "serve[d] as a network and a source of mutual support for female MPs" and worked to address barriers to women's participation in electoral politics, including "parliamentary decorum and electoral reform" (93).

Taken together, these initiatives suggest a heightened degree of group consciousness among women MPs during the 34th Parliament. Although women were a relatively small cohort in the 34th Parliament (13 per cent of seats), those who led the Subcommittee on the Status of Women were also involved with the creation of the Association of Women Parliamentarians and were the same women who made the most speeches about women in parliamentary debate. Dawn Black from the NDP and Mary Clancy from the Liberal Party made the most speeches about women in the 34th Parliament. Both were founding members of the cross-party women's groups. Progressive Conservative MPs Mary Collins, Barbara McDougall, and Barbara Greene were also involved with these groups and were also among the top twenty-five contributors of speeches about women in the 34th Parliament. This overlap suggests that the MPs who advocated most vocally for women in parliamentary debate were also engaged in pushing for women's equality through these other parliamentary channels.

PATTERNS OF ISSUE ATTENTION IN THE 39TH PARLIAMENT

The proportion of speeches about women also spiked in the 39th Parliament. Stephen Harper's Conservative Party won a minority government in January 2006, with 124 out of 308 seats – the slimmest plurality in House of Commons history (Wells 2013). The party came to power after more than a decade of Liberal governments and significant party system realignment that put the Conservative Party further to the ideological right than their Progressive Conservative predecessors. The 39th Parliament was the second in a string of three successive minority parliaments in the early 2000s and the first Conservative minority following the short-lived Liberal minority led by Paul Martin from 2004 to 2005. The 39th Parliament sat from April 2006 until September 2008 when the prime minister asked the governor general to dissolve the parliament. The Liberals formed the Official Opposition with 106 seats, followed by the Bloc Québécois at fifty-one seats, the NDP at twenty-nine seats, and one Independent. The opposition parties were thus collectively positioned to defeat legislation and bring down the government should the need arise. The proportion of seats held by women had increased somewhat since the 34th Parliament from 13 per cent to 21 per cent. But women's share of seats had hovered around 21 per cent since 1997.[2]

Speech Content

To identify the patterns of issue attention that contributed to this spike I examine the issue focus and content of speeches about women during this period using the Hansard subtopic categorizations. Table 4.2 lists the five issues that were addressed most frequently in speeches about women in the 39th Parliament, according to the Hansard subtopics.

The subtopic with the largest number of speeches about women in the 39th Parliament was the status of women (244 speeches), accounting for nearly a quarter of all speeches about women. As noted in the discussion of speeches about women in the 34th Parliament, this Hansard subtopic captures a wide range of issues pertaining to women. The large number of speeches in this subtopic is consistent with the spike in the number of speeches assigned to the automatically generated "status" topic in the 39th Parliament in chapter 3 (figure 3.1.x). The issues raised in speeches about the status of women in the 39th Parliament vary widely, from the commemoration of International Women's Day to efforts to elect more women. Manual inspection of the content of the speeches, however, reveals a particularly acute focus on the Conservative government's changes to funding and eligibility criteria for Status of Women Canada, including the removal of gender equality from the mandate of the Women's Program. At least three-quarters of speeches in this subtopic made direct reference to the Conservative government's cuts and changes to Status of Women Canada.

Of the 244 speeches about the status of women, three quarters (182 speeches) were made during question period. Of those 182 speeches, 143 (79 per cent) focused directly on the government's cuts and changes to Status of Women Canada, with questions often taking an adversarial partisan tone. For example, Liberal MP Maria Minna (2006b) asked:

> Mr. Speaker, the minority Conservative government is anti-women. It has cut off at the knees all organizations working for women's equality in Canada. The criteria [have] been changed so that no organization fighting for women's equality will receive funding. The Conservatives have put tape over women's mouths to shut them up. This is not democracy. When will the minister stop attacking women and give them back their voice?

Table 4.2
Speeches about women in the 39th Parliament by Hansard subtopic

Subtopic	*Number of speeches*	*Proportion of speeches about women*
Status of women	244	23.6%
Business of supply	231	22.3%
Committees of the House	74	7.1%
Petitions	46	4.4%
Sitting resumed	39	3.8%

Conservative responses to opposition questions and critiques of the government's cuts to Status of Women Canada rejected the premise that women require government supports or programs. In one response, Minister Responsible for the Status of Women Bev Oda (2006b) stated: "Mr. Speaker, we have to stop this narrative of victimhood. We as women and as Canadians do not see women as victims. We know they are leaders. We know they have aspirations. We want to give them the opportunities that they deserve."

In addition to oral questions, twelve of the speeches were made during private members' business, and the lengthier speeches included in this category were all in response to motions that called on the government to reinstate equality in the mandate of the Women's Program. The remaining speeches were made as statements by members (forty-six speeches) and tended to cluster around dates such as International Women's Day, Persons Day, and the anniversary of the UN Convention on the Elimination of Discrimination against Women (CEDAW), and more than half of these (twenty-four speeches) connected these major events and anniversaries to the Conservative government's actions relating to Status of Women Canada. Four speeches were part of routine proceedings at the time of the Equal Voice challenge to the parties to nominate more women to increase women's numbers in parliament. Even in the context of a discussion about electing more women, all opposition speeches made a connection to the government's cuts.

The next largest share of speeches about women was categorized as "business of supply" (231 speeches) – a category that includes debate on opposition motions and on motions pertaining to financial estimates for various ministries (Bosc and Gagnon 2017, ch. 18).

Like the petitions subtopic in the 34th Parliament, this subtopic is procedurally focused rather than issue focused; there is thus no parallel topic generated by the unsupervised machine learning model. Manual inspection of the 231 speeches in this subtopic reveals that nearly all the speeches (86 per cent) were made as part of five key debates, four of which were opposition motions and one of which was the debate on estimates for the Department of Canadian Heritage within which Status of Women Canada operated at the time. Speeches in the debate on estimates included technical questions and answers focused on the department's planned expenditures and activities over the coming year – for example, "Mr. Chair, has an analysis … been done on the potential accessibility or the lack thereof of the change in program delivery of the status of women?" (Neville 2007). However, speeches in this debate also included more rhetorical, partisan interventions:

> In 2007, the women of Quebec and Canada have to continue fighting for their causes, but this government has done nothing but roll back the clock on women's equality. Already, with barely 14 female members elected, the Conservatives have set back parity in this House further than ever. How can the minister turn her back on her own sex and embrace the outdated thinking of her party, whose sole aim is to silence the voices of those who have a different vision? Is it because the minister feels that the fight for equality between men and women is really over? (Demers 2007)

This framing suggests a clear attempt to characterize the Conservative Party as uniquely hostile to women's equality.

The four opposition motions that were debated under the business of supply subtopic all criticized the Conservative government's record on women's equality. A May 2007 motion introduced by then Liberal deputy leader Michael Ignatieff critiqued the government's record overall. During the debate on this motion, speeches by seven opposition MPs focused on matters including childcare and cuts to funding for the Women's Program. The three other opposition motions focused directly on women's equality policy issues. A September 2006 motion introduced by Maria Minna, a Liberal MP and critic for the status of women, objected to the government's cuts to funding for the Women's Program (sixty-four speeches). A November 2007 motion, also introduced by Minna, called on the government to take action on women's economic security and pay equity (nineteen speeches). In March 2008 Minna introduced a motion calling for the reinstatement of the Court Challenges Program, restoration of funding for research and advocacy activities under the Women's Program, the creation of new childcare spaces, and the reopening of shuttered Status of Women Canada's regional offices (forty-eight speeches).

Liberal motions were generally supported by the other opposition parties, but debates on these motions were characterized by distinctly partisan conflict. They revealed a critique of the governing Conservatives as well as differences among opposition parties. For example, in a speech that was otherwise supportive of a Liberal motion calling on "the government to develop a strategy to improve the economic security of all women in Canada and present this strategy to the House by February 1, 2008" (Minna 2007), NDP MP Catherine Bell critiqued the previous Liberal government for failing to act on the same issue:

> The Liberal track record on pay equity and other supports for women is dismal, at best. While it may appear that they supported women in our fight for pay equity, they were busy over the past 13 years that they were in government, of which 12 years I might add were in a majority position, dismantling programs for women ... The hypocrisy is that the Liberals would choose an opposition day to put forward a motion to call on the Conservative government to do something they should have done when they were in government. (Bell 2007)

Hostilities among opposition parties went both ways. The text of Liberal MP Maria Minna's March 2008 motion calling for the government to take action on a range of women's equality issues concluded with the following partisan jab:

> that, therefore, the House condemn the irresponsible and self-serving actions on November 28, 2005, by the New Democratic Party and the Bloc Québécois which led to the installation of a government that is hostile to the rights and needs of vulnerable Canadians. (Minna 2008)

This framing of the motion meant that NDP and Bloc Québécois speeches in debate on this motion supported the substance of the policy position it outlined; however, these speeches were characterized by cross-partisan attacks.

Opposition motions have no direct impact on government policy-making and are not binding on the House. But, like question period or private members' business (Soroka et al. 2009; Blidook 2010), they serve to raise the profile of an issue by focusing parliamentary attention and attempting to place the issue on the government's agenda. In the context of a minority parliament, as was the case in the 39th, a House united in its opposition to the government's agenda can also use these motions to signal areas in which legislative policy change is likely to fail.

The third largest share of speeches about women related to committees of the House (seventy-four speeches). Again, there is no parallel topic generated by the unsupervised machine learning model, but this subtopic highlights an important procedural strategy used by parliamentarians to represent women in this parliament. Speeches in this subtopic addressed concurrence motions concerning four reports from the Standing Committee on the Status of Women. If passed, concurrence motions adopt the recommendations of committee reports as orders or resolutions of the House, although the resolutions are non-binding (Bosc and Gagnon 2017, ch. 10). Debates on these concurrence motions therefore provided an opportunity for the Standing Committee on the Status of Women to bring their committee's concerns to the attention of the House of Commons as a whole for sustained debate and consideration. Speeches in the committees of the House subtopic tended to be longer and focused on the substantive issue raised by each report. For example, in debate on a motion based on a committee report calling on the government to introduce pay equity legislation, NDP MP Dawn Black's remarks highlighted the report's content:

> The evidence to support pay equity is before us. We have it in this report. It is clear what we need to do. What we need now is the political will to implement legislation that does have targets, timetables and effective enforcement mechanisms. We leave far too many women behind with this antiquated compaint based system. Far too many women are left without a process to advance their own human rights in terms of pay equity. It is really past the time for the government to take this issue seriously and implement legislation that will work to close the wage gap for Canadian women. (Black 2008)

In addition to the report on pay equity (nine speeches), reports from the Standing Committee on the Status of Women considered by the House focused on cuts to funding for the Women's Program (thirty-five speeches), funding for Indigenous women's shelters (fourteen speeches), and calls for the creation of an equality commissioner who would be responsible for gender-based budgeting and analysis as an independent officer of parliament (twelve speeches).

The frequency of House of Commons debates on reports from the Standing Committee on the Status of Women suggests its members used the committee structure to push back against government initiatives that undermined previous equality gains and to press for measures to improve women's equality. This is consistent with expectations in the parliamentary literature, which identifies committees as a potentially important venue through which parliamentarians can attempt to influence policymaking (Franks 1987; Docherty 1997). Notably, this subtopic does not appear among the top five most frequent subtopics in any other parliaments. Although the Subcommittee on the Status of Women played an active and important role in the substantive representation of women in the 34th Parliament (Young 1997), it was an ad hoc subcommittee of another parliamentary committee and, thus, not empowered to report directly to the House (Bosc and Gagnon 2017, ch. 20). The 39th Parliament was thus distinctive insofar as opposition MPs used the parliamentary standing committee structure to bring committee issues to bear on debates in the House of Commons.

The fourth largest share of speeches about women was petitions. The forty-six speeches in this subtopic are grouped together on the basis of procedural similarity rather than substantive issue content. Speeches in this topic nonetheless shared a focus on two core social conservative issues – same-sex marriage and abortion. Eighteen speeches called on the government to reopen the debate on same-sex marriage, undoing the progress towards marriage equality made in the previous parliament. Twelve speeches were related to abortion, nine of which expressed support for a private member's bill that would have created an additional offence under the Criminal Code when harm is done to a pregnant woman. Had it passed, this bill would have effectively provided legal personhood to foetuses and established a foundation for undermining women's ability to access abortions in Canada. Three of the twelve petitions on the issue expressed opposition to that bill. As noted above, the MP who introduces a petition does not need to endorse its content. Nonetheless, only male Conservative and Liberal MPs introduced petitions that supported a private member's bill that undermined abortion rights. Conservative MP Ken Epp introduced several petitions in support of this bill and his accompanying remarks suggested that he supported the proposed legislation:

> Mr. Speaker, I am encouraged by the number of people who are responding positively to Bill C-484, the bill that would provide protection for unborn children when they, as well as their mothers, are victims of a criminal attack ... This petition contains another 735 signatures today. I am very proud to present the petition. (Epp 2008)

Among speeches about women in this subtopic, the only petitions that opposed the bill were read in by a woman New Democrat (Mathyssen 2008a, 2008b).

The fifth largest share of speeches about women was categorized into the "sitting resumed" Hansard subtopic. The thirty-nine speeches in this subtopic were a continuation of the debate on the November 2007 opposition motion about pay equity categorized into the "business of supply" subtopic discussed above. The speeches made in debate on this motion were categorized into the "sitting resumed" subtopic due to an interruption in proceedings and were made following a recess taken due to a technical problem with the simultaneous translation provided to MPs.

Women's Equality Policymaking Context

In addition to the focus on the government's proposed cuts and changes to Status of Women Canada in parliamentary debate, the 39th Parliament was also characterized by an active cross-party women's group, as in the 34th Parliament. The 39th Parliament witnessed a flurry of activity led by the parliamentary Standing Committee on the Status of Women (SCSW), as indicated by the large number of speeches in the committees of the House subtopic. The SCSW was established under the Standing Orders of the House of Commons in 2004 and followed in the path forged by the Subcommittee on the Status of Women that was created during the 34th Parliament (Standing Committee on the Status of Women 2019). It enjoyed more permanent standing than did the former subcommittee and provided a channel through which parliamentarians could respond to government initiatives and raise the profile of women's issues and concerns in parliament. The SCSW was empowered "to study and report to the House of Commons ... on policy relevant to the 'status of women' as well as on the administration and implementation of programmes under the department's purview" (Grace 2016, 835–6). This stands in contrast to the narrower remit of the 34th Parliament's subcommittee, which had a time-limited mandate and requirement to report to the standing committee under which it was established (Young 1997; Bosc and Gagnon 2017, ch. 20; Standing Committee on the Status of Women 2019). Membership in the SCSW was drawn from all parties, but, unlike most parliamentary committees, "the Chair [was] selected from the Official Opposition," which gave the opposition increased power to set the committee's direction (Grace 2016, 835). In the minority 39th Parliament, the committee was made up of five Conservative members, four Liberals, two Bloc Québécois, and one NDP MP, which meant that, in addition to being chaired by an opposition MP, the opposition members collectively held a majority on the committee (Standing Committee on the Status of Women 2007a).

The SCSW addressed a wide range of issues pertaining to women's equality throughout the 39th Parliament. Topics they addressed included human trafficking, women's economic security and pay equity, parental leave benefits, gender-based analysis in federal policymaking, the cancellation of the Court Challenges Program, issues affecting Indigenous women, and the impact of cuts to Status of Women Canada (Standing Committee on the Status of Women 2007b). On several of these issues, the committee undertook extensive studies that heard from witnesses from stakeholder organizations and government departments and drafted reports that were presented to the House of Commons for consideration. Committee reports calling for increased funding for Status of Women Canada, action on pay equity, restoration of the Court Challenges Program, and increased support for shelters for Indigenous women were brought to the House of Commons for consideration and extensive debate through concurrence motions. More concretely, the committee's work on gender-based analysis (GBA) was successful in bringing about "a commitment by Status of Women Canada ... to 'put a particular focus on working toward strengthening the overall federal approach to GBA'" (Grace 2016, 838).

Although the SCSW was active, its ability to force issues onto the government's agenda does not appear to have been as robust as was that of their counterparts in the 34th Parliament. Whereas members of the subcommittee in the 34th Parliament appear to have been able to push the government to take on new initiatives on violence against women and breast cancer, members of the SCSW in the 39th Parliament found themselves for the most part responding to and pushing back against more hostile government initiatives. Nonetheless, the Standing Committee on the Status of Women, led by opposition women, worked to hear the equality concerns of women in Canada and to bring these issues to the attention of parliament and the government.

ASSESSING THE FINDINGS

The preceding review of the content of speeches about women and broader policymaking context allows us to assess patterns of issue attention that contributed to the spikes in attention to women in parliamentary debate in the 34th and 39th Parliaments. The results presented above show that, in the 34th Parliament, the issues most frequently discussed in parliamentary speeches about women covered several substantive issues, including violence against women, abortion, and funding for women's centres. This suggests that the spike in the number of speeches about women during this parliament was driven (1) by external events – namely, the Montreal Massacre – that focused parliamentarians' attention on the issue of violence against women and (2) by attempts by the Mulroney government to roll back previous women's equality gains, most significantly the recriminalization of abortion through Bill C-43.

The procedural contexts within which MPs made speeches on these issues provides preliminary insight into the mechanisms through which MPs represented women in debate and the ways in which the content of parliamentary debate relates to policy action. In the case of the proposed changes to the Criminal Code on the issue of abortion, MPs for the most part made speeches about women during debate on proposed government legislation. These interventions ensured that women's perspectives and concerns were articulated in the process of legislative policymaking – often articulating opposition and resistance to the government's effort to recriminalize abortion. For the other issues, the connection between parliamentary debate and government policy action was indirect. In the case of the motion calling for the reinstatement of funding for women's centres and the related questions in question period, speeches about women were made as a reaction against and critique of government policy. In the case of violence against women, speeches about women were made during question period and in members' statements to draw attention to an issue that had come to prominence due to shocking external events, to put it on the government's agenda, and to incite policy action. Efforts to force government policy action pertaining to violence against women leveraged the institutional structure of the Subcommittee on the Status of Women to achieve some small policy wins for women.

In the 39th Parliament, the issue most frequently discussed in parliamentary speeches about women across multiple subtopics was the government's cuts and changes to the federal women's policy agency, Status of Women Canada. The subtopics with the largest number of speeches were more indicative of the procedural context in which speeches were made rather than of the specific issue content of those speeches. But manual inspection of the content of speeches in each category reveals a consistent issue focus. This suggests that the spike in the number of speeches about women during this parliament was the result of parliamentarians' response to the Harper government's measures to retrench previous equality gains, particularly through cuts and changes to Status of Women Canada.

The procedural contexts within which MPs made speeches about the government's proposed cuts and changes to Status of Women Canada again provide an initial indication of how speech and policy action were related. There was no focused piece of legislation with which MPs could engage to push back against the Status of Women cuts, so MPs leveraged multiple other indirect tools to register their objections on the official record. This included the use of shorter oral questions (under the status of women subtopic) as well as more focused debate using opposition day motions (under the business of supply subtopic). The large number of speeches in the committees of the House subtopic shows that MPs also leveraged the standing committee structure to represent women's interests and to object to the government's attempt to retrench previous equality gains.

The patterns of issue attention and the procedural avenues used by parliamentarians in the 34th and 39th Parliaments confirm the initial finding from chapter 3 that increases in attention to women's policy issues in parliamentary debate tend to reflect moments of policy action in one of two ways: first, as a direct response to government policy action on an issue, as with legislation on abortion and changes to Status of Women Canada and women's programs and, second, through attempts by MPs to put an issue on the political agenda to compel a government to act, as with efforts to put violence against women on the government agenda. The analysis in this chapter adds to our understanding of the connection between speech and policy action by showing that direct responses to government policy action are not confined to engagement in debate on a focused piece of legislation on an issue but, rather, can include a range of other procedural mechanisms, such as opposition motions, oral questions, and, importantly, the committee system. Governments are still primarily responsible for setting policy agendas, but those who would speak and advocate for women have a range of options at their disposal in terms of how they will respond to and either support or push back against these agendas.

POLICY CASE SELECTION

The analysis of patterns of issue attention, speech content, and procedural strategies used by MPs to represent women in parliamentary debate in the 34th and 39th Parliaments provides us with the big picture of how speech and policy action are connected. But to understand how policy change happens, the strategies MPs use, and whether they are effective, we need to dig into specific instances of policy action through closer qualitative analysis. Building on the analysis above, we can now identify cases for closer investigation.

In the 34th Parliament, government policymaking on abortion warrants closer scrutiny. Multiple issues were addressed in this parliament, and the Criminal Code subtopic was not the one most frequently addressed. It was, however, the most frequently addressed subtopic that engaged with a concrete government policy initiative and was an important contributor to the increase in speeches about women during this parliament. The status of women and petitions subtopics addressed multiple policy issues; and, although the violence against women subtopic attracted the most attention, this reflected parliamentarians' response to shocking external events. MPs did attempt to force government action on issues relating to violence against women, and, indeed, the government established a task force on violence against women, but the concrete policy actions that followed from that initiative were limited.

Policy action on abortion, therefore, is the most suitable case through which to examine how the substantive representation of women in policy action occurred in the 34th Parliament. The government's proposed legislation (Bill C-43, An Act Respecting Abortion) constituted a clear, focused, and neatly bounded attempt to withdraw an equality gain for women. Moreover, since abortion was categorized as a conscience issue, parliamentarians outside cabinet were allowed a free vote on the legislation (Pal 1991; Tatalovich 1997). Instances of free votes such as this offer a unique opportunity to examine the influence of individual legislators under conditions in which the constraints imposed by party discipline are somewhat weakened. Chapter 5 examines the Mulroney government's legislative policymaking on abortion and the role played by women parliamentarians in opposing and ultimately blocking legislation that would have recriminalized abortion and rolled back women's equality.

In the 39th Parliament, the government's cuts and changes to Status of Women Canada warrant closer investigation. This policy issue was the clear driver behind this parliament's spike in speeches about women. Unlike the government's attempt to recriminalize abortion in the 34th Parliament, there was no focused piece of legislation around which policy action on this issue centred; rather, the issue was part of the government's larger budget process and ended up being raised by MPs across Hansard subtopics and through multiple procedural avenues. The case therefore provides an opportunity to understand the ways in which parliamentarians can influence government policy and decision making outside the confines of debate and voting on issue-specific bills. Moreover, Status of Women Canada was central to women's equality policymaking and initiatives. Strong women's agencies are seen by feminist policy scholars as a crucially important tool for using the state to promote women's social and economic equality (McBride and Mazur 2010). The Harper government's changes to Status of Women Canada, which diminished the stature and capacity of the agency to support organizations that work to promote equality, thus constitutes a significant government intervention in the policymaking landscape in Canada. Chapter 6 examines the Harper government's efforts to weaken Status of Women Canada, the multiple strategies used by women MPs to push back against these efforts, the extent to which they were successful, and the factors that contributed to their success.

Increases in attention to women's policy issues in parliamentary debate are clearly tied to moments of policy action on those issues – either through responses to government initiatives or through efforts to put new issues on the political agenda. The details of how policy change on these issues happens and the role elected women might play in bringing about these changes still need to be further explored. The chapters that follow examine the processes through which the substantive representation of women in policy advocacy and outcomes occurred in the 34th and 39th Parliaments.

5

The Mulroney Government and the Recriminalization of Abortion

In January 1991, a tie vote left the Canadian Senate momentarily perplexed. Senators were voting on a government bill that would recriminalize abortion, three years after the Supreme Court ruled that sections of the Criminal Code restricting abortion access violated women's Charter rights. Reports suggest that when the tie "was announced, a collective gasp rippled through the Senate, as virtually no one appeared to know what it meant" (Walker 1991). Following a brief consultation with the clerk, the acting speaker announced that a tie constituted a defeat and the chamber erupted into "whoops of joy and laughter" (ibid.). This narrow defeat was a major win for advocates of women's equality and reproductive freedom. This outcome was the culmination of a long legislative process in which women legislators intervened at multiple stages and through a variety of means to advocate on behalf of women, pushing back against the government's proposals to recriminalize abortion and roll back previous gains. This chapter examines the details of that legislative process and the role women parliamentarians played in advocating for women throughout it.

Up until this point, the analysis of the substantive representation of women in the Canadian parliament has focused largely on substantive representation as expressed in parliamentary debate. The content of parliamentary debate, however, only tells part of the story of women's representation. The substantive representation of women must be understood to include a range of activities and outcomes – speaking for women, advocating for women, and achieving policy outcomes for women. To properly understand the impact women parliamentarians have on the substantive representation of women in Canadian politics, we must consider all three of these dimensions. In this chapter, then, we turn our attention to the substantive representation of women as expressed in advocacy and policy outcomes, focusing on the details of legislative policymaking on abortion in the 34th Parliament. As identified in chapter 4, this is a policy case related to women's equality that contributed to the increased attention to women in parliamentary debate. This chapter investigates the process through which the substantive representation of women occurred in this case. What were the key milestones in the process of the Mulroney government's attempt to recriminalize abortion? Who were the primary advocates of women's equality? What strategies did they use to advocate for women and to influence policymaking? What impact did their interventions have on eventual outcomes? And why were some actors able to influence outcomes while others were not?

IDENTIFYING CRITICAL ACTORS

The analysis in this chapter is grounded in the critical actors framework introduced in chapter 1. This framework posits that the substantive representation of women, expressed in advocacy and policy outcomes, happens through the efforts of a few key individuals who are willing at a relatively low threshold to take action to address women's interests (Childs and Krook 2009). In this chapter and the chapter that follows, the focus is on the substantive representation of women in advocacy and outcomes oriented towards the promotion of women's equality. Although critical actors are not necessarily women – indeed, men can "play a role in advancing women's policy concerns" (138) – there are good reasons to expect that women MPs will take on this role. Feminist political science has long theorized that women are best equipped to represent women's interest by virtue of a shared experience and perspective (Phillips 1995; Mansbridge 1999). Because of this shared experience, women MPs are likely to have a particular sensitivity to and sense of responsibility for representing women as what Mansbridge (2003, 523) refers to as "surrogate representatives." Thinking about the substantive representation of women as being driven by critical actors recognizes that not all women will act as surrogate representatives of women's interests: women's inclination and ability to act on behalf of women's interests is not uniform. Moreover, feminist critical actors need not be thought of as acting exclusively to introduce new policy initiatives for women's equality. They can also be engaged in defensive actions that seek to protect women's equality against hostile policy initiatives that attempt to undermine previous equality gains. The analysis in this chapter therefore focuses on identifying critical actors who tried to defend women's interests against the Mulroney government's attempt to pass legislation that would have recriminalized abortion. It also focuses on understanding the strategies and institutional pathways these critical actors used to do so.

To build a clear picture of how the substantive representation of women occurred in this case and to identify critical actors in this process, I draw on qualitative evidence from documentary sources, including parliamentary debate transcripts, unsealed cabinet minutes, media reports, biographies, and secondary literature. Parliamentary speeches and voting records were accessed through the Parliament of Canada website and through the Linked Parliamentary Data project. Confidential cabinet documents are made public after twenty years through requests under the Access to Information Act. Journalist Stanley Tromp made a request for all cabinet documents containing discussions of abortion between 1988 and 1990. The documents resulting from this request were compiled and made available online. Media reports relevant to the two cases were retrieved through the ProQuest Canadian Newsstream database with keyword and date range search parameters in the advanced search function. Published biographical material about key actors offers additional insight into strategies and motivations for action.

These sources make it possible to determine (1) who the critical actors were who advocated for women's equality and pushed back against the government's attempt to recriminalize abortion and (2) whether their actions shaped government policy decision making and outcomes. How do we know if someone was a critical actor? I look for evidence of actors who spoke frequently on behalf of women's reproductive rights in parliamentary debate or who advocated for women's equality in cabinet discussions. I also look for references in media accounts, biographies, and the secondary literature that an actor was an advocate or champion for women on the abortion issue during this period. How do we know if the efforts of critical actors shaped government policy? I look for evidence that their actions were decisive for policy outcomes based on an assessment of the sequencing of actions and events. I also look for references in media reports, biographies, cabinet documents, or secondary literature that certain actions were influential. Following the principle of triangulation, I look for confirmation from multiple sources.

A BRIEF OVERVIEW OF ABORTION POLICY IN THE 34TH PARLIAMENT

Before delving into an examination of how the substantive representation of women occurred throughout the legislative policymaking process around abortion, it is helpful to review the conditions that precipitated the government's introduction of proposed legislation recriminalizing abortion and to establish the main milestones in the bill's legislative journey. Before the Supreme Court's 1988 *Morgentaler* decision, section 251 of the Criminal Code prohibited abortions "except when performed in an accredited hospital with permission of a therapeutic abortion committee" comprised of three doctors (other than the one performing the procedure) who had to confirm that pregnancy would endanger the life or health of the woman (Saurette and Gordon 2015, 105). After section 251 was struck down, no Criminal Code restrictions limited abortion access in Canada. This constituted a major gain for women's movement activists who had long identified the removal of abortion from the Criminal Code as a core demand. The *Morgentaler* decision decriminalized abortion, but the Court signalled it was parliament's responsibility to develop a new legal framework around abortion. Parliament was left to develop new legislation that would balance "the state's 'legitimate' interest in the foetus and the constitutional protection guaranteed to Canadian women under the Charter" (126).

Over the course of its two mandates from 1984 to 1988 and from 1988 to 1993, the Progressive Conservative (PC) government of Brian Mulroney made several attempts to take up the Court's direction to develop a new legislative framework for abortion. The government initiated a series of parliamentary debates in summer 1988 to identify a legislative approach to abortion (Brodie 1992). The outcome of the debate did not provide clear direction on how to move forward, and the abortion issue fell off the parliamentary agenda for the rest of the 33rd Parliament (Saurette and Gordon 2015; Johnstone 2017).

After the Mulroney government won re-election in November 1988, a series of high-profile court cases forced the abortion issue back onto the government's agenda. During the summer of 1989, several men attempted to use the courts to prevent their former partners from obtaining abortions (Brodie 1992). The court decisions and public attention to these cases "convinced the Mulroney government that it could no longer postpone introducing a new abortion law" (96).

On 3 November 1989, following extensive cabinet deliberations, Mulroney's justice minister Doug Lewis introduced Bill C-43, An Act Respecting Abortion. The proposed legislation would have prohibited abortion "unless the abortion [was] induced by or under the direction of a medical practitioner who [was] of the opinion that, if the abortion were not induced, the health or life of the female person would be likely to be threatened" (Pal 1991, 302). The bill defined health loosely and "ambiguously as physical, mental and psychological health" (ibid.). Anyone found to be performing an abortion outside these conditions would be liable to imprisonment for up to two years (Pal 1991). The bill was intended as a "much-needed compromise" that could satisfy both sides of the issue if they were willing "to accept concessions" (Saurette and Gordon 2015, 133). In practice, it was met with resistance and opposition from all sides. Anti-abortion campaigners said the bill did not go far enough in restricting abortion access, while pro-choice advocates decried the fact that the bill put abortion back in the Criminal Code except under very specific circumstances (Brodie 1992; Johnstone 2017). The proposed legislation was treated as government policy and cabinet ministers were required to vote with the government as it made its way through the legislative process. Other members of the PC caucus were allowed a free vote.

Bill C-43 passed second reading in the House of Commons on 28 November 1989 by a margin of 164 to 114. The entire NDP caucus voted against the bill, consistent with the party's official pro-choice stance (Pal 1991; Young 2000). The Liberal caucus was divided, with sixty members voting against the bill, including all Liberal women (Brodie 1992). Within the PC ranks, the bill was opposed by twelve PC backbenchers, all of them hardline anti-abortion men who saw the bill as too permissive; women in the PC caucus and cabinet unanimously voted in support of the bill (Brodie 1992). Many MPs who voted in favour of the bill at second reading did so to ensure that it made its way to committee, where they hoped it could be changed (Delacourt 1989). But although the bill spent months in committee, it was eventually returned to the House for third reading without amendments (Pal 1991).

When Bill C-43 was considered for third reading in May 1990, there was opposition to it from those on both the pro-choice and the anti-abortion sides of the issue. Despite this widespread opposition, the bill passed third reading by a narrow margin of 140 to 131 (Brodie 1992). The vote on 29 May split almost perfectly along party lines, with only PC MPs and two Liberals (both men) voting in support. The remaining Liberal MPs, all NDP MPs, and thirteen PC MPs (again, mainly anti-abortion men who saw the bill as too permissive) voted against it (Vienneau 1990). None of the women in the PC caucus broke ranks with the party.

After languishing for months while the Senate dealt with the passage of the government's Goods and Services Tax (GST) legislation, Bill C-43 made its way to the Senate for consideration in late October 1990. The Senate was deeply divided on the issue, and senators were permitted a free vote on the bill (Brodie 1992). In an unprecedented tie-vote on 31 January 1991, the Senate defeated Bill C-43.[1] Following the bill's defeat, abortion remained legal in Canada, as it had been since the *Morgentaler* decision in 1988.

CRITICAL ACTORS AGAINST THE RECRIMINALIZATION OF ABORTION

With the key moments of the legislative process established, we can now turn our attention to an examination of how the substantive representation of women occurred at each stage. Who advocated for women and what strategies did they use to try to influence government decision making? At several crucial stages, women parliamentarians played a central role in opposing and ultimately blocking the passage of Bill C-43. As I show, these women attempted to influence legislative outcomes on abortion using the tools available to them based on their roles within the institution – in cabinet, on the backbenches, in opposition, or in an unelected upper house. Ultimately, the efforts of women MPs and cabinet ministers were unable to defeat the government's legislation, but the efforts of pro-choice PC women senators in coordination with other Senate women helped block the bill that would have recriminalized abortion. In this case, women in the Senate acted as an important last line of defence capable of blocking legislation that would have undermined women's equality.

Legislative Development

Prior to the introduction of Bill C-43 in the House of Commons, cabinet discussions informed the development of the government's proposed legislation. Throughout these discussions Barbara McDougall, the minister of employment and immigration and minister responsible for the status of women, consistently advocated for women. As the sole woman on the government's powerful Committee on Priorities and Planning, which plays a key role in establishing the government's legislative agenda, McDougall made clear to her colleagues that the abortion issue "was a decisive one for women" (Cab. Doc. 3-88 CMPP, 1988) and gave voice to women's perspective in these deliberations.

The Committee on Priorities and Planning considered several approaches before finalizing the government's proposed legislative framework. At each stage of the process, McDougall advocated a legislative option that would allow as much free choice for women as possible. When a three-stage legislative model was being considered – in which abortions would have been allowed as a decision between a woman and her doctor in the early stages of pregnancy, with moderate conditions relating to a woman's health in a second stage and more stringent conditions after foetal viability – McDougall signalled her displeasure with the proposed policy regime, which, in her view, constituted a major loss for women since it recriminalized abortion in the later gestational stages. She noted that the proposed legislative solution constituted a significant compromise position for her personally and for pro-choice women in general (Cab. Doc. 17-89 CBPP, 1989).

When an even more restrictive two-stage model was considered, in which abortions would be allowed only if the woman's health required it up to twenty weeks of pregnancy with even more stringent requirements after twenty weeks, McDougall expressed disappointment that the government was moving in this direction (Cab. Doc. 18-89 CBPP, 1989). In a meeting of the full cabinet, McDougall attempted to convince other ministers that the two-stage approach should not be adopted. She appealed to pragmatic political justifications, including the likelihood that the legislation would attract court challenges and would generate strong opposition among women voters (Cab. Doc. 15-89 CBM, 1989). Her exhortations ultimately went unheeded as the more restrictive two-stage model was deemed to have a greater likelihood of passing the House.

Defence of a pro-choice legislative approach was not taken up by all women in Mulroney's cabinet. Kim Campbell, who would go on to inherit the justice portfolio and responsibility for Bill C-43 in a February 1990 cabinet shuffle, stated her preference for the two-stage approach because it: "codifies what currently exists and the only issue that remains is who is best placed to make the decision" (Cab. Doc. 15-89 CBM, 1989).

This stated preference is notable given that Campbell self-identified as a defender of a pro-choice position (Brodie 1992). All other pro-choice voices in the PC cabinet lined up in support of the three-stage approach, which provided for a period in which women could gain access to abortions without restrictions and thus would have preserved a woman's right to choose more than would any of the other options (Cab. Doc. 15-89 CBM, 1989). Campbell's willingness to accept the more restrictive option despite her self-identification as a feminist and defender of pro-choice views suggests a greater readiness than McDougall to compromise on these preferences.

Notably, Prime Minister Mulroney urged his ministers to give McDougall's views and insights serious consideration (Cab. Doc. 17-89 CBPP, 1989). He cautioned that the composition of the Priorities and Planning Committee, which counted McDougall as its sole female member, "was not representative of the general population" and that this numerical underrepresentation had the potential to skew decision making on an issue of great importance to women (Cab. Doc. 17-89 CBPP, 1989). Implicit in the prime minister's effort to amplify McDougall's voice is a recognition that the presence of women in decision-making processes is important for the substantive representation of women's interests in policy outcomes because they bring distinctive insight and perspective to these discussions. Moreover, it highlights the critical role that sympathetic men willing to amplify women's perspectives can play in facilitating the substantive representation of women. Despite Mulroney's efforts to highlight McDougall's views, the anti-abortion position within the caucus and cabinet – driven predominantly by men – proved more influential.

The legislative approach adopted in the final version of the bill was a significant departure from all previous options that had been considered (Cab. Doc. 21-89 CBPP, 1989). The government shifted its approach late in the cabinet deliberation process following a period of caucus consultations that revealed that a large group of anti-abortion MPs would be unwilling to accept legislation that allowed for any period of time in which abortion could be accessed without restrictions since this approach violated their central tenet that life begins and warrants protection at the moment of conception. Ultimately, the government's desire to introduce a bill it was certain could be passed with the support of a predominantly anti-abortion caucus in a free vote in the House overrode all other considerations. The pro-choice contingent within the PC caucus was outnumbered. In a meeting of the Comittee on Priorities and Planning, McDougall emphasized that "the women in cabinet would be bitterly disappointed" with the decision to introduce a bill that did not allow women unrestricted access to abortions at any stage of pregnancy (Cab. Doc. 24-89 CBPP, 1989). Despite her objections to the final version of the bill, McDougall conceded that she and the other women in cabinet would vote in support to ensure cabinet solidarity (Cab. Doc. 24-89 CBPP, 1989).

Throughout the legislative development process, McDougall consistently emphasized that the adoption of legislation that failed to allow women as much unrestricted choice as possible would have significant political and electoral consequences for the PCs since it would alienate women voters and solidify their opposition to the party. McDougall's effort to link the government's policy decisions on abortion to electoral support among women was unsuccessful in the face of a political and legislative calculation shaped by anti-abortion men. Although McDougall acted as a strong substantive representative of women, her advocacy failed to block the introduction of legislation unfavourable to women's equality. As the lone documented advocate for a pro-choice option in cabinet discussions, she had fewer allies among the party membership and federal caucus than did PC anti-abortion advocates. The introduction of a restrictive bill, however, cannot be linked to a lack of effort by McDougall.

House of Commons Debate

Once Bill C-43 was introduced in the House, the opportunities for MPs to influence the legislative outcome were limited. Liberal and NDP women, along with several NDP men, used question period to decry the government's proposed legislation and the recriminalization of abortion. In their interventions during second and third reading debate, women in these opposition parties – as well as several NDP and Liberal men – consistently articulated a pro-choice perspective. But speeches voicing opposition cannot block or change legislation. As noted above, the NDP caucus and most Liberals, including all Liberal women, voted against the bill in addition to speaking out against it in debate. But in the absence of additional votes to form a majority against the government – an unlikely prospect when the government forms a majority – opposition votes were inadequate to change legislative outcomes. There is no evidence that women reached across party lines to coordinate to block the legislation's passage.

In one case, an opposition MP's efforts went beyond speeches and voting. In the final hours of third reading debate, Dawn Black, who led the NDP charge in speaking out against the bill in debate, attempted to use procedural tools to block its passage (Black 1990). Noticing that there were only NDP members present in the chamber, she sought unanimous consent for a motion calling for the bill to be withdrawn. This effort might have succeeded in blocking the bill, but a Conservative MP "who had been relaxing in the members' lobby and following the debate on television, went racing into the House to shout 'No,'" which stopped the motion from passing (Canadian Press 1990). Black used the tools at her disposal to advocate for women and to try to block the bill's passage, but, given the limited tools available to her based on her institutional position, she was unable to influence policy outcomes.

Like women in the opposition parties, many PC women MPs "preferred policy options on the pro-choice end of the spectrum" (Pal 1991, 283) and generally expressed this preference in their statements in legislative debate. For example, Barbara McDougall's statements in parliamentary debate reflected the position she defended in cabinet deliberations. During second reading debate, she stated: "in the view of many women including myself the absence of legislation [on abortion] appeared to respect what I believe, that the judgment of women faced with a difficult decision and their capacity to make a better decision than anyone in this chamber on their behalf was respected in that environment" (McDougall 1989). Her opposition to the recriminalization of abortion is clear: "Many women, including myself, wanted legislation outside the Criminal Code ... Once again, after lengthy discussion our conclusion was that our powers were limited to the Criminal Code. This is not a happy conclusion for me, not by a long way" (ibid.).

The dissatisfaction with Bill C-43 that many PC women articulated in parliamentary debate did not translate into votes. Recall that cabinet ministers were required to vote with the government and that backbenchers were allowed a free vote. But at both second and third readings, PC women voted unanimously in support of the bill. In their speeches during debate, they justified their votes by suggesting the bill was an imperfect compromise but that it was still the best available solution given the deep divide between the two perspectives on the issue (e.g. Collins 1989; Bourgault 1989; Martin 1989). They also indicated that the government had a responsibility to establish a legislative framework following the legal void that was created after the *Morgentaler* decision (Bourgault 1989; Vézina 1989; Bertrand 1989; Collins 1989; Martin 1989). In several cases, PC women suggested that the proposed legislation provided women with access to abortions under a range of circumstances, despite the restrictions created by the bill, and thus left some space for women to make decisions about their reproductive health (e.g. McDougall 1989; Collins 1989; Feltham 1989; Landry 1989; Greene 1989; Bourgault 1989; Campbell 1989). Although several referred to the views and preferences of their constituents in their speeches in debate, it was evident that opinion among their constituents was divided and thus did not provide clear direction for their votes (Vézina 1989; Bernatchez-Tardif 1989; Martin 1989).

Despite the free vote for backbenchers, even the PC women who had articulated dissatisfaction with the proposed legislation during debate toed the party line when it came time to vote. There was no real evidence of critical actors within the PC caucus at this stage of the legislative process. The willingness of pro-choice PC women ministers and backbenchers to vote in support of Bill C-43 even though they were opposed to its content speaks to the power of partisanship as an important factor in their decision-making calculus and behaviour – even when the formal powers of the party whip are not exercised.

Senate Resistance

Ultimately, it was the unprecedented tie vote in the Senate in January 1991 that blocked the passage of Bill C-43 and preserved women's access to legal abortions. Opposing votes by three PC women senators – Pat Carney, Mira Spivak, and Janis Johnson – were especially noteworthy and their actions in opposition to the proposed legislation were central to the defeat of the bill. Eighty-six of 110 senators participated in the final vote on Bill C-43. At the time of the vote, PC senators enjoyed a recently achieved narrow majority over the Liberals following Prime Minister Mulroney's September 1990 decision to use an obscure constitutional provision to appoint eight new PC senators to win a vote on the new Goods and Services Tax (Docherty 2002, 36). Senator Johnson was among the eight emergency appointees, and Senator Carney had been appointed to her post less than one month before that.

With a numerical advantage in the upper house, the government stood a reasonable chance of securing the bill's passage through the

Senate. The Senate vote was not whipped, and senators were free to vote their conscience. The government leader in the Senate, Lowell Murray, is nonetheless reported to have worked hard to persuade PC senators to vote in support of the bill, and he was assisted by pressure emanating from the Prime Minister's Office (Vienneau 1991c; York 1991). Despite efforts by the government to persuade its senators to support the bill, seven PC senators voted against their government. In addition to the three women identified above, four PC men voted against the bill – Norman Atkins, Wilbert Keon, Finlay MacDonald, and John Macdonald. As the final vote tally in table 5.1 shows, voting otherwise split largely along party lines. All other PC senators voted in favour of the bill, with support from only two Liberals – Allan MacEachen and Norbert Thériault.

Without the votes of any one of the forty-three senators who opposed the legislation, Bill C-43 would have passed into law. But the decisions of three PC women senators to vote against their government were especially important as instances of the substantive representation of women. As I explain in greater detail below, the three PC women senators were critical actors in this case because their efforts were motivated by their pro-choice commitments, they staked out their position publicly, and they coordinated behind the scenes with pro-choice allies across party lines. Although four PC men also voted against their government and these votes were indeed important to the result, as I show, their motivations and efforts did not demonstrate an active commitment to the promotion of women's equality.

All three PC women senators who voted against the bill were firmly pro-choice. As a cabinet minister in the first Mulroney government, Pat Carney was the lone PC MP to join Tories for Choice, a group created to oppose anti-abortion interests in the party (Bercovici 1988). Senator Janis Johnson was a long-standing women's equality advocate whose work as a policy and communications consultant focused on women's health and equality issues (Johnson 2013a). Johnson's speech during debate on the bill unequivocally articulated a pro-choice position that defended women's reproductive rights as a central issue for women's equality (Johnson 1991). Johnson directly attributed her decision to oppose Bill C-43 to her prior experience as a women's health and equality advocate (Johnson 2013b). Senator Mira Spivak articulated a clear pro-choice position in legislative debate and was consistently identified alongside Senator Johnson as one of the key pro-choice Progressive Conservative opponents of the bill in the Senate

Table 5.1
Results of the Senate third reading vote on Bill C-43

	Yeas	*Nays*
Progressive Conservative	40	7
Liberal	2	35
Reform/Independent	1	1
Total	**43**	**43**

(Spivak 1991; Ferguson 1991; Vienneau 1991b; Walker 1991). All three women were on the public record as pro-choice opponents of the government's proposed legislation – either through their parliamentary speeches or through media reports that consistently identified them as pro-choice defenders of women's equality rights.

Carney's decision to vote against the bill was particularly important in tipping the count against the bill. Carney had informed the Senate leadership that she would not attend the vote because she was in Vancouver seeking physiotherapy treatment for severe arthritis (Fraser 1991). At the last minute, however, she decided to fly to Ottawa specifically to vote against the legislation without notifying the Senate whip's office that she would be there. Her presence for the vote thus took the government by surprise (Nichols 1991).

Although the bill was opposed by both pro-choice and anti-abortion senators, cross-party coordination among women committed to a pro-choice position on both sides of the Senate was crucial in facilitating the bill's defeat. Senator Joyce Fairbairn, a senior Liberal committed to a pro-choice position, coordinated opposition by making telephone calls to other pro-choice senators to secure their votes (Sharpe 1994; Haussman 2001). One report suggests that Fairbairn was supported in these cross-party coordination efforts by Liberal senator and past president of the National Action Committee on the Status of Women, Lorna Marsden (Gray 1991). Following the vote, Fairbairn confirmed that "there were 'many, many connections across the floor' between opponents of the legislation in both parties" (York 1991). In this case, pro-choice senators were able to do what their pro-choice colleagues in the House of Commons could not: they engaged in issue-based cross-party cooperation to secure a policy outcome that defended women's equality.

Available evidence suggests that the motivations and efforts of the four PC men who voted against the bill in the Senate do not reveal the same degree of commitment or willingness to take initiative to act in defence of women's equality as was the case among women. Senator John Macdonald's decision to vote against Bill C-43 was motivated by anti-abortion commitments, an unwavering belief that life begins at conception, and a refusal to accept any form of legislation that allows for abortion under any circumstances – a position he made clear in his speech during second reading debate on the bill in the Senate (Macdonald 1990). None of the three other PC men spoke during Senate debate on the bill, and the precise motivation behind their votes is not well known. A report in *The Interim*, an anti-abortion social conservative publication, suggests in passing that Finlay MacDonald also voted against the bill because he "supported the pro-life stand" (Eady 1991).

There are no public statements or media reports that provide a clear indication of where the other two PC men stood on the issue or why they voted against the proposed legislation.[2] Wilbert Keon and Norman Atkins appear not to have participated in any of the cross-party coordination prior to the final Senate vote. Senator Keon is reported to have "steadfastly refused to say how he [would] vote" in the lead up to the final Senate vote on the bill, suggesting a lack of coordination with fellow senators (Vienneau 1991a). One report suggests that the decision of Senator Atkins, a long-time PC party organizer, to vote against the bill came as a surprise to the government (Gray 1991), but it was not only the government that was surprised. Nearly twenty years after the vote, Mira Spivak recalled in a speech commemorating Atkins's retirement from the Senate: "When the vote [on Bill C-43] was called, and no one knew how it would go, I looked up in surprise to see Norman Atkins voting his conscience" (Spivak 2009).[3] The fact that no one knew in advance how these men would vote on the bill suggests that they were not actively involved in cross-party collaboration and did not actively participate in the efforts led by pro-choice women to block the proposed legislation's passage. Therefore, although these four men's votes undoubtedly made a critical contribution to the bill's defeat in the Senate, they were less actively engaged than were their women colleagues in advocating and organizing to secure its defeat in defence of women's equality. Their votes were thus critical, but these men were not necessarily critical actors.

ANALYZING THE IMPACT OF CRITICAL ACTORS

The evidence examined above indicates that there were advocates for women's equality at each stage of the legislative process, but pro-choice PC women in the Senate were the only successful critical actors whose efforts were decisive in blocking legislation that would have recriminalized abortion. The willingness of these three women to vote against the government that appointed them helped prevent the retrenchment of previously won equality gains. Why were these women in the Senate able to advocate for and achieve a policy outcome for women while their counterparts in the House of Commons were not?

First, there are important differences between the two houses in terms of the operation of party discipline (Rayment and McCallion 2023). Recall from chapter 1 that party discipline is a consequence of the institutional structure of Westminster parliaments, the central operating principle of which is that the government must maintain the confidence of the majority of members in the legislature in order to remain in power. Governments must be able to count on the votes of everyone in their caucus to ensure their agenda is passed. Parties maintain discipline through the promise of career advancement and the threat of sanctions. But it is important to keep in mind that these mechanisms for discipline do not apply equally in the House of Commons and Senate. First, the government only needs to maintain the confidence of the lower house to stay in power (see Druckman et al. 2005; Russell 2012) – that is, the defeat of a government bill in the Senate would not have the same implications for the confidence convention as would the defeat of a government bill in the House. Moreover, because senators are appointed to serve until age seventy-five and typically do not serve in cabinet, there are fewer rewards and sanctions a government can wield to incentivize compliance with the party line. In the House of Commons, MPs can be strong-armed into voting the party line through a promise of a cabinet position or a threat to block their candidacy in the next election, but these tactics hold less suasion over senators.

Senators faced fewer risks or sanctions for breaking ranks with their party and voting against the government than did government MPs in the House of Commons. Bill C-43 was introduced as government legislation, and all members of the cabinet were required to maintain solidarity and vote with the government or be prepared to resign their cabinet position. Although backbench MPs were free to vote their conscience, the requirement that cabinet ministers vote in support of the bill likely influenced backbenchers who aspired to join the political executive. For backbenchers, voting against the bill could mean sacrificing any future aspirations to cabinet. And the penalty for pro-choice cabinet members who voted against the legislation would have been even more severe, with expulsion from cabinet, which is typical when members of the executive are unable to support the government's legislative agenda. For pro-choice PC MPs, their decision making and opportunities to act for women were thus constrained by the operation of party discipline in the House of Commons – even when the formal powers of the whip were not being exercised.

In the Senate, the threat of party discipline did not loom as large. Voting on the legislation was only whipped for cabinet ministers, and the only member of cabinet in the Senate was Lowell Murray, the government leader in the Senate. All other senators were allowed a free vote. Because the vote in the Senate was not whipped, there were fewer opportunities for the government to sanction those who voted against the bill. Pressure on Tory senators to vote in support of the bill would thus have been lower in the Senate than in the House. Senators were subject to social pressure, but they were more insulated from the power of the prime minister and whip than were their colleagues in the Commons.

In addition to weaker party discipline in the Senate, the political circumstances that formed the backdrop for legislative action had shifted by the time Bill C-43 made its way to the upper house. There was increasing public opposition to Bill C-43 and a growing recognition within the government that the legislation was problematic. Medical doctors across the country had begun to stop providing abortions out of fear of prosecution under the soon-to-be passed law (Brodie 1992). Public opinion also appeared to have solidified against the proposed legislation. A December 1990 poll found that 66 per cent of Canadians "did not favour recriminalizing abortion" (ibid.). These factors appear to have led ministers to see the legislation as problematic, with Justice Minister Campbell publicly committing not to proclaim the bill into law "until the concerns and fears of Canadian doctors have been addressed" (*Toronto Star* 1991).

By the time the bill reached the Senate, the Mulroney government's commitment to getting Bill C-43 passed appears to have softened. Members of the Mulroney cabinet confirmed years later that the bill was not a good piece of legislation but that it was the best that could be put forward given divisions within the PC caucus and the country more broadly (Tromp 2013). A growing sense that the proposed legislation was hard to defend may have released some of the pressure on PC senators to pass the bill. Justice Minister Campbell did not appear to be upset that the bill was defeated (Vienneau 1991c), and her staff are reported to have telephoned Senator Joyce Fairbairn's office following the vote to inform them that Campbell "was pleased [the bill] was defeated" (Sharpe 1994, 210).

Taken together, these conditions made it somewhat easier for senators than MPs to advocate successfully on behalf of women. These critical actors in the Senate were able to seize the opportunity created by the institutional context and political conditions under which they operated. Would-be critical actors in the House of Commons, however, had to navigate a different set of opportunities and constraints than did their Senate colleagues. The strategies MPs used and their ability to influence outcomes depended on their role and position in the House of Commons – in opposition, on the backbenches, or in cabinet. The evidence discussed above suggests that women MPs overall preferred a more pro-choice approach and defended that position in parliamentary speeches, but their ability to convert those preferences into successful policy action varied dramatically.

Why did these differently positioned women face such divergent prospects for action and impact? In this case, advocating for women was low risk for opposition MPs, but their ability to shape outcomes was limited. Given that the substantive representation of women in this case required resistance to a government legislative policy initiative that threatened to curtail previously won equality gains, advocating for women was unproblematic for opposition MPs. For New Democrat Dawn Black, for example, the risk associated with advocating for women and defending equality by opposing Bill C-43 was virtually nil. In her speeches during debate on the bill, she consistently critiqued the government's proposed legislation and highlighted the negative impacts it would have for women if passed. She also leveraged the procedural tools of parliament to stymie the bill's progress through the House. As an opposition legislator, she risked no negative consequences for voting against a government bill or trying to block its passage – in fact, such behaviour was expected given her role. Since the NDP had officially adopted a pro-choice stance, Black's active defence of women's access to legal abortions was consistent with party policy, expected by her fellow New Democrats, and far from controversial. The risk of opposing the government's legislation to recriminalize abortion was thus low for opposition women, but their ability to influence government policy decision making as opposition MPs in a majority parliament was virtually non-existent without the support of at least a handful of PC MPs willing to oppose the official government position in a legislative vote. Black's preference for a pro-choice position therefore translated unproblematically into action – both in House of Commons debate and voting – but her capacity to influence outcomes was limited.

By contrast, women in the PC caucus and cabinet who were inclined to advocate for women had greater opportunities to influence government policy but doing so came with greater risks because it required opposition to the party line. For example, as a member of the government's Committee on Priorities and Planning, Barbara McDougall was able and willing to leverage her powerful position to attempt to influence the development of the legislation by pushing for a more pro-choice approach. Because this advocacy occurred behind closed doors in cabinet discussions that informed the development of the government's bill, her efforts stood a reasonable chance of influencing government decision making with relatively limited risk to her political career. Once the cabinet decided to proceed with a legislative option that restricted access to legal abortions, McDougall was willing to oppose the government in her statements on the official parliamentary record, registering her objections to the legislation. But voting against the bill and breaking cabinet solidarity would have come at great personal cost through the loss of her cabinet position. Such a demotion would also have weakened her ability to represent women's interests in the future. Moreover, without the support of other women in the PC caucus and pro-choice supporters in the other party caucuses, there was no guarantee that such a risk would have paid off and defeated the bill. Given the risk involved in defying the party whip, she chose not to break ranks with her party by voting against the bill. Women on the PC backbenches appear to have made the same calculation.

It was thus easier for women in the opposition parties to take a stand against PC threats to women's equality than it was for their colleagues in government. Yet opposition MPs had fewer opportunities to influence policy decisions and outcomes than did those on the other side of the House. By contrast, it was riskier for women in the government caucus to defend women's equality by voting against the government's legislation. But as relative insiders they had access to more opportunities to influence policy options earlier in the legislative process than did their colleagues across the aisle.

IMPLICATIONS

In the 34th Parliament, women parliamentarians were at the forefront of pushing back against the Mulroney government's attempt to recriminalize abortion. With varying prospects for impact, elected women intervened through the means available to them given their position and role in parliament to push back against the government's proposed legislation – through advocacy around legislative drafting, through speeches, and through procedural tactics. Pitted against a large and vocal contingent of predominantly male and predominantly Progressive Conservative anti-abortion MPs, pro-choice women MPs from all parties were unable to block the government's bill to recriminalize abortion. The actions of the three PC women senators who voted against Bill C-43, however, demonstrated that, under some conditions, a commitment to the substantive representation of women can prevail over other factors and lead to outcomes that preserve women's equality. Bill C-43 was defeated by the narrowest possible margin, facilitated in part by cross-party coordination among pro-choice women in the Senate and the willingness of Senators Mira Spivak, Janis Johnson, and Pat Carney to defy the government that appointed them and vote against the bill. The capacity of women parliamentarians to influence policymaking in defence of women's interests was shaped by the opportunities and constraints created by the institutional context, political conditions, and parliamentary role in which they operated.

The findings from this chapter suggest two important implications for how the substantive representation of women occurs. First, previous research highlights the importance of "the presence of women in the right places within the legislature" for ensuring women-friendly policy outcomes (Childs and Withey 2006, 20). Although Barbara McDougall was strategically well placed and leveraged her position in the Mulroney cabinet to advocate on behalf of women, her efforts on their own were insufficient to stop or even to soften the government's attempt to recriminalize abortion. The presence of women "in the right places" is thus important – indeed, McDougall's efforts ensured that the voices and concerns of women were heard as the government's legislation was developed – but it provides no guarantee of achieving policy outcomes that promote and protect women's equality if other factors militate against this goal.

Second, the Canadian Senate is often dismissed as an undemocratic institution that fails to exercise its full legislative powers and falls short on the representation of regions for which it is responsible (Docherty 2002; Macfarlane 2021). However, the successful efforts of women senators to coordinate across party lines to block the passage of the PC government's bill to recriminalize abortion demonstrates that, whatever its institutional limitations, the Senate has the potential to play an important role in the substantive representation of women. This potential is especially clear when representation takes the form of defending women's equality in response to government proposals that would seek to undermine previously won gains. Consideration of these defensive cases offers a more comprehensive understanding of how and under what conditions the substantive representation of women occurs. More broadly, this case demonstrates senators' capacity to engage in more issue-based cross-party cooperation than is possible in the House of Commons. In light of recent reforms to the Senate appointment process that appear to have reduced partisanship in the upper house (VandenBeukel at al 2021; McCallion 2022), senators' capacity to act as substantive representatives of women is likely to increase.

In the 34th Parliament, women in the House of Commons advocated against Bill C-43, An Act Respecting Abortion, using the procedural tools available to them based on their position within the parliamentary institution – whether it was behind the scenes in cabinet discussions, on the parliamentary record, or through obscure procedural means. Ultimately, their efforts were unable to block the bill's passage in the House. Pro-choice women in the Senate, however, faced somewhat weaker pressures from party discipline and a more favourable political context, and they were able to win for women by blocking the government's proposed legislation. The insights from this case into the strategies MPs use and the constraints they face are instructive. Details from an additional case allow us to build a clearer picture of how MPs navigate their institutional context to advocate and win for women. In chapter 6, the analysis of the response to the Harper government's attempt to cut funding to Status of Women Canada helps to round out our understanding of the strategies and mechanisms through which women MPs advocate and potentially win for women.

6

The Harper Government and Cuts to Status of Women Canada

After more than a year of relentless critique by opposition MPs, the Harper government restored the principle of equality to the mandate of the federal Women's Program in February 2008. This change was implemented on the same day the House of Commons was scheduled to debate Liberal MP Sue Barnes's private member's motion on this very topic. Surprised by the timing, Barnes (2008a) noted in her remarks during debate: "We must be one effective opposition and that must be one desperate government." This reversal followed the government's earlier attempt to cut funding to Status of Women Canada and to change funding eligibility requirements and the mandate of the agency's Women's Program. The government's subsequent decision to reverse some of these initial changes was not a major victory for gender equality, but it did forestall further erosion of the federal bureaucracy's gender equality policy infrastructure and thus can be counted as a win. This outcome was a response to the cumulative pressure created by Liberal, NDP, and Bloc Québécois women MPs who effectively leveraged the procedural and political tools available to them, given their parliamentary role, to pressure the government to change course. This chapter examines the details of the policy decision-making process around Status of Women Canada and the mechanisms through which women MPs advocated for women throughout this process.

The investigation in this chapter adds to our understanding of the process through which feminist substantive representation of women in policy advocacy and outcomes occurs and complements the examination of legislative policymaking on abortion in the 34th Parliament in chapter 5. Substantive representation must be understood to include multiple dimensions – speaking for women, advocating for women, and achieving policy outcomes for women. By focusing on processes of policy advocacy and outcomes on specific issues, this chapter, together with chapter 5, contributes to a more complete understanding of the impact women parliamentarians have on the substantive representation of women in Canadian politics.

To guide the analysis, this chapter asks the same questions that were used to analyze the process of legislative policymaking on abortion in the 34th Parliament. What were the key milestones in the Harper government's attempt to cut funding, change funding eligibility rules, and modify the mandate of the federal gender equality policy bureaucracy? Who were the primary advocates for women's equality throughout this process? What strategies did they use to advocate for women and to influence policymaking? What impact did their interventions have on eventual outcomes? And why were some actors able to influence outcomes while others were not?

IDENTIFYING CRITICAL ACTORS

The analysis in this chapter is again grounded in the critical actors framework, which conceives of the substantive representation of women in advocacy and policy outcomes as resulting from the efforts of a few actors willing to take action on behalf of women at a relatively low threshold (Childs and Krook 2009). Again, the focus in this chapter is on the substantive representation of women in advocacy and outcomes oriented towards the promotion of women's equality. These actions on behalf of women's equality can be initiated by women or men, but there are good reasons to expect that women legislators are more likely to emerge as critical actors than are their male colleagues (Phillips 1995; Mansbridge 1999, 2003). Moreover, these actions can be oriented towards making policy progress, but they can also be defensive. Advocating and winning for women can include resistance to policy initiatives that would erode previous equality gains. The critical actors framework is useful for the analysis of how the substantive representation occurs because it recognizes that not all women legislators will be equally inclined to advocate for women. It also acknowledges that an MP's position within parliament will shape the extent to which they are able to advocate for and achieve results.

To build a clear picture of whether and how women MPs advocated for women in response to the Harper government's attempt to cut funding and change the mandate of Status of Women Canada in the

39th Parliament, I again draw on qualitative evidence from documentary sources, including parliamentary debate transcripts, media reports, biographies, and secondary literature. I use these documentary sources to assess (1) who was involved in advocating for women's equality and (2) whether and to what extent their actions influenced government policy direction. To make these assessments I look for evidence of actors who spoke frequently or initiated measures in defence of Status of Women Canada in parliamentary debate transcripts. I look for confirmation of these activities or other references that an actor was an advocate for preserving Status of Women Canada in media reports, biographies, and the secondary literature. To determine whether these actors' interventions were decisive in shaping policy outcomes, I look for references to certain actions being influential and make assessments that account for pressures and sequencing of events. In each case, I look for confirmation of evidence from multiple sources.

A BRIEF OVERVIEW OF STATUS OF WOMEN CANADA IN THE 39TH PARLIAMENT

Before turning to an assessment of the Harper government's attempt to weaken Status of Women Canada, it is helpful to clarify the role of this policy agency within the federal bureaucracy. In the 1970s, the federal government began building a robust "network of gender-based policy machinery" designed to support women's equality in Canadian society (Brodie and Bakker 2007, 31). The Women's Program was established in 1972 to provide core funding to women's movement organizations across the country (Brodie 2008). In 1973, the Canadian Advisory Council on the Status of Women (CACSW) was created to provide policy advice to the federal government on gender equality issues and to liaise between movement organizations and the federal government (Brodie and Bakker 2007). In 1976, Status of Women Canada was established as a stand-alone federal agency responsible for coordinating across government departments, and it was given a minister responsible for the status of women in the federal cabinet (Brodie 2008). Taken together, these government programs and structures supported the Canadian women's movement, provided a formal link between movement actors and the federal policy process, and created structures within the federal bureaucracy tasked with addressing gender equality issues across government.

When it was first created, this gender-based policy machinery was one of the best-developed in the world. It worked to advocate for gender equality in government policymaking and linked academic and civil society networks with government policy structures (Brodie and Bakker 2007). By the early 1980s, the federal government leveraged Status of Women Canada to work collaboratively with women's organizations and movement actors on key equality issues, including pay equity, violence against women, and childcare (Brodie 2008). During this period, women's movement organizations together with the federal gender-based policy structures enjoyed a reasonable degree of prominence and policy influence in Canada (Brodie 2008; Rodgers and Knight 2011). This collaborative model was short-lived. Under the Progressive Conservative government of Brian Mulroney, first elected in 1984, funding for the Women's Program began to decline (Brodie 2008; Rodgers and Knight 2011). Further erosion of this policy infrastructure continued under Jean Chrétien's Liberal government, first elected in 1993 (Knight and Rodgers 2012; Brodie 2008). The proposed cuts and changes to Status of Women Canada under the Harper government in 2006 were thus significant but can be seen as part of what Brodie (2008, 157) describes as "a prolonged war of attrition" that aimed to undermine the influence of feminist interests.

Less than a year into their first minority mandate in September 2006, the Harper Conservative government announced cuts to operational funding for Status of Women Canada. These cuts were part of a larger $2 billion cost cutting exercise that affected a wide range of programs, from tourism to museums to research, despite the government's projected $13 billion surplus (Whittington and Campion-Smith 2006). Status of Women Canada faced a $5 million cut to its total annual budget of $23 million beginning in the 2007–08 fiscal year (Whittington and Campion-Smith 2006). These cuts would be realized through the closure of twelve of the agency's sixteen regional offices, leaving only four regional centres open across the country in Ottawa; Edmonton, Montreal, and Moncton, respectively (*Toronto Star* 2006; *National Post* 2006).

Days after the cuts to Status of Women Canada were announced, the Harper government announced changes to the funding rules and mandate of the Women's Program. Since its inception, the Women's Program had been mandated to "advance equality for women by addressing women's economic, social, political and legal situation" (Canada 2007c, 3; Ditchburn 2006a). In late 2006, the mandate was changed so that the program was focused on "facilitat[ing] women's participation in Canadian society by addressing their economic, social and cultural situation through Canadian organizations" (Canada 2007c, 3; Ditchburn 2006a). Changes to the eligibility rules for grants allocated through the Women's Program were also changed so that funding could no longer support "advocacy work, lobbying of the government or general research" (Ditchburn 2006a; see also Canada 2007c, 4). Changes to eligibility criteria also broadened the rules under which groups could receive funding through the Women's Program so that for-profit organizations could receive funds for business-oriented events and mentorship initiatives (Brodie 2008). Along with these mandate and eligibility changes, the government also eliminated Status of Women Canada's Policy Research Fund, which provided funding for women's organizations to undertake "policy research on gender equality issues" (Canada 2007c, 7; see also Brodie 2008).

As an instance of policymaking related to women's equality, the Harper-era changes to Status of Women Canada differed from the Mulroney government's attempt to recriminalize abortion discussed in chapter 5, both in terms of substantive issue content and the process by which the changes were proposed. The Mulroney government's effort to recriminalize abortion in the 34th Parliament was a concrete, high-profile, and high-stakes issue of women's equality rights. The issue was addressed through a focused government bill that had to be passed by the House and Senate to become law. Passage of Bill C-43, An Act Respecting Abortion, would have constituted a clear and decisive loss of an important women's right. The Progressive Conservatives held a majority in parliament, but voting on the bill was nominally free for backbench MPs; cabinet ministers were required to vote with the government.

By contrast, the Harper government's efforts to pick apart Status of Women Canada in the 39th Parliament constituted a more incremental change, part of an ongoing longer-term process of undermining feminist advocacy in Canada. Implementation of the government's proposed changes would not have been a concrete or decisive loss but, instead, would have continued to erode the influence of equality-seeking women's movements. The proposed changes were introduced during a minority parliament, meaning the government had to secure the support of opposition MPs to pass any legislation. Procedurally, however, the government's proposed changes to Status of Women Canada were not confined to a single piece of legislation. The funding cuts were part of the government's larger budget process, and the mandate and funding eligibility changes occurred at the discretion of the minister. With the exception of the budget bill (the defeat of which would have brought down the government), there was no single focused bill opposition MPs could vote against to block the full suite of proposed changes. MPs who opposed the government's policy direction on Status of Women Canada therefore had to engage through whatever means they could to influence government decision making. Despite these differences, both cases constitute instances of a government attempt to reverse prior equality gains and an opportunity for critical actors to advocate for women in a pro-equality direction by pushing back against those efforts.

CRITICAL ACTORS AGAINST CUTS TO STATUS OF WOMEN CANADA

Given that the government's efforts to erode Status of Women Canada were not contained within a single piece of legislation, how did the substantive representation of women occur in this case? Who advocated for women in response to the government's policy changes and what strategies did they use to influence government decision making? As I show, opposition women MPs together with movement actors outside parliament took the lead on pushing back against government efforts to undermine Status of Women Canada. These MPs – especially shadow cabinet critics for the status of women in all three opposition parties and members of the Standing Committee on the Status of Women – used oral questions, motions, and the parliamentary committee structure to raise the profile of the government's cuts and to pressure ministers to reverse their decision. Women in the Conservative cabinet and caucus, however, did not participate in this resistance – indeed, they defended their government's direction on the public record, with no public indication of internal party dissent. Ultimately, the efforts of opposition women to raise the public profile of the government's plans and bring feminist concerns to parliament created an environment within which the government felt compelled to soften, if not completely reverse, some of its initial policy changes.

Government Decision Making

There is no evidence that women in the Harper cabinet opposed the government's changes to Status of Women Canada in the 39th Parliament. This stands in contrast to patterns of behaviour identified in chapter 5, wherein Barbara McDougall, the minister of employment and immigration and minister responsible for the status of women in the Mulroney cabinet, consistently advocated for women behind the scenes and in cabinet discussions as her government developed its legislative approach to abortion in the 34th Parliament. Cabinet documents from the 39th Parliament remain sealed, so it is impossible to know with certainty whether or how any of the five women in the twenty-four-member Conservative cabinet – Carol Skelton, Rona Ambrose, Diane Finley, Bev Oda, and Josée Verner – advocated for women around the cabinet table while decisions about Status of Women Canada were being made. Evidence from the 34th Parliament suggests that MPs' parliamentary statements are a reasonably good indicator of their issue positions. Recall, for example, that Barbara McDougall defended women's equality in parliamentary debate, even if she voted with the government. We can therefore look to Conservative women's parliamentary statements in the 39th Parliament as a preliminary indication of where they stood on this issue.

Of the five women in the Harper cabinet, only the women who held the status of women portfolio – Bev Oda from February 2006 to August 2007, and Josée Verner from August 2007 to July 2008 – addressed the government's proposed cuts in debate.[1] Oda and Verner both consistently defended the government's position, using framing that insisted that the Conservative government was committed to women but rejected the need for government intervention or support to achieve gender equality. For example, during debate on an opposition motion critiquing the government's cuts to Status of Women Canada, Minister Oda stated:

> I want the House and all Canadians to know that neither I nor any member of this new Conservative government believes that all Canadian women by nature are weak, frail or vulnerable. They are strong, determined and industrious individuals who want a chance to contribute to their families and their communities and succeed in their ambitions and dreams. Society will have those who will need the help of others

> and this government will be there for them, but this government will not characterize all Canadian women as the frail and the vulnerable. (Oda 2006a)

Women on the Conservative backbenches who spoke during debate on the cuts and changes to Status of Women Canada defended their government's position using similar framing. For example, in debate on the same motion, Helena Guergis stated:

> Unlike the Liberals, we do not characterize our daughters and our granddaughters as weak and vulnerable. Rather, we know that they are confident and full of potential. When I look around the House I see many strong and successful women who worked hard to get where they are today. What I have been hearing from so many women is that they are fed up with being portrayed as victims. (Guergis 2006a)

These statements articulate the perspective that women as a group do not warrant targeted funding or special treatment. Status of Women Canada is thus constructed as an organization that provides unnecessary funding to a self-interested "special interest group" (Brodie 2008, 158–9). This defence of government cuts to Status of Women Canada deployed the language of equality but did so to oppose and undermine the legitimacy of policy interventions by equality-seeking women's movements.

Conservative women's defence of their government's cuts in parliamentary debate, however, does not necessarily confirm that these women did not question the government's decision to cut funding for Status of Women Canada, nor that these women were unconcerned with women's issues. For example, Helena Guergis volunteered at her local rape crisis centre (Guergis 2006b), and Rona Ambrose – who occupied the most senior cabinet position among Conservative women at the time of the Status of Women Canada cuts – held a degree in women's studies, had volunteered for women's shelters and sexual assault centres, and self-identified as a feminist (Boesveld 2015). But she also held individualist views in that she believed women could make progress based on their own merit and saw government intervention to promote equality as unnecessary (Taber 2007; Ivison 2006). This orientation is consistent with a tendency among members of the Conservative Party to be attentive to women's issues but to hold views grounded in a commitment to individual opportunity and a refusal to conceive of women as disadvantaged or in need of government intervention or support (Thomas 2017).

The available evidence about the inclination of Conservative women to defend women's equality in cabinet discussions is thus mixed. Absent confirmation from currently unavailable cabinet sources, it is difficult to know conclusively whether MPs' parliamentary statements reflect their genuine views and preferences or are simply the product of strong message control in the governing party.[2] However, given the importance of parliamentary speechmaking as a tool for public position-taking (Proksch and Slapin 2015), we can, at a minimum, be confident that it is unlikely these women would be willing to stand up in the House to defend a position that was directly at odds with their personal preferences.

Opposition Resistance

Whereas Conservative women lined up in support of their government's cuts and changes to Status of Women Canada during debate, women in the opposition parties were active and vocal opponents of the government's proposed changes. Liberal, New Democrat, and Bloc Québécois MPs seized on the proposed cuts to Status of Women Canada as an opportunity to paint the Conservatives as hostile to women's equality interests. A handful of opposition MPs, almost all of them women, used the full range of procedural means available to them as legislators to pressure the government to reverse its decision to cut funding and to change the mandate of Status of Women Canada. The absence of a single piece of legislation on which opposition efforts could focus made the task of forcing a government to reverse its decision particularly challenging. MPs who opposed the government's policy direction therefore used opposition motions, oral questions, and the Standing Committee on the Status of Women, and collaborated with movement actors outside parliament to connect their parliamentary opposition with public sentiment. Each of these strategies is discussed in greater detail below.

Immediately following the government's announcement, Liberal MP and status of women critic Maria Minna introduced an opposition motion on 28 September 2006 objecting to the cuts to Status of Women Canada. The full text of the motion read:

> That, in the opinion of the House, the government fails to recognize the many roles of women in Canadian society and the importance of providing all Canadian women with equal opportunity; and the House objects to the government's partisan and discriminatory cuts in federal support for women's programs and services. (Minna 2006a)

In total, twenty-six MPs participated in the debate. All participating opposition MPs supported the motion, while all Conservative MPs opposed it. Because the vote occurred in a minority parliament, the motion was adopted by the House but had no formal authority to force the government to act to change its policy decision.[3] In a similar vein, but more than a year after the government's cuts and changes were first announced, Liberal MP and justice critic Sue Barnes introduced a private member's motion on 7 February 2008, calling on the government "to reinstate women's equality as the goal of the Women's Program at Status of Women Canada" (Barnes 2008a). Although both motions lacked the power to force the government to act, they nonetheless allowed MPs to formally register their opposition to government intentions and provided an opportunity for cross-party cooperation among opposition MPs. By continuously drawing attention to the issue in parliament, they worked to keep the issue on the public agenda. The women who introduced these motions engaged in the substantive representation of women by advocating for women's equality using the procedural means available to them given their position within the institution.

Opposition MPs also used question period to put pressure on the government. They repeatedly raised the budget cuts, mandate change, regional office closures, and changes to the funding eligibility rules for the Women's Program while also drawing attention to the Conservative Party's track record on gender equality. As the aspect of parliamentary proceedings that attracts the most media attention (Soroka et al. 2009), question period served again to keep the issue on the public radar. Recall from chapter 4 that, of the 182 speeches made during oral questions under the status of women Hansard subtopic, 143 were explicitly about the government's cuts and changes to Status of Women Canada. Of these, seventy-two were questions, more than half of which were asked by a small group of opposition women MPs: Liberal status of women critic Maria Minna, Liberal Women's Caucus chair

Belinda Stronach, NDP status of women critic Irene Mathyssen, Bloc Québécois critic Nicole Demers, and Bloc Québécois member of the Standing Committee on the Status of Women Johanne Deschamps.

The MPs who asked questions about Status of Women Canada most frequently held formal roles related to the representation of women. Notably, however, both the Liberal and NDP leaders raised the issue in question period, signalling firm support for women's equality and its federal policy machinery within both parties. The first question Stéphane Dion asked in question period after assuming the leadership of the Liberal Party in December 2006 concerned the government's cuts and changes to Status of Women Canada (Whittington and Delacourt 2006; Ivison 2006):

> For my first question to a Prime Minister, I feel I must talk about women's rights. When the government is posting multi-billion dollar budget surpluses thanks to the previous Liberal government, why on earth is the Prime Minister closing 12 of the 16 Status of Women offices across Canada if it is not to cripple those who dare challenge his government's neo-conservative ideology? (Dion 2006)

This suggests that funding for Status of Women Canada, and the support for women's equality this funding implied, had become an important political cleavage along which parties could distinguish themselves. The Liberals in particular exploited this cleavage, with the publication of the so-called Pink Book by the Liberal Women's Caucus, which outlined a series of policy proposals on women's economic equality issues, such as maternity and parental leave, pay equity, and childcare (McMurdy 2006).

MPs also used the Standing Committee on the Status of Women as another mechanism through which to scrutinize government action. The committee structure also enabled MPs to bring the voices and perspectives of women's organizations into the parliamentary debate about Status of Women Canada. As noted in chapter 4, membership in the SCSW is drawn from all parties but, unlike most parliamentary committees, "the Chair is selected from the Official Opposition," which gives the opposition increased power to set the committee's direction (Grace 2016, 835). In the minority 39th Parliament, the committee was made up of five Conservative members, four Liberals, two Bloc Québécois, and one NDP MP (Standing Committee on the

Status of Women 2007a). This meant that, in addition to being chaired by an opposition MP, the opposition members collectively held a majority on the committee. The structure and composition of this committee – particularly in a minority parliament – therefore meant that it was strategically well positioned within the parliamentary institution to facilitate opposition women MPs' ability to scrutinize and put pressure on the government. The SCSW seized this opportunity and undertook several initiatives, including ministerial scrutiny, committee motions, public hearings, and formal reports.

On 5 October 2006, Minister Oda appeared before the SCSW to respond to committee reports on core funding for women's organizations and gender-based analysis. In these hearings, opposition MPs grilled the minister on the decision to reduce funding for Status of Women Canada and to remove the principle of equality from the Women's Program's mandate (Canada 2006a). Media reports on the hearings cited opposition claims that the minister was "letting down Canadian women" and noted the ideological distance between the Conservative government's approach to women's equality and that of the opposition parties (Ditchburn 2006b; Greenaway 2006).

Following the hearing with the minister, SCSW co-chair and NDP status of women critic Irene Mathyssen introduced a motion in a committee meeting on 19 October 2006, calling on the government to reverse the announced funding cuts and to restore the Women's Program's previous mandate (Canada 2006d). The motion was passed by a margin of one vote and reported to the House as the recommendation of the committee on 3 November 2006. In a meeting of the SCSW on 26 October 2006, Maria Minna introduced a similar motion condemning the cuts to Status of Women Canada and calling on the government to reverse them and to reinstate the previous funding guidelines for the Women's Program (Canada 2006b). Again, the motion was passed by a thin margin, with all Conservative members of the committee voting against the resolution. The motion was reported to the House as a recommendation of the committee on 22 November 2006, with a dissenting opinion submitted by the Conservative Party (Canada 2006e). In April 2007, Conservative MP and SCSW member Joy Smith introduced a motion calling for Status of Women Canada spending for the upcoming fiscal year to focus on programming relating to violence, women's full participation in society, and women's economic status, with no mention of the promotion of equality or the eligibility of advocacy projects. Bloc Québécois MP and status of women critic Nicole Demers moved an amendment to the motion adding to it equality and advocacy provisions. The amended motion was passed with support from all opposition MPs and was opposed by all Conservative members of the committee, and it was reported to the House as a recommendation of the SCSW (Canada 2007b).

In addition to motions expressing its opinion and recommendations, the SCSW also undertook an extensive analysis of the impact of the government's proposed cuts and program changes. On 7 November 2006, Belinda Stronach introduced a motion calling for the committee to "hold extended meetings to assess the impact the cuts to Status of Women Canada and the extensive changes to the Terms and Conditions of the Women's Program have had on the ability of Status of Women Canada to carry on its important work on behalf of women in Canada" (Canada 2006c). The committee subsequently received written briefs from eighty-two organizations and individuals and heard deputations from twenty-nine organizations (Canada 2007c).

The report resulting from this study was presented to the House on 7 May 2007 and included five recommendations: (1) reversing the decision to close twelve regional offices of Status of Women Canada, (2) maintaining funding for the Policy Research Fund, (3) reinstating women's equality in the mandate of the Women's Program, (4) removing restrictions on advocacy activities for funding recipients, and (5) restricting Women's Program funding to not-for-profit organizations (Canada 2007c, 17). The minister responsible for Status of Women Canada, by this time Josée Verner, responded to the report in a letter to the SCSW chair that defended the government's changes. The letter emphasized additional funding allocated to Status of Women Canada programs for the upcoming fiscal year and the focus on funding for programs that can demonstrate "measurable results," but it provided no indication that any action would be taken in response to the SCSW's report (Canada 2007a).

These motions and the report from the SCSW again constitute instances of the substantive representation of women through advocacy for women's equality. The women who introduced these motions advocated for women and took initiative to defend women's interests using the institutional means available to them. In each case, the motions and reports were passed by the SCSW and brought to the House for consideration as the result of consistent cross-party cooperation among opposition women MPs. Conservative women MPs, however, defended their government's approach rather than finding common ground with women from other parties. The motions from the SCSW called on the government to act, but they lacked the authority to compel the government to implement changes. Nonetheless, they conveyed with a certain degree of formality the official view of the committee and the perspectives of extra-parliamentary movement actors who gave testimony to it (Grace 2016).

In addition to bringing the voices of movement actors into parliament through the committee structure, opposition MPs worked with a coalition of feminist and labour movement actors to condemn the government's cuts and changes to Status of Women Canada, thus raising the public profile of the issue. On 10 December 2006, women MPs from all three opposition parties attended a rally in Ottawa organized by the Coalition for Women's Equality. The coalition brought together nine feminist organizations, including the National Action Committee on the Status of Women and the National Association of Women and the Law – both of which were, by this time, significantly weakened due to years of funding challenges (National Association of Women and the Law 2006a, 2006b). Maria Mourani and Irene Mathyssen, status of women critics for the Bloc Québécois and NDP, respectively, supported the work of the coalition at the rally, as did Liberal women's caucus chair Belinda Stronach. Stronach told a news conference that the government's cuts to Status of Women Canada were part of a broader effort to "cripple – or even abolish – the federal Status of Women department" (*Toronto Star* 2006; *Globe and Mail* 2006). This cross-party support for women's equality advocates outside parliament enabled these women MPs to establish a visible connection between their advocacy for women within parliament and the women in the population they represented. These connections emphasized the extent to which opposition women MPs' parliamentary critiques responded to and reflected the perspectives of women in the voting public.

The efforts and interventions of key opposition MPs discussed above are summarized in Table 6.1. Maria Minna, Belinda Stronach, and Irene Mathyssen emerge as the most frequent advocates against the Conservative government's cuts. All three women held formal roles related to the representation of women – either as their party's shadow cabinet critic for status of women (Minna and Mathyssen) or as their party's women's caucus chair (Stronach). The Bloc Québécois critic role transferred from Nicole Demers to Maria

Table 6.1
Summary of opposition MPs' interventions in the 39th Parliament

	Introduced a motion in the House	*Asked multiple oral questions*	*Introduced a motion in committee*	*Supported movement actors*	*Held a formal role related to women*
Maria Minna (LPC)	✓	✓	✓		Status of Women Critic
Belinda Stronach (LPC)		✓	✓	✓	Women's Caucus Chair
Irene Mathyssen (NDP)		✓	✓	✓	Status of Women Critic
Nicole Demers (BQ)		✓	✓		Status of Women Critic
Maria Mourani (BQ)				✓	Status of Women Critic
Johanne Deschamps (BQ)		✓			SCSW Member
Sue Barnes (LPC)	✓				Women's Caucus member

Mourani in early 2007, otherwise Demers likely would have had as many interventions as did the other top advocates. These opposition women regularly engaged in the substantive representation of women by advocating for women's equality using the tools available to them as opposition members.

Government Response

By early 2008, the Conservative government walked back some of its initially announced changes to Status of Women Canada. The Conservatives' initial announcement included $5 million in administrative cuts and regional office closures, but, according to federal public accounts, they eventually increased funding for the agency's granting program from $10.5 million in 2006–07 to $17.5 million in 2008–09. Although grant funding increased, the regional office closures remained in effect, with only four offices remaining open (Status of Women Canada 2019). By early 2008, reference to equality was restored to the mandate of the Women's Program, such that it was tasked "to advance the equality of women across Canada through the improvement of their economic and social conditions and their participation in democratic life" (Barnes 2008a). However, changes to eligibility criteria for grant recipients prohibiting organizations engaged in advocacy or research from receiving funding and allowing for-profit organizations to receive grants remained in place, and the Policy Research Fund was not reinstated (Bird and Rowe 2013). The Conservative government's measures to weaken Status of Women Canada were therefore scaled back somewhat from their initial proposal.

Collectively, the pressure created by opposition women and extra-parliamentary allies precipitated this partial retreat. There is no clear evidence of a single act that caused the government to increase funding and to restore equality to the mandate of Status of Women Canada. However, Liberal MP Sue Barnes's private member's motion calling for the reinstatement of the principle of equality to the mandate of the Women's Program was introduced immediately before the government announced its decision to adjust its policy direction in early 2008. Unlike most of the other MPs who frequently advocated for women against the government's policy direction on this issue in parliament, Barnes did not occupy a formal role committed to the representation of women. She was nonetheless actively engaged as a member of the Liberal women's caucus (Barnes 2009). Despite not occupying a formal women's equality role in parliament, she was plugged in to a formal institutional structure designed to improve women's representation.

Barnes's motion appears to have influenced the timing of the government's decision to restore equality to the Women's Program mandate. As she noted in the final debate on the motion:

> On the morning of February 7, I came to Parliament and turned on the computer to check whether anything had really changed. If anyone went to the women's program that day, the program mandate read: "The mandate of the WP is to facilitate women's participation in Canadian society by addressing their economic, social and cultural situation through Canadian organizations." It continues, but there is no mention of the word "equality." I was to speak a few hours later. A couple of hours before I spoke, I went to the website and the program mandate miraculously said: "The newly revised mandate of the Women's

> Program is to advance the equality of women across Canada through the improvement of their economic and social conditions and their participation in democratic life." (Barnes 2008b)

Barnes's opposition motion may have affected the timing of government decision making about the Women's Program mandate, but it did not bring about the change on its own. Instead, the government's decision to restore equality to the mandate and to increase funding for the Women's Program is best understood as a response to the cumulative pressure created by women on the opposition benches in collaboration with extra-parliamentary movement actors. Collectively, the efforts of opposition women MPs drew critical public and parliamentary attention to the government's attempt to weaken Status of Women Canada and created an environment within which it was politically challenging for the government to leave all its initial changes in place.

ANALYZING THE IMPACT OF CRITICAL ACTORS

The evidence above shows that the combined efforts of opposition women did not block all Conservative government changes to Status of Women Canada, but they did manage to moderate many of them. These actions demonstrated a commitment to the promotion of women's equality, and, as such, the opposition women who pushed back can be considered critical actors in this case. Much of the opposition response to the Status of Women changes doubtless fell into the category of political posturing. But this posturing was not without impact. Opposition women MPs leveraged the full suite of parliamentary tools available to them – opposition and private members' motions, oral questions, committee work, and collaboration with movement actors outside parliament – to pressure the government to reverse its changes. Their pressure led the government to backtrack on some of its initially proposed measures.

Why were opposition women able to advocate and achieve policy outcomes for women while their counterparts in the Conservative Party were unable or unwilling to speak out against their government's position? First, there are important differences in how the pressures of party discipline operate for government and opposition MPs. Party discipline results from the operational structure of Westminster parliaments and the requirement that the government maintain the confidence of a majority of members in the House of Commons to remain in power. When the government is in a minority position, as was the case in the 39th Parliament, its ability to count on the votes of everyone in its caucus is especially important. A government will always work to secure the support of its caucus, but the mechanisms wielded by a governing party to maintain discipline – the promise of career advancement and the threat of sanctions – would be particularly acute in a minority. Party discipline and internal message control under the Harper government are widely reported to have been notably strict (Martin 2010; Wells 2013; Ibbitson 2015). And in this case, MPs are reported to have been told explicitly in a caucus meeting that if they opposed the government's plans to implement its broad package of funding cuts, their careers would suffer (Smith 2006). Government MPs therefore faced significant risks of sanction if they spoke out against the government's cuts and mandated changes to Status of Women Canada. By contrast, speaking out against the government's policy direction on Status of Women Canada was consistent with opposition MPs' institutional role. Opposition parties are expected to scrutinize and critique government action. In particular, the women who occupied institutional positions relevant to women's equality within parliament rose to the challenge of defending women's equality and opposing the government's cuts.

Second, the advocacy of these opposition women yielded results because their efforts shifted the background political conditions against which the Conservative government made its policy decisions. Women in the opposition parties called attention to the government's cuts and changes to Status of Women Canada through motions, oral questions, and committee work. They used these parliamentary tools to portray the Conservative government as "anti-women" and to position gender equality as a salient partisan issue. For example, following the release of the Liberals' Pink Book, Judy Sgro, the Liberal chair of the Standing Committee on the Status of Women, emphasized the failings of the government position on women's equality, stating, "I think Harper and his Conservative government, based on their policies, would clearly prefer women would stay barefoot and pregnant in the kitchen and move us backwards 40 years" (Canadian Press 2006). In addition to highlighting the government's position to the public to increase the issue's salience, opposition women worked to reflect public sentiment back to the government. By working with outside actors and using the committee structure to bring outside voices into parliament, they emphasized public opposition to the government's proposed cuts. These efforts increased the prominence of an issue on which the Conservative government was already politically vulnerable and reinforced a public perception of the Conservative Party as "anti-women."

This strategy was effective because the Conservative Party suffered from low levels of electoral support among women voters. Data from the Canadian Election Study suggest that women's support for the Conservative Party in the 2006 and 2008 elections was 4 to 6 per cent lower than was men's (Bird and Rowe 2013; see also Gidengil et al. 2003). Because the Conservatives already suffered from weak support among women voters, increasing public awareness of the government's cuts to Status of Women Canada threatened to weaken the party's already low levels of electoral support among women. Opposition efforts thus exploited an existing electoral vulnerability of the Conservative Party. By tapping into that vulnerability, opposition actors shifted the background conditions against which the government assessed the viability of its policy direction. With gender equality on the public radar, a harsh stance on Status of Women Canada would have become more politically challenging for the government to maintain. Opposition efforts to change the background political conditions thus shifted the government's political calculus. The eventual decision to increase the budget allocation for Status of Women Canada allowed the government to "send a relatively low-cost signal that it was concerned about women" (Bird and Rowe 2013, 174). This backtracking can thus be read as an attempt by the Conservative Party to mitigate the political and electoral impact of its initial policy direction on the federal women's policy agency.

Taken together, the direction in which party discipline operated, combined with a focus on exploiting public opposition to the government's cuts, meant that opposition women's advocacy on behalf of women facilitated the government's decision to soften its policy direction. By contrast, there is no publicly available evidence that Conservative women MPs opposed or resisted their government's attempt to weaken Status of Women Canada. What accounts for these divergent approaches and opportunities for action and impact?

In this case, as in the 34th Parliament, there was little to no risk for opposition women MPs to resist the government's cuts and changes to Status of Women Canada, but their ability to influence outcomes was far from guaranteed. As opposition members, using motions, oral questions, and committee proceedings to scrutinize and critique the government aligned with their institutional role as opposition members. Opposition MPs risked no negative consequences for pushing back against the government's policy changes – indeed, their parliamentary roles and the logic of partisan politics demanded it. Opposition women MPs' capacity to affect government policy direction, however, was limited. Once a government decides on a policy direction, it is difficult to force a change in direction. In a minority parliament, opposition parties can band together to defeat an undesirable bill, but, in this case, there was no legislative target for opposition parties to focus on. The funding cuts to Status of Women were included in the government's omnibus budget bill. And although the opposition parties could have voted against the budget bill, defeating a budget – and a government – over a $5 million cut in a multi-billion-dollar budget would have been a wildly disproportionate response. The minority context, however, did create opportunities to leverage public opposition to force the government to modify its policy direction since electoral vulnerabilities are especially pertinent when the timing of the next election is uncertain. Opposition women thus leveraged their institutional role within parliament and the broader political context to pressure the government to reverse course.

By contrast, the risk of speaking out against the government's policy direction would have been much greater for Conservative MPs despite their closer proximity to decision making. For government MPs, defying the whip and breaking ranks to speak out against their party's policy direction would have risked severe career penalties. The threat of these consequences is likely to have been wielded with a heavy hand given the importance for a minority government to be able to count on the support of its own caucus. Cabinet records from the 39th Parliament remain sealed so we cannot know with certainty what was said in cabinet discussions about the Status of Women cuts, but the available evidence is mixed as to whether women in the Conservative cabinet would have been inclined to speak out against the cuts. Even if these five women were inclined to defend Status of Women Canada, reports suggest that opportunities to influence government direction were limited and partisan message control was strict (Smith 2006; Martin 2010; Wells 2013; Ibbitson 2015).

The apparent absence of dissent within the Conservative caucus and cabinet in the 39th Parliament stands in contrast to the behaviour of women in the Progressive Conservative Party in the 34th Parliament. In the 34th Parliament, some Progressive Conservative women defended women's equality interests and spoke out against their government's attempt to recriminalize abortion. Conservative women in the 39th Parliament, however, consistently defended their government's policy direction in public statements reported in the media, in committee meetings, and in parliamentary debate.

What accounts for these divergent patterns of legislator behaviour between the 34th and 39th Parliaments, particularly among Conservative women? There are of course important differences between the substance of the policy issues addressed in these two parliaments and the way in which these issues were positioned in relation to norms of party discipline. For example, in the 34th Parliament cabinet ministers were required to support the government's legislation on abortion while backbenchers were allowed a free vote. This may have created space for cabinet ministers to voice concerns publicly in debate, even if they eventually voted with the government. No similar exemption was made for Conservative backbenchers with regard to the cuts to Status of Women Canada in the 39th Parliament. These differences notwithstanding, the absence of any objections from Conservative women suggests the constraints and pressures created by partisanship were more decisive in the 39th Parliament than in the 34th.

The differences in legislator behaviour between the two cases are also consistent with shifting patterns in the Canadian party system over this period, including increased partisanship and polarization in the Canadian party system and heightened partisan message control (Cochrane 2010; Blidook and Byrne 2013; Marland 2020). These changes may have limited the ideological space available on the political right for pro-equality perspectives. Women in the more moderate Progressive Conservative Party of the 34th Parliament were able to advocate for a feminist perspective. Indeed, research has shown that women in the Mulroney Progressive Conservative Party were committed to women's equality and movement objectives and constituted a "distinctive ideological grouping" within the party (Young 2000, 174). A similar degree of internal ideological diversity was not apparent in the Conservative Party in the 39th Parliament. The ideological space occupied by the political right in Canada shifted following the emergence and integration of the harder right populist Reform and Canadian Alliance formations into the Conservative Party of Canada in 2003. These parties have been less sympathetic to the equality claims of women as a political group (Thomas 2017; Young 2000). This perspective is reflected in the parliamentary statements by women in the Harper government who endorsed an individualist perspective that emphasized equality of opportunity, which was largely incompatible with the collectivist aims of a pro-equality women's movement. These patterns suggest that there was more internal ideological cohesion and less space for women to advocate for feminist aims within the Harper Conservatives than within the Mulroney Progressive Conservatives – or at least stronger internal party message control that limited the ability of those with preferences that deviated from the official party line to advocate for those perspectives.

IMPLICATIONS

In the 39th Parliament, women MPs led the charge against the Harper government's plans for Status of Women Canada, but this resistance came exclusively from the opposition benches. Opposition women defended the preservation of Status of Women Canada, but their concerns were not shared by Conservatives. Irene Mathyssen, Maria Minna, and Belinda Stronach occupied formal roles related to the status of women and used the tools available to them given their institutional role and the political circumstances within which they operated to resist the government's attempt to cut funding and to change the mandate of Status of Women Canada. These women spoke out against the government's actions in question period; they also introduced, spoke, and voted in support of motions condemning the government's cuts and changes to the federal women's policy agency. They leveraged the parliamentary committee structure to amplify the voices of extra-parliamentary feminists and supported the efforts of these actors outside parliament. The cumulative pressure created by these and other opposition women's actions exploited the Conservatives' low voter support among women, and the government backtracked on some of its proposed changes. As was the case in the 34th Parliament, the willingness and ability of women MPs to act in defence of women's equality was shaped by party affiliation, institutional role, and political context.

There are two key implications for our understanding of how the substantive representation of women occurs in the Canadian parliamentary context that follow from this chapter's findings. First is the importance of the committee system as a key site for the substantive representation of women. Parliamentary committees in general have long been recognized as promising sites of opposition and backbench influence in Canada (Franks 1987; Docherty 1997). More recently, Grace (2016) highlights the research, scrutiny, and civil society bridging functions of the Standing Committee on the Status of Women in particular. The findings from this chapter suggest that the Standing Committee on the Status of Women has the potential to play a particularly important role in the substantive representation of women through advocacy by playing a key connective role between parliamentary and movement actors.

Second, the findings from this chapter suggest that the actions of opposition MPs can in fact have an impact, however small, on government decision making. Once a government has decided on a policy direction, there is typically very little that opposition MPs can do to change this direction. Parliamentary speeches alone cannot block or change a government decision, and opposition votes are generally inadequate to block government legislation – although this is not the case in a minority parliament. By mobilizing public opposition to the cuts and leaning into an existing electoral vulnerability, however, opposition women in the 39th Parliament showed that the actions of parliamentarians do not need to operate exclusively through parliamentary channels to have an impact. By shaping the background political conditions against which they operated, opposition MPs were able to shift the government's political calculations and decision making. This suggests that the range of opportunities for opposition MPs to advocate and to achieve policy outcomes for women may be broader than is typically assumed when background political conditions, including the precarity of a minority parliament, can be leveraged.

The details of the types of actors involved and the strategies they used in the 39th Parliament differed from those in the 34th Parliament due to differences in terms of the nature of the government initiative to which MPs were responding and the political conditions under which they operated. Nonetheless, in both cases we see that women were at the forefront of pushing back against government proposals that undermined women's equality interests. In both cases, those who chose to advocate for women sought out opportunities to bring women's perspectives onto the political agenda and to compel a shift in government decision making, leveraging the tools available to them based on their institutional position and political context.

Conclusion

This book began by asking whether parliamentary politics in Canada would look different if women occupied a larger share of seats in the House of Commons. In other words, what difference, if any, might the presence of women in Canadian politics make? This is of course a massive question that defies easy answers. Defining the boundaries of what counts as impact and clarifying why we might expect elected women to behave differently from elected men present conceptual challenges. Even with the conceptual groundwork clarified, identifying how best to measure impact in a comprehensive way is not a straightforward task. And the reality of party discipline and executive dominance of the legislative process in the Canadian parliamentary system means that the role and contributions of individual MPs – or even groups of MPs linked by factors other than party affiliation – are often overlooked. The analysis in the preceding pages tackles these challenges head on by presenting a new conceptual framework for thinking about the substantive representation of women and the impact of elected women that specifies the types of actions involved in acting for women and the factors that shape an MP's ability to do so. It leverages innovative methodological tools and a massive dataset of parliamentary debate transcripts to facilitate a large-scale analysis of patterns of the substantive representation of women in parliamentary speech. And it takes seriously the possibility that individual MPs who are inclined to act on behalf of women might find ways to have an impact on policy decision making and outcomes, even in an institutional context that makes it challenging to do so.

By focusing on patterns of parliamentary speech and two specific instances of policymaking related to women's equality, this book provides answers that address this big picture question and offers valuable insight into how we might think about when, whether, and how the presence of women in parliament matters for the substantive representation of women in Canadian politics. The preceding chapters make the case that the presence of women in parliament does indeed matter for the substantive representation of women's interests – but it matters for slightly different reasons than we might expect. Women's presence does not only matter for driving progress towards equality: it is an important factor in guarding against regress. Elected women find ways to navigate their institutional context in order to have an impact on Canadian politics, particularly during moments of threat. In these final pages, I review the book's major findings, take stock of this new knowledge and why it matters, and reflect on where we might go from here.

WOMEN'S IMPACT ON PARLIAMENTARY DEBATE

The analysis in the preceding chapters is oriented around several key research questions. How, if at all, do women MPs in Canada behave differently from their male colleagues? And if they do act differently, what kind of an impact might these women have on the issues that are addressed in parliamentary debate, the policy decisions that get made, and the outcomes that follow from them?

When it comes to the substantive representation of women in parliamentary debate, the presence of elected women has a clear impact on the issues that get discussed in parliament. Women act differently from their male colleagues when it comes to speaking about women in parliamentary debate. As women's presence in the House of Commons grew, the share of parliamentary speeches about women also increased. Men parliamentarians did tend to make more speeches about women as women's presence in the House grew, but their share of the total number of speeches about women in each parliament was marginal when compared with the number of speeches women were making – a particularly notable observation given that women MPs' share of seats was consistently much smaller than was that of men. The driving force behind the increasing level of attention to women in parliamentary debate was unquestionably women. Women MPs, regardless of party affiliation, made dramatically more speeches about women than did men. An MP's gender was a more important factor in determining whether they would speak about women in debate than was their party affiliation. In an institutional context in which party affiliation exerts a strong influence over legislator behaviour, this last point is especially important and perhaps even a bit surprising.

While the impact of party affiliation on the inclination to make speeches about women was relatively muted, partisanship was not entirely irrelevant in shaping patterns of the substantive representation of women in parliamentary debate and, indeed, presented some unexpected results. Consistent with expectations in the literature that left-leaning political parties are more sympathetic to women's equality claims and thus more likely to act for women (Celis and Childs 2012), left-leaning New Democrat MPs were predicted to be more likely to make more speeches about women than were those in the reference category of Liberal MPs. But right-leaning Conservative MPs were also more likely to make speeches about women. Indeed, Conservative MPs were predicted to make more speeches about women than were MPs from any other partisan group. This pattern suggests a greater willingness among Conservative MPs to engage with women's issues and to make representative claims about women than is typically assumed – a pattern that warrants further attention and to which we return below.

But what were all these speeches concerning women about? What policy issues were put on the agenda as a result of women MPs speaking about women in debate? When MPs spoke about women, they tended to address policy issues that are typically identified as "women's issues" – employment, pay equity, childcare, women's health and reproductive rights, violence against women, Indigenous women, and program funding to support gender equality. This issue focus is consistent with the position held by feminist scholars who view the substantive representation of women in terms of issues that redress gender inequality (Wängnerud 2000; Beckwith and Cowell-Meyers 2007; Kittilson 2008). This approach that pre-determines the issue content of what counts as women's issues has been criticized for failing to account for the diversity of experiences, perspectives, and views held by women (Smooth 2011; Schwindt-Bayer and Taylor-Robison 2011; Celis et al. 2014). But even when using a more inductive, content-neutral approach, the content of representative claims made about women in parliamentary speech confirms that these issues that are oriented around addressing women's equality and autonomy are in fact the issues that are important for the substantive representation of women's interests – albeit with the caveat that MPs differed in terms of how they approached these issues and what they considered to be the appropriate policy solutions.

Although partisanship did not play a decisive role in shaping whether MPs spoke about women, there were some important differences in terms of patterns of issue attention by party. Left and centrist MPs made the most speeches on issues relating to women's social and economic equality, whereas right-leaning Conservative MPs tended to focus on topics that reflected a socially conservative approach to family and gender relations (e.g., same sex-marriage). This suggests that, while gender matters for *whether* an MP will speak about women in parliamentary debate, partisanship matters for *how* they speak about women and the issues they will raise when making representative claims.

WOMEN'S IMPACT ON POLICY DECISION MAKING

The analysis also finds that patterns of parliamentary debate and policy action were connected. Increases in attention to a specific policy issue in parliamentary speech reflect either a response to government action on that issue or an attempt by MPs to put that issue on the political agenda. MPs responded to government proposals through debate on legislation or by raising questions and flagging concerns about a proposal in question period or members' statements. MPs also attempted to put new issues on the parliamentary agenda by raising these issues in question period or through private members' business. Periods of heightened attention to women in the 34th and 39th Parliaments were driven primarily by women MPs' responses to two instances of government policy action that would have undermined women's equality by rolling back policy gains. The spike in the 34th Parliament was driven in part by the Mulroney government's attempt to recriminalize abortion. In the 39th Parliament, it was driven by the Harper government's efforts to cut funding to Status of Women Canada.

When it comes to women's impact on policy decision making and outcomes, women parliamentarians were at the forefront of advocating for women and pushing back against hostile government initiatives. In both cases, the women who led the charge in advocating for women as critical actors had previously worked on women's equality issues or occupied formal institutional roles in parliament focused on the status of women, or both. These women leveraged but were also constrained by the institutional positions they occupied. Their interventions' ability to influence government decision making was shaped by the interaction between the opportunities available to them based on their institutional role and the political conditions under which they operated.

In the 34th Parliament, critical actors in both houses of parliament attempted to stop government legislation recriminalizing abortion. Ultimately it was a tie vote in the Senate and the efforts of three Progressive Conservative women senators working in coordination across party lines with other pro-choice advocates and willing to break ranks with their party that made a key contribution to the bill's defeat. Barbara McDougall served as the minister responsible for the status of women, was committed to a pro-choice position, and was strategically well-positioned in the inner circle of the Mulroney cabinet to shift the government's approach towards a less restrictive option prior to the introduction of legislation in the House of Commons. Her persistent efforts, however, faced opposition from men in the PC cabinet and caucus who wanted a more restrictive approach to abortion. In the House of Commons, Progressive Conservative women who preferred a more pro-choice approach were constrained by party discipline and were unwilling to break ranks with their party to vote against the legislation. In the absence of votes by government MPs against the legislation, opposition objections were insufficient to force the majority government to modify its approach. In the House of Commons, pro-choice MPs were unable to come together across party lines to defeat the bill and would-be critical actors were unable to pressure the cabinet to reverse its approach.

The rare defeat of a government bill in the Senate was made even more stunning by the tie vote that brought it about. This tie was made possible in part by the willingness of three PC women senators to vote against their government. These Senate women broke ranks with their party to defend women's equality due to the weaker constraints imposed by party discipline in the upper house and the sense that, by the time the bill made its way to the Senate, the government's commitment had been weakened by negative public responses to it. The successful defence of women's equality in the 34th Parliament was thus made possible by critical actors outside the political executive rather than by pressure exerted on the government leading to an internal government decision to shift its policy direction.

In the 39th Parliament, the Conservative government retreated from some of its proposed changes to Status of Women Canada in response to cumulative pressure created by critical actors on the opposition benches who leveraged existing government vulnerabilities. Opposition women MPs – especially those serving as their parties' critics for status of women and as members of the Standing Committee on the Status of Women – engaged in a relentless campaign of parliamentary questioning, motions, committee scrutiny, and coordination with extra-parliamentary advocates to raise the profile of the Conservative government's proposed cuts and pressure it to reverse its policy changes. No publicly available evidence indicates that Conservative women acted to preserve the mandate and funding of the women's policy agency.

Opposition women MPs used their positions in the 39th parliament to amplify public displeasure with the government's proposed changes to Status of Women Canada. Their efforts were taken up by the opposition parties more broadly, and by the Liberals in particular, as a politically effective and electorally promising strategy. These actions were effective because they took advantage of the government's existing weaknesses, including a precarious minority government and lower electoral support for the Conservative Party among women voters. The government eventually reversed some of its proposed funding cuts to Status of Women Canada and restored the promotion of women's equality to the agency's mandate, but it left in place changes to program funding eligibility criteria. Thus, despite the limited tools available to them to influence government decisions, opposition women MPs were able to leverage political conditions to indirectly influence government policymaking in defence of women's interests.

CONCEPTUAL AND METHODOLOGICAL INNOVATIONS

The findings summarized above and the theoretical framework within which they are situated offer new conceptual and empirical insights that increase our knowledge about women in Canadian parliamentary politics. Conceptually, the analysis is grounded in a framework that refines how we think about the substantive representation of women. This framework disaggregates the foundational concept of the substantive representation of women into distinct categories based on both the form representation takes (parliamentary speech, policy advocacy, and policy outcomes) and the content and direction of the representation (feminist pro-equality and non-feminist traditional). The framework also explicitly includes actions that defend women's interests against hostile policy interventions in addition to those actions focused on initiating new policies.

What is the benefit of rethinking substantive representation in this way? This reconceptualization offers two key advantages that increase our understanding of whether and how elected women have an impact on politics. First, by disaggregating the substantive representation of women in terms of both form and content, this framework allows for greater conceptual clarity in terms of the actions and orientations that the substantive representation of women consists of and facilitates clearer empirical analysis. By distinguishing between representation through speech, advocacy, and outcomes we can be more precise about the dimensions of substantive representation in which we are interested and the most appropriate ways to measure it. Within this framework, for example, a parliamentary speech that calls on the government to address the crisis of missing and murdered Indigenous women and girls, and success in blocking the passage of legislation that would have restricted abortion access are both instances of the substantive representation of women. These two actions, however, are clearly quite different in terms of what they require of legislators, how they can be achieved, and their impact on the women whose interests they are intended to represent. The ability to distinguish between these two actions while also recognizing that both are instances of the substantive representation of women allows for greater precision and makes it easier to identify different explanatory factors that might help account for each of these types of behaviours.

Additionally, this disaggregation can help account for unexpected patterns of representative behaviour. For example, the finding that Conservative MPs were likely to make more parliamentary speeches about women than were MPs from any other partisan group runs counter to expectations about partisan patterns of the representation of women in parliamentary speech – namely, that members of left-leaning parties will be more likely to represent women than will those on the political right. The fact that Conservative MPs were predicted to make so many speeches about women was thus surprising. Closer inspection of the content of their parliamentary speeches about women, however, reveals that, in many cases, these speeches were not oriented in a pro-equality direction – as with speeches opposing same-sex marriage. But recall that our conceptual framework encompasses speech, advocacy, and policy outcomes in both pro-equality and non-feminist traditional directions and that the task of evaluating the quality of representative claims is an important but separate step from determining whether they count as substantive representation of women. The speeches made by Conservative MPs were thus representative claims about women, but they were not pro-equality feminist claims. The ability to make this distinction in terms of the content of representative claims about women makes it easier to account for complex or unexpected patterns of representative behaviour, such as the tendency for Conservative MPs to be so actively engaged in the substantive representation of women in parliamentary speech. The refined conceptual framework enables a more comprehensive and granular understanding of how and under what conditions the substantive representation of women occurs.

Building on this conceptual clarification, the methodological tools used in this study make it possible to answer questions about the impact of women on Canadian politics on a much larger scale than would previously have been feasible. The disaggregated framework for thinking about the substantive representation of women clarifies and expands the scope of the activities that count as instances of substantive representation. This framework includes patterns of parliamentary speech and issue attention alongside more effort-intensive advocacy efforts and the achievement of policy outcomes. It recognizes that each of these components of substantive representation exists in relation to one another. This framework invites analysis of the content of parliamentary debate. In the Canadian context, where patterns of legislative voting or bill introduction are strictly constrained by political parties and the political executive, parliamentary speech has the potential to reveal nuances in terms of who and how legislators represent. The availability of digitized, machine-readable parliamentary debate transcripts through the Linked Parliamentary Data Project (Beelen et al. 2017) together with computational text analysis tools enable a comprehensive analysis of the substantive representation of women in parliamentary debate.

The large-scale analysis made possible by these tools reveals that, when it comes to the substantive representation of women in parliamentary debate, MPs' gender matters far more than does their party affiliation in shaping patterns of speech. This finding runs counter to the view that party affiliation is the primary explanatory variable in understanding Canadian legislator behaviour. Indeed, when it comes to issues related to women's equality, more room exists for independent MP behaviour than is typically assumed in the literature, with gender playing an outsized role in determining MPs' willingness to speak for women in parliament. Looking at the big picture of patterns of parliamentary speech thus generates new and unexpected knowledge about patterns of legislator behaviour and the impact of elected women on one dimension of political representation.

In addition to generating new insights pertaining to the factors that shape patterns of parliamentary speech, the large-scale analysis also facilitates the identification of cases for qualitative analysis. The computational text analysis and machine learning tools act as a filter capable of sifting through massive amounts of textual data and identifying key moments or individual actors relevant to the substantive representation of women in parliament. By highlighting moments of heightened attention to women's issues in parliamentary debate, the large-scale analysis provides valuable direction in terms of where to look to understand patterns of advocacy on specific policy issues. This mixed methodological approach combines big picture and fine-grained analysis to provide a more comprehensive understanding of the substantive representation of women.

IMPLICATIONS AND LESSONS LEARNED

Even in an institutional context in which there are limited opportunities for individual MPs to influence policy agendas and outcomes, who we elect matters. The presence of more women has an impact on the issues that get discussed and the policy decisions that get made. The connection between presence and impact is neither direct nor guaranteed, but the evidence suggests that parliamentarians nonetheless find opportunities to act for women. This opens up new space for thinking about where and how the substantive representation of women occurs. The women who were inclined to act for women had to navigate an institutional environment that is not designed to facilitate the substantive representation of women over and above representational obligations to political parties or geographical constituents. Despite this inhospitable institutional context, these women nonetheless found ways to identify and exploit the opportunities that do exist to act for women.

This matters for our understanding of how Canadian parliamentary institutions work. The tendency for women MPs to be more likely to make speeches about women, regardless of party affiliation, demonstrates that, despite the constraints of partisanship, there are indeed opportunities for MPs to act as representatives of something other than their political party in parliamentary debate. It also sheds light on how parliamentarians influence policy decision making. By leveraging the tools available to them from their position within parliament, motivated critical actors can in fact influence government policymaking in defence of women's equality. In the two cases examined in this study, critical actors committed to the defence of women's equality managed to forestall government initiatives that would have undermined women's equality despite the constraints created by partisanship and the dominance of the political executive. In the 34th Parliament, Senate women who were somewhat less constrained by party discipline due to their appointed role in the upper house voted against their party to defeat the government's legislation on abortion. In the 39th Parliament, women in the opposition parties leveraged the parliamentary committee structure to amplify public opposition to the government's changes to Status of Women Canada. These efforts tapped into low support for the Conservative Party among women voters to create pressure that forced the government to change course. These findings call into question the policy irrelevance of individual MPs and opposition parties in Canada and contribute to a growing body of literature that examines more closely the ways in which MPs leverage existing parliamentary structures to influence policymaking in executive-dominated parliaments characterized by a high degree of party discipline (Soroka at al. 2009; Blidook 2012; Russell et al. 2016; Russell et al. 2017).

The strategies used by women parliamentarians in these two cases offer important lessons about the institutional venues that serve as promising sites for the substantive representation of women's interests. In both the 34th and 39th Parliaments, gender-focused parliamentary committees emerged as an important institutional venue to advance equality aims and to facilitate cross-party collaboration among women MPs. In the 34th Parliament, the Subcommittee on the Status of Women served as a key venue through which women from all parties worked together to put policy issues relating to violence against women and women's health on the government's legislative agenda. In the 39th Parliament, the Standing Committee on the Status of Women was a central venue through which opposition women parliamentarians pushed back against the Conservative government's cuts to Status of Women Canada (although Conservative women were absent from these efforts).

Parliamentary committees have long been recognized as promising sites of backbench influence in Canada (Franks 1987; Docherty 1997). Grace (2016) examines the specific role of the Standing Committee on the Status of Women as a mechanism through which women's interests can be brought into the legislative policymaking process. The analysis presented in this study confirms the relevance of parliamentary women's committees as an important venue through which MPs can effectively advocate for women's interests. In practical terms, this suggests that MPs and extra-parliamentary actors committed to the advancement of women's interests should look to the Standing Committee on the Status of Women as a site for collaboration and action.

Perhaps more surprisingly, the Senate also emerged as an important site for the substantive representation of women's interests. The Canadian Senate is often seen as an impotent or inconsequential element of Canada's parliamentary institutional structure (Docherty 2002). This was not the case in the 34th Parliament. Critical actors in the Senate were able to collaborate across party lines and vote against their own party to block the passage of a government bill that would have recriminalized abortion. This case was of course unusual, but it demonstrates that, under the right conditions, the Senate can in fact be an important venue through which the substantive representation of women in policymaking can occur (see also Rayment and McCallion 2023). As compared with the House of Commons, party discipline tends to be lower in the Senate. This weaker party discipline made it easier for Senate women committed to women's equality to vote against their government to block the passage of a bill that would have severely curtailed abortion rights in the 34th Parliament.

The potential for the Senate to serve as an important site for the substantive representation of women's interests as it did in the 34th Parliament is likely to increase going forward given recent institutional changes. In 2015, a non-partisan, merit-based process for appointing senators was introduced (Thomas 2019). These changes appear to have weakened the constraints of partisanship in the upper house, with Senators more willing to vote independently and to propose amendments to government legislation (VandenBeukel et al 2021; McCallion 2022). As partisan representational obligations in the Senate diminish, the space available for senators who are inclined to act for women expands. The descriptive representation of women has historically been higher in the Senate than in the House of Commons, briefly reaching gender parity in December 2020 (McCallion 2021). In practical terms, the presence of a sizeable contingent of women in the Senate coupled with decreasing partisan pressures suggests that this upper house has the potential to serve as an important site for the representation of women's interests. This expands the scope of where extra-parliamentary women's equality advocates may want to focus their advocacy efforts. It also suggests that the Senate is a worthwhile site of investigation for researchers interested in understanding the substantive representation of women in Canadian parliamentary institutions.

WHERE DO WE GO FROM HERE?

The findings and analysis presented in this book generate valuable new knowledge about the ways in which elected women have an impact on Canadian parliamentary politics. This study constitutes the first large-scale examination of the substantive representation of women in parliamentary speech in Canada. But the analysis is necessarily a preliminary first cut into an incredibly rich dataset that is ripe for further investigation. Looking ahead, future research could dig deeper with regard to the content of parliamentary speeches, the policy issues addressed in these speeches, and the framing used to address them. The unsupervised topic models used in this study identify a clear set of issues addressed in parliamentary speeches about women – largely issues relating to women's equality and autonomy. Manual inspection of a subset of these speeches reveals variation in how MPs talked about these issues and the approaches to them that they advocated. To establish a more comprehensive understanding of the perspectives articulated on these topics, automated machine learning techniques or qualitative approaches could be used to examine more closely the way in which these issues are discussed. This more detailed examination of the content and direction of speeches about women would allow for a more robust understanding of how these issues are discussed in parliament and could be used to probe the positions articulated by MPs of different parties and genders.

Additionally, the finding that women MPs are more likely to represent women in parliamentary debate regardless of party raises the question of whether similar patterns would hold for other underrepresented groups in Canadian politics. For example, would Indigenous or racialized Canadians be more likely to make representative claims about, and raise issues that are important to, these groups as surrogate representatives in the same way? The conceptual framework and methodological techniques used for studying the substantive representation of women in parliamentary debate could be adapted and applied to investigate these questions and would help to provide a more comprehensive understanding of the ways in which increased descriptive diversity of legislative institutions might matter for Canadian politics.

In addition to identifying questions that build on this study's foundation, the analysis also uncovers new and unexpected findings that warrant further investigation. One of the more puzzling findings to emerge is related to the role of conservative parties in the substantive representation of women in Canada. Conservative parties are typically seen to be disengaged from women's equality issues and incompatible with pro-equality feminist aims (Erickson 1997; Bashevkin 1998; Young 2000; Bryson and Heppell 2010; Celis and Childs 2012). And yet this study finds that Conservative Party MPs were more likely than were those in any other political party to represent women in parliamentary debate, while conservative governments introduced policy initiatives that were at odds with women's equality aims. These findings problematize the perceived incompatibility between conservatism and the representation of women. As noted above, the disaggregated typology of the substantive representation of women that distinguishes between pro-equality and more traditionally oriented actions provides a framework that helps to account for this unexpected finding in terms of patterns of parliamentary speech. When they spoke about women in debate, Conservative MPs often did so in a non-feminist manner, from a perspective less concerned about increasing women's equality outcomes and more committed to the preservation of traditional gender roles than did MPs from other parties. This positioning constitutes an instance of the substantive representation of women in parliamentary speech within the disaggregated typology of the substantive representation of women that treats both feminist and non-feminist claims as manifestations of the substantive representation of women. But the quality of these claims and the extent to which they respond to and are deemed acceptable by the women on whose behalf they are made warrants closer examination. Further research on partisan differences in issue framing in parliamentary speeches about women is also needed to better understand the role conservative parties and MPs play in the substantive representation of women in parliamentary debate.

Additionally, differences in the patterns of policy advocacy among Progressive Conservative MPs in the 34th Parliament and Conservative MPs in the 39th Parliament raise questions about the role different types of conservative parties might play in the substantive representation of women. In the 34th Parliament, some Progressive Conservative women preferred, articulated, and advocated a less restrictive approach to the regulation of abortion than did the legislation their government introduced. Eventually, they all voted in support of the bill but many of them spoke against it in parliament. Barbara McDougall defended a more pro-choice approach in cabinet discussions, and PC women in the Senate joined forces with pro-choice women from other parties to ultimately defeat the government's bill. In the 34th Parliament, Progressive Conservative women could hold and advocate feminist policy preferences quite distinct from those of their male colleagues.

By contrast, in the case of the Conservative government's attempt to cut funding to Status of Women Canada in the 39th Parliament, women in the Conservative Party were less willing to speak in defence of women's equality or to collaborate with other women parliamentarians across party lines to preserve the funding and mandate of Status of Women Canada. Thus, in the 34th Parliament, Progressive Conservative women spoke, advocated, and eventually secured some protection for women's equality, but there is no evidence of a similar internal party dynamic among women in the Conservative Party in the 39th Parliament. Until cabinet documents detailing the contents of cabinet discussions are unsealed, however, this remains a preliminary conclusion.

There appears to be a clear divergence between the Conservative and Progressive Conservative parties in terms of the extent to which women within these parties were inclined and able to advocate for women in a pro-equality direction. This is consistent with research that has suggested the importance of distinguishing among different types of conservative parties to understand the compatibility between conservatism and feminism (Erzeel et al. 2014; O'Brien 2018). This divergence between the two parties' approaches reflects shifting dynamics in the Canadian party system and clear differences in the ideological positions occupied by each party. In the 34th Parliament, the Progressive Conservatives operated within a brokerage model of politics capable of accommodating a diversity of ideological views within an electoral coalition and occupying a more centrist ideological space (Malloy 2003; Cochrane 2010). The emergence of the harder-right Reform Party in the early 1990s led to increased polarization in the Canadian party system (Cochrane 2010). The Conservative Party of Canada that emerged in the early 2000s following the unification of the Reform/Canadian

Alliance and Progressive Conservative parties was thus decidedly more right-wing than its Progressive Conservative predecessor. This shift appears to have narrowed the space available for women in parties on the political right to advocate for feminist aims.

Further research is needed to assess whether and to what extent there is ideological space for the substantive representation of women within the Conservative Party of Canada. Earlier research suggests that Progressive Conservative women were distinct from PC men in their support for women's equality initiatives (Young 2000). More recently, scholars have examined the post-2003 Conservative Party's stance on women's equality issues (Thomas 2017; Bird and Rowe 2013). Future research should investigate more closely the attitudes of Conservative legislators and partisans on issues relating to feminism and women's equality. This would allow for a clearer understanding of whether and to what extent women in the more right-wing Conservative Party can be compared with PC partisans from an earlier period and, in particular, whether there is space within the newer party to hold and defend feminist views.

THE BOTTOM LINE

Given all this, why does it matter if we elect more women? First and foremost, this study shows that the presence of more women in parliament changes the content of parliamentary debate. An MP's gender, more than any other factor, is what matters for whether they will represent women in parliamentary debate. This on its own is important insofar as patterns of issue attention signal parliamentarians' policy priorities and have the potential to shift political agendas. By raising issues related to women in parliamentary debate, elected women ensure that these issues are part of the agenda-setting process.

When it comes to impact on policy advocacy and outcomes, the connection between presence and impact is indeed more contingent, but presence is nonetheless important. First, elected women can indeed have an impact, but it matters which women we elect. That is, the individual backgrounds and prior commitments of the women who are elected matter, as does the partisan banner under which they run for and win office, and the institutional role they occupy in parliament. The inclination to act for women, however conceived, will be shaped by personal policy preferences, while the ability to achieve desired policy outcomes will be facilitated or constrained by positions within the parliamentary institution. Elected women with strong commitments to gender equality may be motivated to push for policy changes that increase women's equality. Yet if they occupy positions far removed from the centre of power, they can speak up for women but there is little they can do to influence policy outcomes. On the flip side, women with no strong commitment to gender equality will be unlikely to push for change even if they do come to occupy positions of power and influence within parliament. But even these women may come to play an important moderating role if governments initiate policy changes that threaten women's previous equality gains. The upshot is that increasing the total number of elected women overall can still matter. It is likely to lead to the inclusion of more women with a range of perspectives, including women with commitments to gender equality, and a greater chance that these women will be elevated to positions of influence in which they have the opportunity to advocate and win for women. If feminist activists and voters in general are interested in substantive policy outcomes that contribute to increasing women's equality, then growing the presence of elected women, particularly those women who are committed to gender equality, can be an important step forward – although it is not a guarantee.

Second, the presence of women may be more important for guarding against the retrenchment of previously won gains than for initiating new policy proposals. That is, the presence of women matters, but it matters for a slightly different reason than we might typically think. Executive-dominated Westminster parliamentary systems make it difficult for individual parliamentarians to initiate policy change. But the findings from this study suggest that elected women's inclination to speak for women in parliamentary debate and to advocate for women through other means is activated when women's equality is under threat. Women parliamentarians may have little interest in pushing for policy changes that increase gender equality. If a government initiates a policy initiative that threatens women's equality, however, women may emerge as reluctant champions willing to speak up and take action to prevent retrenchment. The election of more women thus serves as a safeguard against government initiatives that would roll back hard-won equality gains. This function may not be as exciting as the implementation of new initiatives that advance equality, but it is nonetheless crucially important to the bottom line of gender equality, particularly when governments that are unsympathetic or hostile to women's equality claims come to power.

Appendix 1

Comparison of Measures of Speeches about Women

As a robustness check of the measure for what counts as a speech about women, I compared the proportion of parliamentary speeches about women using measures that set the threshold for what counts as a speech about women at three different levels. Figure A1.1 below shows the parliament-to-parliament variation in the number of speeches about women using these three different thresholds – one mention of women for every 500, 330, and 250 words.

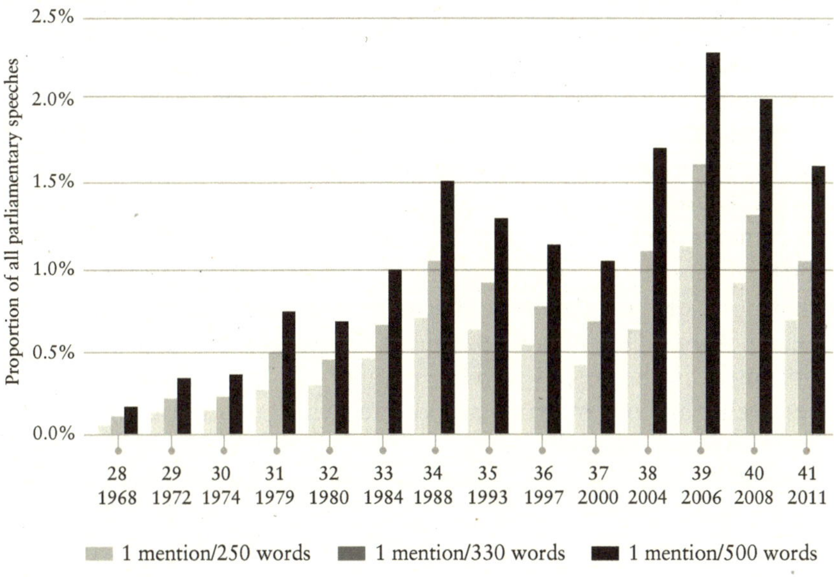

Figure A1.1 Percentage of parliamentary speeches about women at three different thresholds, 1968–2015.

Appendix 2

Unsupervised Topic Model Selection

Two different topic models were considered for the purpose of automatically categorizing speeches about women into a set of issue topics: latent Dirichlet allocation and non-negative matrix factorization. Latent Dirichlet allocation, or LDA, is a complex generative probabilistic model based on the foundational idea that topics are probability distributions over words in a vocabulary and that documents contain words from a variety of topics (Steyvers and Griffiths 2007). The model uses statistical inference to determine the topics (i.e., distributions of words) that are likely to have generated a document based on the words contained in each. Documents can be assigned to a topic based on the estimated probability of a document being generated by a topic.

Non-negative matrix factorization, or NMF, models are based on the decomposition of a term-document matrix (TDM). A TDM indicates the frequency with which every word in a full corpus of documents appears in each document. Through NMF, the complete TDM is decomposed into two smaller matrices, with the constraint that none of the values in either matrix can be negative (Lee and Seung 1999). This process produces one matrix that clusters each document in the corpus into the number of topics specified by the researcher and one matrix that indicates which words are important for each topic (Rheault 2018).

Models were constructed using the scikit-learn package for Python. When specifying the models' parameters, I allow a maximum of two thousand features for both models. The LDA models are based on a TDM that uses a simple count of words from the full corpus that appears in each document. The NMF models use TDMs based on a measure of the weighted frequency of words relative to document length.

Table A2.1
Performance metrics for non-negative matrix factorization (NMF) and latent Dirichlet allocation (LDA) topic models with ten through twenty topics

	NMF		*LDA*	
Number of topics	*Coherence score*	*Log-likelihood*	*Coherence score*	*Log-likelihood*
10	-37.29	-372,838	-44.43	-3,702,511
11	-49.49	-368,845	-52.83	-3,701,269
12	-61.85	-369,598	-70.19	-3,700,883
13	-78.88	-372,483	N/A	-3,702,903
14	-93.03	-380,057	N/A	-3,706,451
15	-111.64	-374,606	N/A	-3,711,211
16	-133.67	-374,532	N/A	-3,711,608
17	-153.30	-376,094	N/A	-3,709,082
18	-176.86	-376,589	N/A	-3,718,459
19	-212.43	-379,441	N/A	-3,723,816
20	-245.56	-378,499	N/A	-3,716,168

Given the size of the corpus and the limited scope of issues likely to be raised given that all speeches must refer to women, an appropriate number of topics is likely to be relatively small. Table A2.1 lists the average coherence scores of the NMF and LDA models with ten through twenty topics. The internal coherence of the topics generated by each unsupervised topic model is measured using the approach described by Mimno et al. (2011), which generates a score based on an analysis of co-occurrence patterns of words in every document assigned to each topic. The closer the score is to zero, the more coherent the topic. The table also lists the log-likelihood scores for models as an indicator of the goodness of each model's fit. A higher score indicates a better fit – that is, a score of -100 is better than a score of -300.

The NMF model was selected because it returned better average coherence scores than did the LDA model. In addition to producing poorer scores, calculations of the coherence metric for the LDA models also tended to produce division by zero errors. These errors signal that none of the speeches in the corpus was assigned to one or more of the topics generated by the model, which suggests that the model and the number of topics included therein do not create an adequate categorization of the speeches in the corpus. In addition to producing better average coherence scores, the NMF models tended to produce a tighter set of topics based on manual inspection of the content of the topics generated by each of the models.

To determine the number of topics to be included in the NMF model, I select a model that generates a strong coherence score, fits the data well, and also ensures that the topics generated by the model are substantively meaningful when their features are assessed qualitatively. The coherence scores do become consistently worse as the corpus of text is divided into a larger number of topics. Recall, however, that the goal when determining the number of topics to be included in an unsupervised machine learning model is not simply to select the model with the best average coherence score, since topics that contain many commonly used words will produce inflated coherence scores. We must therefore turn to a qualitative assessment of the substance of the features in each model together with a consideration of the fit of each model.

Models with a smaller number of topics tended to produce a concise list of topics that collapsed multiple issues together. Models with a larger number of topics, by contrast, generated more granular, disaggregated topics – for instance, separating pay equity from maternity leave from employment or disaggregating women's health into breast health and reproductive health. However, models with more topics also included topics with no discernable issue focus, characterized either by an assortment of generic terms, or multiple topics that were essentially indistinguishable from one another. When more than twenty topics were included in the model, at least 20 per cent of the topics the model generated could not be linked to a distinct issue focus. When the number of topics was set below ten, relevant and distinct topics disappeared and were collapsed into more general categories. The goal then was to select a model that maximized the specificity of the issue focus implied by each topic and, at the same time, minimized the number of topics for which no clear or distinct issue focus could be identified.

Qualitative review of the topics showed that models with thirteen or more topics included at least one topic for which the distinguishing features were so generic that no clear issue focus could be discerned. Log-likelihood scores measuring the goodness of fit of each model suggested that the models with eleven and twelve topics fit best. The

Log-likelihood score for the model with eleven topics was slightly better than was that for twelve topics, but the eleven-topic model collapsed one-fifth of all speeches into the International Women's Day category and failed to distinguish between employment issues generally and pay equity more specifically, suggesting that the categorization of speeches was not as precise as it could be. The difference in the log likelihood scores between the eleven- and twelve-topic models was negligible, so the twelve-topic model was selected.

Notes

CHAPTER TWO

1 The analyses in this chapter were run using both this narrow measure – that is, speeches that mention the words "woman" or "women" – as well as a broader measure. The broad measure counted a speech as being about women if it included any of the following words that refer to women: "woman," "women," "female," "widow," "mother," "girl," "wife," "wives," "sister," "daughter," "lady," "ladies," "maternal," "maternity," "feminine," "feminist," "feminism." The search captures all variations of the words listed above – for example, "woman's," "females," or "grandmothers" would each count as an appearance of the terms "woman," "female," and "mother," respectively. The results using the narrow and broad measures follow the same patterns. For simplicity, I only report the results using the narrow measure here, and I use this narrow measure for all subsequent analysis in the chapters that follow.

2 As I show in chapter 3, these were parliaments in which a sizeable share of speeches about women were speeches opposing same-sex marriage – a topic on which debate was dominated by men and right-leaning MPs. This suggests that men MPs prioritized speaking about women in order to advocate for a policy that undermined equality.

3 As an additional robustness check, the relationship between the frequency of legislative speeches about women and the proportion of parliamentary seats held by NDP MPs only was also examined. Again, there was no clear relationship between these two factors.

4 Men first appear on the list at the 28th and 29th ranked positions – Brian Mulroney, who served as prime minister in the 33rd Parliament when the

Morgentaler decision decriminalized abortion, and Lloyd Axworthy, who served as minister responsible for the status of women in the 32nd Parliament.

5 Poisson regression, which is also an appropriate model for this type of dependent variable, was also considered. However, tests for overdispersion in the dependent variable (the count of speeches about women by MP) came back positive, making negative binomial regression the more appropriate choice. As an additional robustness check, the same analysis was run using logit models that estimate the probability that any speech an MP makes will be a speech about women. Results were consistent with the negative binomial results.

6 For simplicity, the dataset treats the Reform Party and Canadian Alliance as a single category. The dataset excludes MPs from the Social Credit Party and Green Party as well as Independents because their numbers were too small.

CHAPTER THREE

1 To remove the standard English language stop words, I use the stop word module in the Natural Language Tool Kit (NLTK) package for Python. The list of Canadian parliament-specific stop words includes: "canada," "canadian," "canadians," "speaker," "mr," "s," "member," "members," "bill," "government," "opposition," "liberal," "conservative," "ndp," "liberals," "conservatives," "minister," "house," "commons," "prime," "said," "asked," "motion," "amendment", "like," and "people."

2 Latent Dirichlet allocation models were also considered for this task, but the NMF models performed better, as reported in appendix 2.

3 A more detailed rationale for the model selection, including coherence scores for the NMF and LDA models, is outlined in appendix 2.

4 Although it was passed by parliament in March 2009, the Public Sector Compensation Act was never brought into force because "supporting regulations were never completed" (Treasury Board Secretariat 2017). In February 2016, the Liberal government of Justin Trudeau announced that it would not bring the act into force (Treasury Board Secretariat 2017). In October 2018, the Trudeau government introduced proactive pay equity legislation for all federally regulated employers ten or more employees (Employment and Social Development Canada 2018).

CHAPTER FOUR

1 Details of parliamentary composition compiled by the author based on data available on the Parliament of Canada website (Parliament of Canada n.d.).

2 Ibid.

CHAPTER FIVE

1 Under section 36 of the Constitution Act, "if a vote is tied in the Senate, the motion is defeated" (Senate of Canada 2016).

2 One could speculate that, as a former heart surgeon, Senator Keon may have shared the Canadian Medical Association's concerns with the criminal implications of the bill for those in the medical profession.

3 Spivak's language in this speech implies that Senator Atkins shared a pro-choice perspective, but this is not articulated explicitly.

CHAPTER SIX

1 In response to a question about the government's cuts to Status of Women Canada, Diane Finley, who served as minister of human resources and social development, insisted that "the government has not cut any program spending on women, none. We have cut administration because that does not help women on the ground. Our programming is going to continue" (Finley 2006). She did not otherwise engage with this issue in debate.

2 Interviews with these women might appear to be a solution to this challenge. However, the principle of cabinet secrecy would technically still apply and prohibit anyone who participated in these cabinet discussions from divulging details about their content (Campagnolo 2017). Even if a former cabinet member were willing to ignore cabinet secrecy, the temporal distance of the events in question means that post-hoc accounts of cabinet discussions from 2006 are unlikely to provide reliable insight into events.

3 Motions, once adopted by the House, are resolutions that that are "a declaration of opinion or purpose, [but they do] not require that any action be taken, nor [are they] binding" (Bosc and Gagnon 2017, ch. 12).

References

Abji, Salina, Anna C. Korteweg, and Lawrence H. Williams. 2019. "Culture Talk and the Politics of the New Right: Navigating Gendered Racism in Attempts to Address Violence against Women in Immigrant Communities." *Signs: Journal of Women in Culture and Society* 44 (3): 797–822.

Agocs, Carol. 2014. "Introduction: Perspectives on Employment Equity in Canada." In *Employment Equity in Canada: The Legacy of the Abella Report*, ed. Carol Agocs, 3–12. Toronto: University of Toronto Press.

Ashton, Niki. 2015. "National Action Plan to Address Violence against Women." Edited Hansard. 41st Parliament, 2nd Session, 28 April 2015. Retrieved from LiPaD: The Linked Parliamentary Data Project website: https://www.lipad.ca/full/permalink/4636057.

Atchison, Amy. 2015. "The Impact of Female Cabinet Ministers on a Female-Friendly Labour Environment." *Journal of Women, Politics and Policy* 36: 388–414.

Atchison, Amy, and Ian Down. 2009. "Women Cabinet Ministers and Female-Friendly Social Policy." *Poverty and Public Policy* 1 (2): 1–23.

Bäck, Hanna, Marc Debus, and Jorge M. Fernandes. 2021. "The Politics of Legislative Debates: An Introduction." In *The Politics of Legislative Debates*, ed. Hanna Bäck, Marc Debus and Jorge M. Fernandes, 2–20. Oxford: Oxford University Press.

Barnes, Sue. 2008a. "Status of Women." Canada. Parliament. House of Commons. Edited Hansard. 39th Parliament, 2nd Session, 7 February 2008. Retrieved from LiPaD: The Linked Parliamentary Data Project website: https://www.lipad.ca/full/permalink/4383556.

– 2008b. "Status of Women." Canada. Parliament. House of Commons. Edited Hansard. 39th Parliament, 2nd Session, 14 March 2008.

Retrieved from LiPaD: The Linked Parliamentary Data Project website: https://www.lipad.ca/full/permalink/4389998.

– 2009. Interview by Alison Loat (Samara Centre for Democracy). Transcript. London, ON, 12 October 2009.

Barnes, Tiffany. 2016. *Gendering Legislative Behaviour: Institutional Constraints and Collaboration.* Cambridge: Cambridge University Press.

Bashevkin, Sylvia. 1993. *Toeing the Lines: Women and Party Politics in English Canada.* 2nd ed. Toronto: Oxford University Press.

– 1994. "Confronting Neo-Conservatism: Anglo-American Women's Movements under Thatcher, Reagan and Mulroney." *International Political Science Review* 15 (3): 275–96.

– 1996. "Losing Common Ground: Feminists, Conservatives and Public Policy in Canada during the Mulroney Years." *Canadian Journal of Political Science* 29 (2): 211–42.

– 1998. *Women on the Defensive: Living through Conservative Times.* Chicago: University of Chicago Press.

Baumgartner, Frank R., and Bryan D. Jones, eds. 2002. *Policy Dynamics.* Chicago: University of Chicago Press.

Beckwith, Karen, and Kimberly Cowell-Meyers. 2007. "Sheer Numbers: Critical Representation, Thresholds and Women's Political Representation." *Perspectives on Politics* 5 (3): 553–65.

Beelen, Kaspar, Timothy Alberdingk Thijm, Christopher Cochrane, Kees Halvemaan, Graeme Hirst, Michael Kimmins, Sander Lijbrink, Maarten Marx, Nona Naderi, Ludovic Rheault, Roman Polyanovsky, and Tanya Whyte. 2017. "Digitization of the Canadian Parliamentary Debates." *Canadian Journal of Political Science* 50 (3): 849–64.

Bell, Catherine. 2007. "Business of Supply." Canada. Parliament. House of Commons. Edited Hansard. 39th Parliament, 2nd Session, 1 November 2007. Retrieved from LiPaD: The Linked Parliamentary Data Project website: https://www.lipad.ca/full/permalink/4374232.

Bercovici, Vivian. 1988. "Pro-Choice Tories Seek to Influence MPs' Votes." *Globe and Mail,* 18 July 1988, A1.

Bernatchez-Tardif, Monique. 1989. "Criminal Code." Canada. Parliament. House of Commons. Edited Hansard. 34th Parliament, 2nd Session, 23 November 1989. Retrieved from LiPaD: The Linked Parliamentary Data Project website: https://lipad.ca/full/permalink/3802965.

Bertrand, Gabrielle. 1989. "Criminal Code." Canada. Parliament. House of Commons. Edited Hansard. 34th Parliament, 2nd Session, 21 November 1989. Retrieved from LiPaD: The Linked Parliamentary Data Project website: https://www.lipad.ca/full/permalink/3802628.

Bill C-8. 2009. An Act Respecting Family Homes Situated on First Nation Reserves and Matrimonial Interests or Rights in or to Structures and Lands Situated on Those Reserves. 40th Parliament, 2nd Session. https://www.parl.ca/LegisInfo/BillDetails.aspx?Language=E&billId=3635116.

Bill C-47. 2008. An Act Respecting Family Homes Situated on First Nation Reserves and Matrimonial Interests or Rights in or to Structures and Lands Situated on Those Reserves. 39th Parliament, 2nd Session. https://www.parl.ca/LegisInfo/BillDetails.aspx?Language=E&billId=3314226.

Bill S-2. 2013. An Act Respecting Family Homes Situated on First Nation Reserves and Matrimonial Interests or Rights in or to Structures and Lands Situated on Those Reserves. 41st Parliament, 2nd Session. https://www.parl.ca/LegisInfo/BillDetails.aspx?Language=E&billId=5138145.

Bill S-4. 2010. An Act Respecting Family Homes Situated on First Nation Reserves and Matrimonial Interests or Rights in or to Structures and Lands Situated on Those Reserves. 40th Parliament, 3rd Session. https://www.parl.ca/LegisInfo/BillDetails.aspx?Language=E&billId=4398583.

Bird, Karen. 2005. "Gendering Parliamentary Questions." *Political Studies* 7: 353–70.

Bird, Karen, and Andrea Rowe. 2013. "Women, Feminism, and the Harper Conservatives." In *Conservatism in Canada*, ed. James Farney and David Rayside, 165–83. Toronto: University of Toronto Press.

Black, Dawn. 1990. "Criminal Code." Canada. Parliament. House of Commons. Edited Hansard. 34th Parliament, 2nd Session, 24 May 1990. Retrieved from LiPaD: The Linked Parliamentary Data Project website: https://www.lipad.ca/full/permalink/3830469.

– 2008. "Committees of the House." Canada. Parliament. House of Commons. Edited Hansard. 39th Parliament, 1st Session, 7 November 2008. Retrieved from LiPaD: The Linked Parliamentary Data Project website https://www.lipad.ca/full/permalink/4342969.

Blaxill, Luke, and Kaspar Beelen. 2016. "A Feminized Language of Democracy? The Representation of Women at Westminster since 1945." *Twentieth Century British History* 27 (3): 412–49.

Blidook, Kelly. 2010. "Exploring the Role of 'Legislators' in Canada: Do Members of Parliament Influence Policy." *Journal of Legislative Studies* 16 (1): 32–56.

– 2012. *Constituency Influence in Parliament: Countering the Centre.* Vancouver: UBC Press.

Blidook, Kelly, and Matthew Byrne. 2013. "Constant Campaigning and Partisan Discourse in the House of Commons." In *Parties, Elections, and the Future of Canadian Politics*, ed. Amanda Bittner and Royce Koop, 46–66. Vancouver: UBC Press.

Boesveld, Sarah. 2015. "The Chatelaine Q&A: Opposition Leader Rona Ambrose." *Chatelaine*, 23 December 2015. https://www.chatelaine.com/living/the-chatelaine-qa-opposition-leader-rona-ambrose.

Bosc, Marc, and André Gagnon, eds. 2017. *House of Commons Procedure and Practice*. 3rd ed. Ottawa: House of Commons. http://www.ourcommons.ca/About/ProcedureAndPractice3rdEdition/Index-e.html.

Bourgault, Lise. 1989. "Criminal Code." Canada. Parliament. House of Commons. Edited Hansard. 34th Parliament, 2nd Session, 23 November 1989. Retrieved from LiPaD: The Linked Parliamentary Data Project website: https://www.lipad.ca/full/permalink/3803158.

Bratton, Kathleen. 2002. "The Effect of Legislative Diversity on Agenda-Setting: Evidence from Six State Legislatures." *American Politics Research* 30 (2): 115–42.

Bratton, Kathleen A., and Leonard P. Ray. 2002. "Descriptive Representation, Policy Outcomes and Municipal Day-Care Coverage in Norway." *American Journal of Political Science* 46 (2): 428–37.

Brodie, Ian. 2018. *At the Centre of Government: The Prime Minister and the Limits of Political Power*. Montreal and Kingston: McGill-Queen's University Press.

Brodie, Janine. 1992. "Choice and No Choice in the House." In *The Politics of Abortion*, ed. Janine Brodie, Shelley A. M. Gavigan, and Jane Jenson, 57–116. Toronto: Oxford University Press.

– 2008. "We Are All Equal Now: Contemporary Gender Politics in Canada." *Feminist Theory* 9 (2): 145–64.

Brodie, Janine, and Isabella Bakker. 2007. "Canada's Social Policy Regime and Women: An Assessment of the Last Decade." Ottawa: Status of Women Canada. http://publications.gc.ca/collections/collection_2007/swc-cfc/SW21-156-2007E.pdf.

Browes, Pauline. 1990. "Funding for Women's Centres." Canada. Parliament. House of Commons. Edited Hansard. 34th Parliament, 2nd Session, 6 April 1990. Retrieved from LiPaD: The Linked Parliamentary Data Project website: https://www.lipad.ca/full/permalink/3822812.

Bryson, Valerie, and Timothy Heppell. 2010. "Conservatism and Feminism: The Case of the British Conservative Party." *Journal of Political Ideologies* 15 (1): 31–50.

Cab. Doc. 3-88 CMPP. 1988. "Abortion." 2 February 1988. Cabinet Documents released under the Access to Information Act.
Cab. Doc. 15-89 CBM. 1989. "General Discussion – Abortion." 21 September 1989. Cabinet Documents released under the Access to Information Act.
Cab. Doc. 17-89 CBPP. 1989. "Items – Abortion." 13 and 14 September 1989. Cabinet Documents released under the Access to Information Act.
Cab. Doc. 18-89 CBPP. 1989. "Abortion – Discussion." 19 September 1989. Cabinet Documents released under the Access to Information Act.
Cab. Doc. 21-89 CBPP. 1989. "Items – Abortion." 10 October 1989. Cabinet Documents released under the Access to Information Act.
Cab. Doc. 24-89 CBPP. 1989. "Items – Abortion." 31 October 1989. Cabinet Documents released under the Access to Information Act.
Campagnolo, Yan. 2017. "The Political Legitimacy of Cabinet Secrecy." *Reviue juridique Thémis de l'Université de Montréal* 51. CanLIIDocs 3560. https://www.canlii.org/en/commentary/doc/2017CanLII Docs3560.
Campbell, Kim. 1989. "Criminal Code." Canada. Parliament. House of Commons. Edited Hansard. 34th Parliament, 2nd Session, 21 November 1989. Retrieved from LiPaD: The Linked Parliamentary Data Project website: https://www.lipad.ca/full/permalink/3802613.
– 1991. "Violence against Women." Canada. Parliament. House of Commons. Edited Hansard. 34th Parliament, 3rd Session, 19 June 1991. Retrieved from LiPaD: The Linked Parliamentary Data Project website: https://www.lipad.ca/full/permalink/3873649.
Campbell, Rosie, Sarah Childs, and Joni Lovenduski. 2010. "Do Women Need Women Representatives?" *British Journal of Political Science* 40: 171–94.
Canada. 2006a. Parliament. House of Commons. Standing Committee on the Status of Women. Meeting 15 – Evidence. 39th Parliament, 1st Session. http://www.ourcommons.ca/DocumentViewer/en/39-1/FEWO/meeting-15/evidence.
– 2006b. Parliament. House of Commons. Standing Committee on the Status of Women. Meeting 19 – Minutes of Proceedings. 39th Parliament, 1st Session. http://www.ourcommons.ca/DocumentViewer/en/39-1/FEWO/meeting-19/minutes.
– 2006c. Parliament. House of Commons. Standing Committee on the Status of Women. Meeting 22 – Minutes of Proceedings.

39th Parliament, 1st Session. http://www.ourcommons.ca/DocumentViewer/en/39-1/FEWO/meeting-22/minutes.

– 2006d. Parliament. House of Commons. Standing Committee on the Status of Women. Report 9 – Funding cuts announced September 25, 2006 and the new mandate of Status of Women Canada. 39th Parliament, 1st Session. http://www.ourcommons.ca/DocumentViewer/en/39-1/FEWO/report-9.

– 2006e. Parliament. House of Commons. Standing Committee on the Status of Women. Report 10 – Cuts to Status of Women Canada. 39th Parliament, 1st Session. http://www.ourcommons.ca/DocumentViewer/en/39-1/FEWO/report-10.

– 2007a. Parliament. House of Commons. Standing Committee on the Status of Women. Government response to the eighteenth report of the Standing Committee on the Status of Women. 39th Parliament, 1st Session. http://www.ourcommons.ca/DocumentViewer/en/39-1/FEWO/report-18/response-8512-392-228.

– 2007b. Parliament. House of Commons. Standing Committee on the Status of Women. Meeting 48 – Minutes of Proceedings. 39th Parliament, 1st Session. http://www.ourcommons.ca/DocumentViewer/en/39-1/FEWO/meeting-48/minutes.

– 2007c. Parliament. House of Commons. Standing Committee on the Status of Women. Report 18 – The impacts of funding and program changes at Status of Women Canada. 39th Parliament, 1st Session. http://www.ourcommons.ca/Content/Committee/391/FEWO/Reports/RP2876038/feworp18/feworp18-e.pdf.

Canadian Press. 1990. "NDP Abortion Ploy Irks Tories, Liberals." *Globe and Mail*, 26 May 1990, A5.

– 2006. "Tories Prefer Canadian Women to 'Stay Barefoot and Pregnant,' Say Liberals." *Canadian Press NewsWire*, 27 November 2006.

Carroll, Susan J. 1994. *Women Candidates in American Politics*. Bloomington: Indiana University Press.

– 2002. "Representing Women: Congresswomen's Perceptions of Their Representational Roles." In *Women Transforming Congress*, ed. Cindy Simon Rosenthal, 50–68. Norman, OK: University of Oklahoma Press.

Catalano, Ana. 2009. "Women Acting for Women? An Analysis of Gender and Debate Participation in the British House of Commons, 2005–2007." *Politics and Gender* 5: 45–68.

Celis, Karen. 2006. "Substantive Representation of Women: The Representation of Women's Interests and the Impact of Descriptive

Representation in the Belgian Parliament, 1900–1979." *Journal of Women, Politics and Policy* 28 (2): 85–114.

Celis, Karen, and Sarah Childs. 2012. "The Substantive Representation of Women: What to Do with Conservative Claims?" *Political Studies* 60: 213–25.

– 2018. "Conservatism and Women's Political Representation." *Politics and Gender* 12 (1): 5–26.

– 2020. *Feminist Democratic Representation*. Oxford: Oxford University Press.

Celis, Karen, Sarah Childs, Johanna Kantola, and Mona Lena Krook. 2014. "Constituting Women's Interests through Representative Claims." *Politics and Gender* 10: 149–74.

Chaney, Paul. 2006. "Critical Mass, Deliberation and the Substantive Representation of Women: Evidence from the UK's Devolution Programme." *Political Studies* 54: 691–714.

Childs, Sarah, and Mona Lena Krook. 2006. "Should Feminists Give Up on Critical Mass? A Contingent Yes." *Politics and Gender* 2 (4): 522–30.

– 2009. "Analysing Women's Substantive Representation: From Critical Mass to Critical Actors." *Government and Opposition* 44 (2): 125–45.

Childs, Sarah, and Julie Withey. 2004. "Women Representatives Acting for Women: Sex and the Signing of Early Day Motions in the 1997 British Parliament." *Political Studies* 52: 552–64.

– 2006. "The Substantive Representation of Women: The Case of the Reduction of VAT on Sanitary Products." *Parliamentary Affairs* 59 (1): 10–23.

Clancy, Mary Catherine. 1992. "Status of Women." Canada. Parliament. House of Commons. Edited Hansard. 34th Parliament, 3rd Session, 26 February 1992. Retrieved from LiPaD: The Linked Parliamentary Data Project website: https://www.lipad.ca/full/permalink/3896934.

Clayton, Amanda, and Pär Zetterberg. 2018. "Quota Shocks: Electoral Gender Quotas and Government Spending Priorities Worldwide." *Journal of Politics* 80 (3): 916–32.

Cochrane, Christopher. 2010. "Left/Right Ideology and Canadian Politics." *Canadian Journal of Political Science* 43 (3): 583–605.

Cochrane, Christopher, Jean-François Godbout, and Jason VandenBeukel. 2021. "Canada: Predictors of Floor Access in the House of Commons, 1988-2019." In *The Politics of Legislative Debates*, ed. Hanna Bäck, Marc Debus and Jorge M. Fernandes, 193–213. Oxford: Oxford University Press.

Collier, Cheryl. 2006. "Governments and Women's Movements: Explaining Child Care and Anti-Violence Policy in Ontario and British Columbia, 1970–2000." PhD diss., University of Toronto.

Collier, Cheryl, and Rianne Mahon. 2008. "One Step Forward, Two Steps Back: Child Care Policy from Martin to Harper." In *How Ottawa Spends, 2008–2009: A More Orderly Federalism?*, ed. Allan M. Maslove, 119–42. Montreal and Kingston: McGill-Queen's University Press.

Collins, Mary. 1989. "Criminal Code." Canada. Parliament. House of Commons. Edited Hansard. 34th Parliament, 2nd Session, 22 November 1989. Retrieved from LiPaD: The Linked Parliamentary Data Project website: https://www.lipad.ca/full/permalink/3802847.

Crown-Indigenous Relations and Northern Affairs Canada. 2016. "Background on the Inquiry." https://www.rcaanc-cirnac.gc.ca/eng/1449240606362/1534528865114.

Delacourt, Susan. 1989. "MPs Back Abortion Bill, Warn Obstacles Remain." *Globe and Mail*, 29 November 1989, A1.

Demers, Nicole. 2007. "Business of Supply." Canada. Parliament. House of Commons. Edited Hansard. 39th Parliament, 1st Session, 16 May 2007. Retrieved from LiPaD: The Linked Parliamentary Data Project website: https://www.lipad.ca/full/permalink/4364787.

Dietrich, Bryce, Matthew Hayes, and Diana Z. O'Brien. 2019. "Pitch Perfect: Vocal Pitch and the Emotional Intensity of Congressional Speech." *American Political Science Review* 113 (4): 941–62.

Dion, Stephane. 2006. "Status of Women." Canada. Parliament. House of Commons. Edited Hansard. 39th Parliament, 1st Session, 4 December 2006. Retrieved from LiPaD: The Linked Parliamentary Data Project website. https://lipad.ca/full/permalink/4346677.

Ditchburn, Jennifer. 2006a. "No Money for Women's Lobby Groups: Conservatives Target Status of Women – 'Equality' Dropped from Agency Goals." *Toronto Star*, 5 October 2006, A7.

– 2006b. "Women Let Down, MPs Tell Oda: Conservative Funding Cuts Denounced – Minister Deflects Call for Resignation." *Toronto Star*, 6 October 2006, A6.

Dittmar, Kelly, Kira Sanbonmatsu, and Susan Carroll. 2018. *A Seat at the Table: Congresswomen's Perspectives on Why Their Presence Matters*. New York: Oxford University Press.

Docherty, David. 1997. *Mr. Smith Goes to Ottawa: Life in the House of Commons*. Vancouver: UBC Press.

– 2002. "The Canadian Senate: Chamber of Sober Reflection or Loony Cousin Best Not Talked About." *Journal of Legislative Studies* 8 (3): 27–48.
– 2005. *Legislatures*. Vancouver: UBC Press.
– 2014. "Parliament: Making the Case for Relevance." In *Canadian Politics*, ed. James Bickerton and Alain-G. Gagnon, 153–75. Toronto: University of Toronto Press.

Dovi, Suzanne. 2002. "Preferable Descriptive Representatives: Will Just Any Woman, Black, or Latino Do?" *American Political Science Review* 96 (4): 729–43.

Druckman, James N., Lanny W. Martin, and Michael F. Thies. "Influence without Confidence: Upper Chambers and Government.' *Legislative Studies Quarterly* 30 (4): 529–48.

Eady, Robert. 1991. "Back from the Brink: C-43 Dead Pro-Life Experts Denounce Legalized Abortion." *Interim*, 5 March1991. https://www.theinterim.com/issues/abortion/back-from-the-brink-c-43-dead-pro-life-experts-denounce-legalized-abortion.

Employment and Social Development Canada. 2018. "Government of Canada Introduces Historic Proactive Pay Equity Legislation." https://www.canada.ca/en/employment-social-development/news/2018/10/government-of-canada-introduces-historic-proactive-pay-equity-legislation.html.

Epp, Ken. 2008. "Petitions." Canada. Parliament. House of Commons. Edited Hansard. 39th Parliament, 2nd Session, 9 May 2008. Retrieved from LiPaD: The Linked Parliamentary Data Project website: https://www.lipad.ca/full/permalink/4396506.

Erickson, Lynda. 1997. "Might More Women Make a Difference? Gender, Party, and Ideology among Canada's Parliamentary Candidates." *Canadian Journal of Political Science* 30 (4): 663–88.

Erzeel, Silvia. 2012. "Women's Substantive Representation in the Belgian Chamber of Representatives: Testing the Added Value of a Claims Making Approach." *World Political Science Review* 8 (1): 28–47.
– 2015. "Explaining Legislators' Actions on Behalf of Women in the Parliamentary Party Group: The Role of Attitudes, Resources and Opportunities." *Journal of Women, Politics and Policy* 36: 440–63.

Erzeel, Silvia, Karen Celis and Didier Caluwaerts. 2014. "Are Conservatism and Feminism Mutually Exclusive? A Study of 'Feminist Conservative' Voters in Belgium." In *Gender, Conservatism and Political Representation*, ed. Karen Celis and Sarah Childs, 273–86. Colchester: ECPR Press.

Feltham, Louise. 1989. "Criminal Code." Canada. Parliament. House of Commons. Edited Hansard. 34th Parliament, 2nd Session, 22 November 1989. Retrieved from LiPaD: The Linked Parliamentary Data Project website: https://www.lipad.ca/full/permalink/3802872.

Ferguson, Jonathan. 1991. "Bill's Defeat Pleases Critics." *Toronto Star*, 1 February 1991, A12.

Finley, Diane. 2006. "Government Programs." Canada. Parliament. House of Commons. Edited Hansard. 39th Parliament, 1st Session, 16 October 2006. Retrieved from LiPaD: The Linked Parliamentary Data Project website. https://lipad.ca/full/permalink/4338355.

Franceschet, Susan. 2011. "Gendered institutions and substantive representation: Female legislators in Argentina and Chile." In *Gender, politics and institutions: Towards a feminist institutionalism*, ed. Mona Lena Krook, and Fiona Mackay. London: Palgrave Macmillan.

Franceschet, Susan, and Jennifer M. Piscopo. 2008. "Gender Quotas and Women's Substantive Representation: Lessons from Argentina." *Politics and Gender* 4: 393–425.

Franks, C.E.S. 1987. *The Parliament of Canada*. Toronto: University of Toronto Press.

Fraser, Graham. 1991. "Carney Loses Panel Post." *Globe and Mail*, 4 February 1991, A1.

Gidengil, Elisabeth, André Blais, Richard Nadeau, and Neil Nevitte. 2003. "Women to the Left? Gender Differences in Political Beliefs and Policy Preferences." In *Gender and Electoral Representation in Canada*, ed. Manon Tremblay, and Linda Trimble, 140–59. Don Mills: Oxford University Press.

Globe and Mail. 2006. "MPs Join Fight to Restore Women's Aid Funding." 11 December 2006, A5.

Godbout, Jean-François. 2020. *Lost on Division: Party Unity in the Canadian Parliament*. Toronto: University of Toronto Press.

Grace, Joan. 2016. "Presence and Purpose in the Canadian House of Commons: The Standing Committee on the Status of Women." *Parliamentary Affairs* 69: 830–44.

Gray, Charlotte. 1991. "Results of Legislative Drama Likely Mean Abortion a Dead Political Issue." *Canadian Medical Association Journal* 144 (6): 780–4.

Greenaway, Norma. 2006. "Oda 'Letting Women Down,' NDP MP Says." *National Post*, 6 October 2006, A7.

Greene, Barbara. 1989. "Criminal Code." Canada. Parliament. House of Commons. Edited Hansard. 34th Parliament, 2nd Session,

23 November 1989. Retrieved from LiPaD: The Linked Parliamentary Data Project website: https://www.lipad.ca/full/permalink/3803140.
Grimmer, Justin, and Brandon M. Stewart. 2013. "Text as data: The Promise and Pitfalls of Automatic Content Analysis Methods for Political Texts." *Political Analysis* 21 (3): 267–97.
Guergis, Helena. 2006a. "Business of Supply." Canada. Parliament. House of Commons. Edited Hansard. 39th Parliament, 1st Session, 28 September 2006. Retrieved from LiPaD: The Linked Parliamentary Data Project website. https://lipad.ca/full/permalink/4336425.
– 2006b. "Business of Supply." Canada. Parliament. House of Commons. Edited Hansard. 39th Parliament, 1st Session, 28 September 2006. Retrieved from LiPaD: The Linked Parliamentary Data Project website. https://lipad.ca/full/permalink/4336427.
Haussman, Melissa. 2001. "Of Rights and Power: Canada's Federal Abortion Policy 1969–1991." In *Abortion Politics, Women's Movements, and the Democratic State: A Comparative Study of State Feminism*, ed. Dorothy McBride Stetson, 63–86. Oxford: Oxford University Press.
Holli, Anne Maria. 2008. "Feminist Triangles: A Conceptual Analysis." *Representation* 44 (2): 169–85.
Hough, Richard. 2012. "Do Legislative Petitions Systems Enhance the Relationship between Parliament and Citizen?" *Journal of Legislative Studies* 18 (3–4): 479–95.
House of Commons. 2019. "Debates (Hansard)." Compendium of Procedure, Parliamentary Publications. https://www.ourcommons.ca/About/Compendium/ParliamentaryPublications/c_d_debateshansard-e.htm.
Howlett, Michael. 1998. "Predictable and Unpredictable Policy Windows: Institutional and Exogenous Correlates of Canadian Federal Agenda-Setting." *Canadian Journal of Political Science* 31 (3): 495–524.
Hunter, Lynne. 1990. "Allotted Day, S.O. 81 – Funding for Women's Centres." Canada. Parliament. House of Commons. Edited Hansard. 34th Parliament, 2nd Session. 6 April 1990. Retrieved from LiPaD: The Linked Parliamentary Data Project website. https://lipad.ca/full/permalink/3822530.
Htun, Mala, and S. Laurel Weldon. 2018. *The Logics of Gender Justice: State Action on Women's Rights around the World.* Cambridge: Cambridge University Press.
Ibbitson, John. 2015. *Stephen Harper.* Toronto: McLelland and Stewart.
Indigenous and Northern Affairs Canada. 2015. "Government of Canada Launches Inquiry into Missing and Murdered Indigenous Women and

Girls." https://www.canada.ca/en/indigenous-northern-affairs/news/2015/12/government-of-canada-launches-inquiry-into-missing-and-murdered-indigenous-women-and-girls.html.

Ivison, John. 2006. "Tories Plan to Policy Pay Equity on Gender: Caucus Divided by Labour Minister's Proposal." *National Post*, 31 October 2006, A1.

Johnson, Janis. 1991. "Abortion." Canada. Parliament. Senate. Senate Debates. 34th Parliament, 2nd Session, vol. 5: 5281–2, 31 January 1991. http://parl.canadiana.ca/view/oop.debates_SOC3402_05/545?r=0&s=1.

– 2013a. "About Senator Johnson." https://janisjohnson.ca/about (link defunct).

– 2013b. "Protecting a Woman's Right to Choose." https://janisjohnson.ca/my-work-over-the-years/protecting-a-womans-right-to-choose (link defunct).

Johnstone, Rachael. 2017. *After Morgentaler: The Politics of Abortion in Canada*. Vancouver: UBC Press.

Kam, Christopher. 2001. "Do Ideological Preferences Explain Parliamentary Behaviour? Evidence from Great Britain and Canada." *Journal of Legislative Studies* 7 (4): 89–126.

– 2009. *Party Discipline and Parliamentary Politics*. Cambridge: Cambridge University Press.

Kenny, Meryl. 2014. "A Feminist Institutionalist Approach." *Politics and Gender* 10 (4): 679–84.

Kingdon, John. 1995. *Agendas, Alternatives and Public Policies*. 2nd ed. Boston: Little Brown.

Kittilson, Miki Caul. 2008. "Representing Women: The Adoption of Family Leave in Comparative Perspective." *Journal of Politics* 70 (2): 323–34.

Knight, Melanie, and Kathleen Rodgers. 2012. "'The Government Is Operationalizing Neo-Liberalism': Women's Organizations, Status of Women Canada, and the Struggle for Progressive Social Change in Canada." NORA – *Nordic Journal of Feminist and Gender Research* 20 (4): 266–82.

Koop, Royce, Heather Bastedo, and Kelly Blidook. 2018. *Representation in Action: Canadian MPs in the Constituencies*. Vancouver: UBC Press.

Ladner, Keira. 2017. "Taking the Field: 50 Years of Indigenous Politics in the CJPS." *Canadian Journal of Political Science* 50 (1): 163–79.

LaMarsh Judy. 1969. *Memoirs of a Bird in a Gilded Cage*. Toronto: McClelland and Stewart.

Landry, Monique. 1989. "Criminal Code." Canada. Parliament. House of Commons. Edited Hansard. 34th Parliament, 2nd Session, 22 November 1989. Retrieved from LiPaD: The Linked Parliamentary Data Project website: https://www.lipad.ca/full/permalink/3802876.

Layton, Jack. 2006a. "Status of Women." Canada. Parliament. House of Commons. Edited Hansard. 39th Parliament, 1st Session, 6 December 2006. Retrieved from LiPaD: The Linked Parliamentary Data Project Website: https://lipad.ca/full/permalink/4347271.

– 2006b. "Status of Women." Canada. Parliament. House of Commons. Edited Hansard. 39th Parliament, 1st Session, 6 December 2006. Retrieved from LiPaD: The Linked Parliamentary Data Project Website: https://lipad.ca/full/permalink/4347273.

Lieberman, Evan S. 2005. "Nested Analysis as a Mixed-Method Strategy for Comparative Research." *American Political Science Review* 99 (3): 435–52.

Lovenduski, Joni, and Pippa Norris. 2003. "Westminster Women: The Politics of Presence." *Political Studies* 51: 84–102.

Macdonald, John M. 1990. "Abortion Bill." Canada. Parliament. Senate. Senate Debates. 34th Parliament, 2nd Session, vol. 2: 1932–3, 13 June 1990. http://parl.canadiana.ca/view/oop.debates_SOC3402_02/928?r=0&s=1.

MacDonald, Martha. 2009. "Income Security for Women: What about Employment Insurance?" In *Public Policy for Women: The State, Security, and Labour Market Issues*, ed. Marjorie Griffin Cohen and Jane Pulkingham, 251–70. Toronto: University of Toronto Press.

Macfarlane, Emmett. 2021. *Constitutional Pariah: Reference re Senate Reform and the Future of Parliament*. Vancouver: UBC Press.

Mackay, Fiona. 2008. "'Thick' Conceptions of Substantive Representation: Women, Gender and Political Institutions." *Representation* 44 (2): 125–39.

Mackay, Fiona, Meryl Kenny, and Louise Chappell. 2010. "New Institutionalism through a Gender Lens: Towards a Feminist Institutionalism?" *International Political Science Review* 31 (5): 573–88.

Maheu, Shirley. 1990. "Status of Women." Canada. Parliament. House of Commons. Edited Hansard. 34th Parliament, 2nd Session, 26 March 1990. Retrieved from LiPaD: The Linked Parliamentary Data Project Website: https://www.lipad.ca/full/permalink/3819904.

Malloy, Jonathan. 2003. "High Discipline, Low Cohesion? The Uncertain Patterns of Canadian Parliamentary Parties." *Journal of Legislative Studies* 19 (1): 32–45.

Mansbridge, Jane. 1999. "Should Blacks Represent Blacks and Women Represent Women? A Contingent Yes." *Journal of Politics* 6 (3): 628–57.
– 2003. "Rethinking Representation." *American Political Science Review* 97 (4): 515–28.
Marland, Alex. 2020. *Whipped: Party Discipline in Canada*. Vancouver: UBC Press.
Martin, Lawrence. 2010. *Harperland*. Toronto: Viking Canada.
Martin, Shirley. 1989. "Criminal Code." Canada. Parliament. House of Commons. Edited Hansard. 34th Parliament, 2nd Session, 23 November 1989. Retrieved from LiPaD: The Linked Parliamentary Data Project website: https://www.lipad.ca/full/permalink/3803169.
Mathyssen, Irene. 2008a. "Petitions." Canada. Parliament. House of Commons. Edited Hansard. 39th Parliament, 2nd Session, 26 May 2008. Retrieved from LiPaD: The Linked Parliamentary Data Project Website: https://www.lipad.ca/full/permalink/4397847.
– 2008b. "Petitions." Canada. Parliament. House of Commons. Edited Hansard. 39th Parliament, 2nd Session, 26 May 2008. Retrieved from LiPaD: The Linked Parliamentary Data Project Website: https://www.lipad.ca/full/permalink/4398974.
Mazur, Amy G. 2002. *Theorizing Feminist Policy*. Oxford: Oxford University Press.
McBride, Dorothy E., and Amy Mazur. 2010. *The Politics of State Feminism: Innovation in Comparative Research*. Philadelphia: Temple University Press.
McCallion, Elizabeth. 2021. "The Canadian Senate Briefly Reached Gender Parity: Here's Why It Matters." *The Conversation Canada*. https://theconversation.com/the-canadian-senate-briefly-reached-gender-parity-heres-why-it-matters-153525.
– 2022. "From Private Influence to Public Amendment? The Senate's Amendment Rate in the 41st, 42nd, and 43rd Canadian Parliaments." *Canadian Journal of Political Science* 55 (3): 583–99.
McDermott, Patricia. 1996. "Pay and Employment Equity: Why Separate Policies?" In *Women and Canadian Public Policy*, ed. Janine Brodie, 89–104. Toronto: Harcourt Brace.
McDougall, Barbara Jean. 1989. «Criminal Code.» Canada. Parliament. House of Commons. Edited Hansard. 34th Parliament, 2nd Session, 8 November 1989. Retrieved from LiPaD: The Linked Parliamentary Data Project website: https://www.lipad.ca/full/permalink/3801636.

McLaughlin, Audrey. 1991. "Violence against Women." Canada. Parliament. House of Commons. Edited Hansard. 34th Parliament, 3rd Session, 6 December 1991. Retrieved from LiPaD: The Linked Parliamentary Data Project Website: https://www.lipad.ca/full/permalink/3890457.

McMurdy, Deirdre. 2006. "Pink Book Puts Hefty Price on Improving Status of Women." *Ottawa Citizen*, 28 November 2006, A5.

Mimno, David, Hanna M. Wallach, Edmund Talley, Miriam Leenders, and Andrew McCallum. 2011. "Optimizing Semantic Coherence in Topic Models." Proceedings of the 2011 Conference on Empirical Methods in Natural Language Processing, 262–72.

Minna, Maria. 2006a. "Business of Supply." Canada. Parliament. House of Commons. Edited Hansard. 39th Parliament, 1st Session, 28 September 2006. Retrieved from LiPaD: The Linked Parliamentary Data Project website. https://www.lipad.ca/full/permalink/4336350.

– 2006b. "Status of Women." Canada. Parliament. House of Commons. Edited Hansard. 39th Parliament, 1st Session, 28 September 2006. Retrieved from LiPaD: The Linked Parliamentary Data Project website: https://www.lipad.ca/full/permalink/4337894.

– 2007. "Business of Supply." Canada. Parliament. House of Commons. Edited Hansard. 39th Parliament, 2nd Session, 1 November 2007. Retrieved from LiPaD: The Linked Parliamentary Data Project website: https://lipad.ca/full/permalink/4373958.

– 2008. "Business of Supply." Canada. Parliament. House of Commons. Edited Hansard. 39th Parliament, 2nd Session, 6 March 2008. Retrieved from LiPaD: The Linked Parliamentary Data Project website: https://www.lipad.ca/full/permalink/4387760.

Mitchell, Margaret Anne. 1990. "Funding for Women's Centres." Canada. Parliament. House of Commons. Edited Hansard. 34th Parliament, 2nd Session, 6 April 1990. Retrieved from LiPaD: The Linked Parliamentary Data Project website: https://www.lipad.ca/full/permalink/3822819.

– 1992. "Status of Women." Canada. Parliament. House of Commons. Edited Hansard. 34th Parliament, 3rd Session, 13 March 1992. Retrieved from LiPaD: The Linked Parliamentary Data Project website: https://www.lipad.ca/full/permalink/3899135.

Mulroney, Martin Brian. 1990. "Status of Women." Canada. Parliament. House of Commons. Edited Hansard. 34th Parliament, 2nd Session, 5 March 1990. Retrieved from LiPaD: The Linked Parliamentary Data Project website: https://www.lipad.ca/full/permalink/3815472.

National Association of Women and the Law. 2006a. "Coalition for Women's Equality." http://archive.nawl.ca/en/issues/entry/coalition-for-women8217s-equality-coalition-pour-legalite-des-femmes (link defunct).
– 2006b. "Conservative Government Trying to Silence Women's Groups." http://nawl.ca/en/issues/entry/conservative-government-trying-to-silence-women8217s-groups-le-gouvernement (link defunct).
– 2009. "Public Sector Equitable Compensation Act." http://nawl.ca/en/library/entry/public-sector-equitable-compensation-act-loi-sur-lequite-dans-la-remunerati (link defunct).
National Post. 2006. "12 Status of Women Centres to Shrink to Four Regional Offices by April 1." 30 November 2006, A5.
Neville, Anita. 2007. "Business of Supply." Canada. Parliament. House of Commons. Edited Hansard. 39th Parliament, 1st Session, 16 May 2007. Retrieved from LiPaD: The Linked Parliamentary Data Project website: https://lipad.ca/full/permalink/4364835.
Nichols, Marjorie. 1991. "Carney the Author of Her Own Misfortune." *Ottawa Citizen*, 7 February 1991, A3.
O'Brien, Diana Z. 2018. "'Righting' Conventional Wisdom: Women and Right Parties in Established Democracies." *Politics and Gender* 14: 27–55.
Och, Malliga. 2018. "Conservative Feminists? An Exploration of Feminist Arguments in Parliamentary Debates of the Bundestag." *Parliamentary Affairs* 72 (2): 353–78.
Oda, Bev. 2006a. "Business of Supply." Canada. Parliament. House of Commons. Edited Hansard. 39th Parliament, 1st Session, 28 September 2006. Retrieved from LiPaD: The Linked Parliamentary Data Project website: https://www.lipad.ca/full/permalink/4336374.
– 2006b. "Oral Questions." Canada. Parliament. House of Commons. Edited Hansard. 39th Parliament, 1st Session, 6 October 2006. Retrieved from LiPaD: The Linked Parliamentary Data Project website: https://www.lipad.ca/full/permalink/4338144.
O'Regan, Valerie. 2000. *Gender Matters: Female Policymakers' Influence in Industrialized Nations*. Westport, CT: Praeger.
Osborn, Tracy. 2012. *How Women Represent Women: Political Parties, Representation and Gender in the State Legislatures*. New York: Oxford University Press.
Osborn, Tracy, and Jeanette Morehouse Mendez. 2010. "Speaking as Women: Women and Floor Speeches in the Senate." *Journal of Women, Politics and Policy* 31 (1): 1–21.

Pal, Leslie A. 1991. "How Ottawa Dithers: The Conservatives and Abortion Policy." In *How Ottawa Spends, 1991–91: The Politics of Fragmentation*, ed. Frances Abele, 269–306. Ottawa: Carleton University Press.

Parliament of Canada. n.d. "Parliamentarians." https://lop.parl.ca/sites/ParlInfo/default/en_CA/People/parliamentarians.

Pearson, Kathryn, and Logan Dancey. 2011. "Speaking for the Underrepresented in the House of Representatives: Voicing Women's Interests in a Partisan Era." *Politics and Gender* 7: 493–519.

Philips, Susan D. 1989. "Rock-a-Bye Brian: The National Strategy on Child Care." In *How Ottawa Spends, 1989–90*, ed. Katherine A. Graham, 165–208. Ottawa: Carleton University Press.

Phillips, Anne. 1995. *The Politics of Presence.* New York: Clarendon Press.

Pitkin, Hanna. 1967. *The Concept of Representation.* Berkeley: University of California Press.

Porter, Ann. 2003. *Gendered States: Women, Unemployment Insurance, and the Political Economy of the Welfare State in Canada, 1947–1997.* Toronto: University of Toronto Press.

Proksch, Sven-Oliver, and Jonathan B. Slapin. 2015. *The Politics of Parliamentary Debate: Parties, Rebels and Representation.* Cambridge: Cambridge University Press.

Public Service Alliance of Canada. 2013. "Pay Equity: New Law Compromises Equal Pay for Women in the Federal Public Sector." http://psacunion.ca/pay-equity-new-law-compromises-equal-pay-women.

Rayment, Erica, and Elizabeth McCallion. 2023. "Contexts and Constraints: The Substantive Representation of Women in the Canadian House of Commons and Senate." *Representation.* http://doi.org/10.1080/00344893.2023.2173283.

Rayside, David. 2008. *Queer Inclusions, Continental Divisions: Public Recognition of Sexual Diversity in Canada and the United States.* Toronto: University of Toronto Press.

Rheault, Ludovic. 2018. "Automated Textual Analysis of Parliamentary Debates." Workshop delivered at the McMaster Conference on Substantive Representation, 6 December 2018. https://github.com/lrheault/mcmaster/blob/master/Module1.ipynb.

Roach, Kent. 2015. "Vandalizing the Criminal Code with Irrational and Arbitrary Restrictions on Provocation." *Criminal Law Quarterly* 62 (4): 403–6.

Rodgers, Kathleen, and Melanie Knight. 2011. "'You Just Felt the Collective Wind Being Knocked Out of Us': The Deinstitutionalization of Feminism and the Survival of Women's Organizing in Canada." *Women's Studies International Forum* 34: 570–81.

Russell, Meg. 2012. "Elected Second Chambers and Their Powers: An International Survey." *Political Quarterly* 83 (1): 117–29.

Russell, Meg, and Philip Cowley. 2016. "The Policy Power of the Westminster Parliament: The 'Parliamentary State' and the Empirical Evidence." *Governance: An International Journal of Policy, Administration, and Institutions* 29 (1): 121–37.

Russell, Meg, Daniel Gover, and Kristina Wollter. 2016. "Does the Executive Dominate the Westminster Legislative Process? Six Reasons for Doubt." *Parliamentary Affairs* 69: 286–308.

Russell, Meg, Daniel Gover, Kristina Wollter, and Meghan Benton. 2017. "Actors, Motivations and Outcomes in the Legislative Process: Policy Influence at Westminster." *Government and Opposition* 52 (1): 1–27.

Saurette, Paul, and Kelly Gordon. 2015. *The Changing Voice of the Anti-Abortion Movement: The Rise of "Pro-Woman" Rhetoric in Canada and the United States*. Toronto: University of Toronto Press.

Savoie, Donald J. 1999. "The Rise of Court Government in Canada." *Canadian Journal of Political Science* 32 (4): 635–64.

Schwindt-Bayer, Leslie, and William Mishler. 2005. "An Integrated Model of Women's Representation." *Journal of Politics* 67 (2): 407–28.

Schwindt-Bayer, Leslie, and Michelle M. Taylor-Robison. 2011. "The Meaning and Measurement of Women's Interests: Introduction." *Politics and Gender* 7 (3): 417–18.

Senate of Canada. 2016. "Voting." Senate Procedural Notes, no. 4. https://sencanada.ca/media/106257/procedural-note-4.pdf.

Sharpe, Sydney. 1994. *The Gilded Ghetto: Women and Political Power in Canada*. Toronto: Harper Collins.

Smith, Charlie. 2006. "Women Kick Harper's Ass." *Georgia Straight*, 13 December 2006. https://www.straight.com/article/women-kick-harpers-ass.

Smith, Jennifer. 2003. "Debating the Reform of Canada's Parliament." In *Reforming Parliamentary Democracy*, ed. Leslie Seidle and David Docherty, 150–68. Montreal and Kingston: McGill-Queen's University Press.

Smooth, Wendy. 2011. "Standing for Women? Which Women? The Substantive Representation of Women's Interests and the Research Imperative of Intersectionality." *Politics and Gender* 7 (3): 436–41.

Soroka, Stuart, Erin Penner, and Kelly Blidook. 2009. "Constituency Influence in Parliament." *Canadian Journal of Political Science* 42 (3): 563–91.

Spivak, Mira. 1991. "Abortion Bill." Canada. Parliament. Senate. Senate Debates. 34th Parliament, 2nd Session, vol. 5: 5213–16, 29 January 1991. http://parl.canadiana.ca/view/oop.debates_SOC3402_05/477?r=0&s=1.

Standing Committee on the Status of Women. 2007a. "Committee members as of January 30, 2007." https://www.ourcommons.ca/Committees/en/FEWO/Members?parl=39&session=1&membershipOn=2007-01-30#committeeMembersPanel.

– 2007b. "Work – Reports." https://www.ourcommons.ca/Committees/en/FEWO/Work?show=reports&parl=39&session=1.

– 2019. "About – History." https://www.ourcommons.ca/Committees/en/FEWO/About.

Status of Women Canada. 2019. "Programs Branch – Regional Offices." https://swc-cfc.gc.ca/contact/index-en.html#regional (link defunct).

Stewart, Margaret, and Doris French. 1959. *Ask No Quarter: A Biography of Agnes Macphail.* Toronto: Longmans, Green and Company.

Steyvers, Mark, and Tom Griffiths. 2007. "Probabilistic Topic Models." In *Handbook of Latent Semantic Analysis*, ed. Thomas K. Landauer, Danielle S. McNamara, Simon Dennis, and Walter Kintsch, 427–48. London: Routledge

Sutherland, S. L. 1991. "Responsible Government and Ministerial Responsibility: Every Reform Is Its Own Problem." *Canadian Journal of Political Science* 24 (1): 91–120.

Swers, Michele L. 2002. *The Difference Women Make.* Chicago: University of Chicago Press.

– 2005. "Connecting Descriptive and Substantive Representation: An Analysis of Sex Differences in Co-Sponsorship Activity." *Legislative Studies Quarterly* 30 (3): 407–33.

– 2013. *Women in the Club: Gender and Policymaking in the Senate.* Chicago: University of Chicago Press.

Taber, Jane. 2007. "Silence of the Lamb." *Globe and Mail*, 2 June 2007, F3.

Tatalovich, Raymond. 1997. *The Politics of Abortion in the United States and Canada: A Comparative Study.* Armonk, NY: M.E. Sharpe.

Thomas, Melanee. 2017. "Equality of Opportunity But Not Result: Women and Federal Conservatives in Canada." In *The Blueprint: Conservative Parties and Their Impact on Canadian Politics*, ed. J.P. Lewis and Joanna Everitt, 129–49. Toronto: University of Toronto Press.

Thomas, Paul G. 2019. *Moving toward a New and Improved Senate.* Institute for Research on Public Policy. https://irpp.org/research-studies/moving-toward-new-improved-senate.

Thomas, Sue. 1994. *How Women Legislate.* Oxford: Oxford University Press.

Thompson, Debra. 2008. "Is Race Political?" *Canadian Journal of Political Science* 41 (3): 525–47.

Tiessen, Rebecca. 2015. "'Walking Wombs': Making Sense of the Muskoka Initiative and the Emphasis on Motherhood in Canadian Foreign Policy." *Global Justice: Theory Practice Rhetoric* 8 (1): 74–92.

Timpson, Annis May. 2001. *Driven Apart: Women's Employment Equality and Child Care in Canadian Public Policy.* Vancouver: UBC Press.

Tolley, Erin. 2019. "Who You Know: Local Party Presidents and Minority Candidate Emergence." *Electoral Studies* 58: 70–9.

Toronto Star. 1991. "Campbell Vows to Shield MDs from Bill on Abortion." 17 January 1991, A11.

– 2006. "Push on Tories to Restore Programs." 11 December 2006, A10.

Treasury Board Secretariat. 2017. "FAQ: Pay Equity Reform." https://www.canada.ca/en/treasury-board-secretariat/services/innovation/equitable-compensation/frequently-asked-questons-pay-equity-reform.html.

Tremblay, Manon. 1998. "Do Female MPs Substantively Represent Women? A Study of Legislative Behaviour in Canada's 35th Parliament." *Canadian Journal of Political Science* 31 (3): 435–65.

– 2003. "Women's Representational Role in Australia and Canada: The Impact of Political Context." *Australian Journal of Political Science* 38 (2): 215–38.

– 2007. "Electoral Systems and Substantive Representation of Women: A Comparison of Australia, Canada and New Zealand." *Commonwealth and Comparative Politics* 45 (3): 278–302.

Tremblay, Manon, and Réjean Pelletier. 2000. "More Women or More Feminists? Descriptive and Substantive Representations of Women in the 1997 Canadian Federal Election." *International Political Science Review* 21 (4): 381–405.

Trimble, Linda. 2006. "When Do Women Count? Substantive Representation of Women in Canadian Legislatures." In *Representing Women in Parliament: A Comparative Study*, ed. Marian Sawer, Manon Tremblay and Linda Trimble, 120–33. London and New York: Routledge.

Tromp, Stanley. 2013. "Mulroney-Era Documents Reveal Detailed Debate of Canada's Abortion Laws." *Globe and Mail*, 17 November 2013. https://www.theglobeandmail.com/news/national/mulroney-era-documents-reveal-detailed-debate-of-canadas-abortion-laws/article15476897.

VandenBeukel, Jason, Christopher Cochrane, and Jean-François Godbout. 2021. "Birds of a Feather? Loyalty and Partisanship in the Reformed Canadian Senate." *Canadian Journal of Political Science*, online first, 1–20. http://doi.org/10.1017/S0008423921000548.

Vargas, Virginia, and Saskia Wieringa. 1998. "The Triangle of Empowerment: Processes and Actors in the Making of Public Policy for Women." In *Women's Movements and Public Policy in Europe, Latin America and the Caribbean*, ed. Geertje Lycklama à Nijeholt, Virginia Vargas, and Saskia Wieringa, 3–24. New York and London: Garland.

Vézina, Monique. 1989. "Criminal Code." Canada. Parliament. House of Commons. Edited Hansard. 34th Parliament, 2nd Session, 21 November 1989. Retrieved from LiPaD: The Linked Parliamentary Data Project website: https://www.lipad.ca/full/permalink/3802581.

Vienneau, David. 1990. "Row Erupts as MPs Pass Abortion Bill." *Toronto Star*, 30 May 1990, A12.

– 1991a. "Abortion Bill Faces Senate Hurdle." *Toronto Star*, 20 January 1991, B4.

– 1991b. "Abortion Bill Nears Final Vote." *Toronto Star*, 24 January 1991, A14.

– 1991c. "Abortion Bill Still in Doubt Senator Says." *Toronto Star*, 25 January 1991, A2.

Walker, William. 1991. "Senate Kills Abortion Bill by a Tie Vote." *Toronto Star*, 1 February 1991, A1.

Wängnerud, Lena. 2000. "Testing the Politics of Presence: Women's Representation in the Swedish Riksdag." *Scandinavian Political Studies* 23 (1): 67–91.

– 2009. "Women in Parliaments: Descriptive and Substantive Representation." *Annual Review of Political Science* 12: 51–69.

Webb, Paul, and Sarah Childs. 2012. "Gender Politics and Conservatism: The View from the British Conservative Party Grassroots." *Government and Opposition* 47 (1): 21–48.

Wells, Paul. 2013. *The Longer I'm Prime Minister: Stephen Harper and Canada, 2006–*. Toronto: Random House Canada.

Whittington, Les, and Bruce Campion-Smith. 2006. "Tories Cut $1B Despite Surplus: Wide Range of Programs Lose Funding Critics Say Targets Based on 'Ideology.'" *Toronto Star*, 26 September 2006, A1.

Whittington, Les, and Susan Delacourt. 2006. "Dion Faces Same-Sex Debate: Won't Say if He'll Force Liberal MPs to Vote against Tory Motion." *Toronto Star*, 5 December 2006, A1.

Women's Legal Education Action Fund. 2009. "Pay Equity." https://www.leaf.ca/wp-content/uploads/2011/01/PayEquityFactSheet.pdf.

York, Geoffrey. 1991. "Senators Kill Abortion Bill with Tied Vote." *Globe and Mail*, 1 February 1991, A1.

Young, Iris Marion. 2002. *Inclusion and Democracy*. New York: Oxford University Press.

Young, Lisa. 1997. "Fulfilling the Mandate of Difference: Women in the Canadian House of Commons." In *In the Presence of Women: Representation in Canadian Governments*, ed. Jane Arscott, and Linda Trimble, 82–106. Toronto: Harcourt Brace.

– 2000. *Feminists and Party Politics*. Vancouver: UBC Press.

Index

Page numbers followed by (t) and (f) indicate references to tables and figures.